Quicken 4 For Windows For Dummies

COMPUTER
BOOK SERIES
FROM IDG

D0488613

Speedy shortcuts that'll save you scads of time

Shortcut	Why you should try darn hard to remember this
Ctrl+S	Displays Splits dialog box so that you can use more than one category to describe a payment or deposit.
Shift+Del	Moves the selected text in a field to the Windows Clipboard (so that you can paste it into some other field).
Ctrl+Ins	Copies the selected text in a field to the Windows Clipboard (so that you can paste it into some other field).
Shift+Ins	Pastes what is on the Clipboard into the selected field.
Ctrl+P	Prints the contents of the active window (almost always).
F1	"Help" me, somebody, please!
Alt+Backspace	Yikes! Quicken, please "undo" what I just did.
Ctrl+C	Displays the list of categories.

Some cool date-editing tricks

If the selection cursor is on a date field, you can do this:

Press	What happens
+	Adds 1 day to the date shown
–	Subtracts 1 day from the date shown
y	Changes the date to the first date in the year
r	Changes the date to the last date in the year
m	Changes the date to the first date in the month
h	Changes the date to the last date in the month

A dozen sneaky shortcuts for busy people

The Quicken iconbar is just a row of buttons you click to do things really fast.

Use this button	Quicken does this
Homebase	Displays the Quicken Homebase window. The left side of the window shows a set of financial and system managment tasks. The right side shows a list of the tasks within a selected set.
Registr	Displays the register window so that you can enter transactions.
Accts	Displays a list of accounts already set up.
Recon	Let's reconcile a bank account, dude.
Check	Displays the ol' Write Checks window so that you can record (and print) a check.
Calendar	Shows the Financial Calendar.
Graphs	Draws a chart that shows something financial.
Reports	Prints a report. Now.
Snapshots	Whips up a snapshot report that gives you the pulse of your financial affairs.
Options	Displays the Options dialog box (in case you want to make some changes to the way Quicken works).
Print	Prints the contents of the active window.
Help	An electronic yelp for help. Do this when you get into trouble.
Port	If you created an investment account, Quicken adds the Port button so that you can easily flip to the Portfolio View window.

. . . For Dummies: #1 Computer Book Series for Beginners

Quicken 4 For Windows For Dummies

Cheat Sheet

A dozen Windows tricks you can use in Quicken for Windows — and just about any other Windows program, too

1. To move quickly to list box entries that begin with a specific letter, press the letter.

2. To select a list box entry and choose a dialog box's suggested command button, double-click the entry.

3. To move the insertion bar to the beginning of a field, press Home.

4. To move the insertion bar to the end of a field, press End.

5. To close a window or dialog box, double-click its control menu icon (the little hyphen in a box in the upper left corner).

6. To shrink a window to a tiny picture, click the down-arrow head in the window's upper right corner.

7. To unshrink a window that appears as just a tiny picture, double-click the picture.

8. To maximize the Quicken desktop so that it fills the monitor screen, click the up-arrow head in the application window's upper right corner.

9. To maximize the register so that it fills the Quicken desktop, click the up-arrow head in the register window's upper right corner.

10. To yelp for help from just about anywhere, press F1.

11. To switch to another application — so that you can multitask, dude press Ctrl+Esc so that Windows displays the Task List. Then double-click the Program Manager entry in the Task List (if you want to start another application) or double-click the application (if you've already started it and it shows).

12. To change any document window's or application window's size, position the mouse pointer on the window border and then drag the border. (If you can't see the border because the window has previously been maximized, click on the double-headed arrow in the window's upper right corner.)

Three things that every Quicken user should do

1. Use the Retirement Planner to estimate when and how you can retire.

2. Create a category list that makes it easy to track your spending and tax deductions.

3. Use the Reconcile command to balance bank accounts each month with only a few minutes of effort.

. . . For Dummies: #1 Computer Book Series for Beginners

QUICKEN 4 FOR WINDOWS

FOR

DUMMIES™

QUICKEN 4 FOR WINDOWS FOR DUMMIES™

by Stephen L. Nelson

IDG BOOKS

IDG Books Worldwide, Inc.
An International Data Group Company

San Mateo, California ♦ Indianapolis, Indiana ♦ Boston, Massachusetts

Quicken 4 For Windows For Dummies

Published by
IDG Books Worldwide, Inc.
An International Data Group Company
155 Bovet Road, Suite 310
San Mateo, CA 94402

Library of Congress Catalog Card No.: 94-78900

ISBN: 1-56884-209-0

Printed in the United States of America

10 9 8 7 6 5 4 3 2 1

2D/QZ/SQ/ZU

Distributed in the United States by IDG Books Worldwide, Inc.

Distributed in Canada by Macmillan of Canada, a Division of Canada Publishing Corporation; by Computer and Technical Books in Miami, Florida, for South America and the Caribbean; by Longman Singapore in Singapore, Malaysia, Thailand, and Korea; by Toppan Co. Ltd. in Japan; by Asia Computerworld in Hong Kong; by Woodslane Pty. Ltd. in Australia and New Zealand; and by Transworld Publishers Ltd. in the U.K. and Europe.

For general information on IDG Books in the U.S., including information on discounts and premiums, contact IDG Books at 800-434-3422 or 415-312-0650.

For information on where to purchase IDG Books outside the U.S., contact Christina Turner at 415-312-0633.

For information on translations, contact Marc Jeffrey Mikulich, Foreign Rights Manager, at IDG Books Worldwide; FAX NUMBER 415-286-2747.

For sales inquiries and special prices for bulk quantities, write to the address above or call IDG Books Worldwide at 415-312-0650.

For information on using IDG Books in the classroom, or ordering examination copies, contact Jim Kelly at 800-434-2086.

 is a registered trademark of IDG Books Worldwide, Inc.

About the Author

Steve Nelson is a CPA with a masters degree in finance. As corny as it sounds, Steve truly enjoys writing books that make using personal computers easier and more fun. In fact, a substantiated rumor says Steve has written over 40 computer books.

Steve is the best-selling author on the Quicken product, having sold something like 300,000 books on Quicken.

Welcome to the world of IDG Books Worldwide.

IDG Books Worldwide, Inc., is a subsidiary of International Data Group, the world's largest publisher of business and computer-related information and the leading global provider of information services on information technology. IDG was founded more than 25 years ago and now employs more than 5,700 people worldwide. IDG publishes more than 200 computer publications in 63 countries (see listing below). Forty million people read one or more IDG publications each month.

Launched in 1990, IDG Books is today the fastest-growing publisher of computer and business books in the United States. We are proud to have received 3 awards from the Computer Press Association in recognition of editorial excellence, and our best-selling ...*For Dummies* series has more than 10 million copies in print with translations in more than 20 languages. IDG Books, through a recent joint venture with IDG's Hi-Tech Beijing, became the first U.S. publisher to publish a computer book in the People's Republic of China. In record time, IDG Books has become the first choice for millions of readers around the world who want to learn how to better manage their businesses.

Our mission is simple: Every IDG book is designed to bring extra value and skill-building instructions to the reader. Our books are written by experts who understand and care about our readers. The knowledge base of our editorial staff comes from years of experience in publishing, education, and journalism — experience which we use to produce books for the '90s. In short, we care about books, so we attract the best people. We devote special attention to details such as audience, interior design, use of icons, and illustrations. And because we use an efficient process of authoring, editing, and desktop publishing our books electronically, we can spend more time ensuring superior content and spend less time on the technicalities of making books.

You can count on our commitment to deliver high-quality books at competitive prices on topics customers want to read about. At IDG, we value quality, and we have been delivering quality for more than 25 years. You'll find no better book on a subject than an IDG book.

John J. Kilcullen

John Kilcullen
President and CEO
IDG Books Worldwide, Inc.

Acknowledgments

Hey, reader alot of people spent alot of time working on this book to make Quicken easier for you. You should know who these people are in case you ever meet them in the produce section of the local grocery store squeezing cantaloupe.

The editorial folks are: Mary Bednarek, Diane Steele, Sandra Blackthorn, Tracy Barr, and Colleen Rainsberger. And the production folks are: Beth Jenkins, Tony Augsburger, Valery Bourke, Sherry Dickinson Gomoll, Drew Moore, Carla Radzikinas, Tricia Reynolds, Steve Peake and Kathie Schnorr.

Special thanks to Tom Ware for his technical assistance and superb attention to detail. Also, special thanks to Michael Hart for all his help.

(The publisher would like to give special thanks to Patrick J. McGovern, without whom this book would not have been possible.)

Credits

Publisher
David Solomon

Managing Editor
Mary Bednarek

Acquisitions Editor
Janna Custer

Production Director
Beth Jenkins

Senior Editors
Tracy L. Barr
Sandra Blackthorn
Diane Graves Steele

**Associate
Production Coordinator**
Valery Bourke

Acquisitions Assistant
Megg Bonar

Project Editor
Colleen Rainsberger

Technical Reviewer
Tom Ware

Pre-Press Coordinator
Steve Peake

Production Staff
Tony Augsburger
Paul Belcastro
Sherry Dickinson Gomoll
Drew R. Moore
Carla Radzikinas
Patricia R. Reynolds
Kathie Schnorr
Gina Scott

Proofreader
Sandra Profant

Indexer
Sherry Massey

Book Design
University Graphics

Contents at a Glance

Cartoons at a Glance
By Richard Tennant

page 149

page 49

page 265

page 86

page 293

page 7

page 237

page 213

page 298

page 190

Table of Contents

Introduction

· ·

*Y*ou aren't a dummy, of course. But, here's the deal. You don't have to be some sort of techno-geek or financial wizard to manage your financial affairs on a PC. You have other things to do, places to go, and people to meet. And that's where *Quicken 4 For Windows For Dummies* comes in.

In the pages that follow, I give you the straight scoop on how to use Quicken For Windows, without a lot of extra baggage, goofy tangential information, or misguided advice.

About This Book

This book isn't meant to be read cover to cover like some Robert Ludlum page turner. Rather, it's organized into tiny, no sweat descriptions of how you do the things you'll need to do. If you're the sort of person who just doesn't feel right not reading a book from cover to cover, you can, of course, go ahead and read this thing from front to back.

I can recommend this approach, however, only for people who have already checked the TV listings. There may, after all, be a "Rockford Files" rerun on.

About the Author

If you're going to spend your time reading what I have to say, you deserve to know what my qualifications are. So let me take just a minute or so to do that.

I have an undergraduate degree in accounting and a masters degree in finance and accounting. I am also a certified public accountant (CPA).

I've spent most of the last ten years helping businesses set up computerized financial management systems. I started with Arthur Andersen & Co., which is one of the world's largest public accounting and systems consulting firms. More recently, I've been working as a sole proprietor. When I wasn't doing financial systems work, I served as the controller of a small, 50-person computer software company.

Oh yeah, one other thing. I've used Quicken for my business and for my personal record-keeping for several years.

None of this information makes me sound like the world's most exciting guy, of course. I doubt you'll be inviting me to your next dinner party. Hey, I can deal with that.

But knowing a little something about me should give you a bit more confidence in applying the stuff talked about in the pages that follow. All joking aside, we're talking about something that's extremely important: *your money.*

How to Use This Book

I always enjoyed reading those encyclopedias my parents bought for me and my siblings. You could flip open, say, the E volume, look up *Elephants,* and then learn just about everything you needed to know about elephants for a fifth grade report: where elephants lived, how much they weighed, and why they ate so much.

You won't read anything about elephants here. But you should be able to use this book in the same way. If you want to learn about something, look through the table of contents or index and find the topic — *check printing,* for example. Then flip to the correct chapter or page and read as much as you need or enjoy. No muss. No fuss.

If there's anything else you want to learn about, of course, you just repeat the process.

What You Can Safely Ignore

Sometimes I had to provide step-by-step descriptions of tasks. I felt very bad that I had to do this (but, hey, ya gotta learn somehow). So to make things easier for you, I described the tasks using bold text. That way you'll know exactly what you're supposed to do. I also provided a more detailed explanation in regular text. You can skip the regular text that accompanies the step-by-step descriptions if you already understand the process.

Here's an example that shows what I mean:

1. **Press Enter.**

   Find the key that's labeled *Enter.* Extend your index finger so that it rests ever so gently on the Enter key. In one sure, fluid motion, press the Enter key using your index finger. Then release your finger.

OK, that's kind of an extreme example. I never go into that much detail. But you get the idea. If you know how to press Enter, you can just do that and not read further. If you need help — say with the finger part or something — just read the nitty-gritty details.

Is there anything else you can skip? Let me see now. . . . You can skip the Technical stuff, too. The information I've stuck in these paragraphs is really only here for those of you who like that kind of stuff.

For that matter, I guess the stuff in the Tip paragraphs can safely be ignored, too. If you're someone who enjoys trying it another way, go ahead and read the Tips.

What You Should Not Ignore (Unless You're a Masochist)

Don't skip the Warnings. They're the ones flagged with the picture of the nineteenth-century bomb. They describe some things you really shouldn't do.

Out of respect for you, I'm not going to put stuff in these paragraphs like, "Don't smoke." I figure that you're an adult. You can make your own lifestyle decisions.

So I'll reserve the Warnings for more urgent and immediate dangers — things akin to: "Don't smoke while you're filling your car with gasoline."

Three Foolish Assumptions

I'm going to assume just three things:

- ✔ You've got a PC with Microsoft Windows.
- ✔ You know how to turn it on.
- ✔ You want to use Quicken.

By the way, if you haven't already installed Quicken and need some help, refer to Appendix A. It describes how to install Quicken.

How This Book Is Organized

This book is organized into five mostly coherent parts.

Part I: Zen, Quicken, and the Big Picture

Part I, "Zen, Quicken, and the Big Picture," covers some up-front stuff you need to take care of. I promise I won't waste your time here. I just want to make sure that you get off on the right foot.

Part II: The Absolute Basics

This second part of *Quicken 4 For Windows For Dummies* explains the core knowledge that you need to keep a personal or business checkbook with Quicken: using the checkbook, printing, balancing your bank accounts, and using the Quicken calculators.

Some of this stuff isn't very exciting compared to MTV (especially Cindy Crawford's *House of Style*), so I'll work hard to make things fun for you.

Part III: Home Finances

Part III talks about the sorts of things you may want to do with Quicken if you're using it at home: credit cards, loans, mutual funds, stocks and bonds. You get the idea. If you don't ever get this far — hey, that's cool.

If you do get this far, you'll find that Quicken provides some tools that eliminate not only the drudgery of keeping a checkbook, but also the drudgery of most other financial burdens.

While we're on the subject, I also want to categorically deny that Part III contains any secret messages if you read it backwards.

Part IV: Serious Business

The "Serious Business" section helps people who use Quicken in a business.

If you're pulling your hair out because you're using Quicken in a business, postpone the hair-pulling — at least for the time being. Read Part IV first. It will tell you about preparing payroll, tracking the amounts that customers owe you, and other wildly exciting stuff.

Part V: The Part of Tens

Gravity isn't just a good idea, it's also the law.

By tradition, the same is true for this part of a . . . *For Dummies* book. "The Part of Tens" provides a collection of ten-something lists: ten things you should do if you get audited, ten things you should do if you own a business, ten things to do when you next visit Acapulco — oops, sorry about that last one. Wrong book.

Appendixes

It's an unwritten rule that computer books have appendixes, so I included three. Appendix A tells you how to install Quicken in ten easy steps. Appendix B gives you a quick and dirty overview of the Microsoft Windows operating environment. Appendix C is a glossary of key financial and Quicken terms.

Conventions Used in This Book

To make the best use of your time and energy, you should know about the following conventions used in this book.

When I want you to type something such as **Hydraulics screamed as the pilot lowered his landing gear**, I'll put it in bold letters. When I want you to type something that's short and uncomplicated, such as **Jennifer**, it will still appear in bold type.

By the way, with Quicken you don't have to worry about the case of the stuff you type. If I tell you to type **Jennifer**, you can type **JENNIFER**. Or you can follow e. e. cummings lead and type **jennifer**.

Whenever I describe a message or information that you'll see on the screen, I present it as follows:

```
Surprise! This is a message on-screen.
```

You can choose menus and commands and select dialog box elements with the mouse or the keyboard. To select them with the mouse, you just click them. To select them with the keyboard, you press Alt and the underlined letter in the menu, command, or dialog box. For example, the letter F in File and the letter O in Open are underlined, so you can choose the File Open command by pressing Alt+F, O. (I also identify the keyboard selection keys by underlining them in the text.) You can choose many commands by clicking icons on the iconbar as well.

Special Icons

Like many computer books, this book uses icons, or little pictures, to flag things that don't quite fit into the flow of things. ...*For Dummies* books use a standard set of icons that flag little digressions, such as:

 This icon points out nerdy technical material that you may want to skip (or read, if you're feeling particularly bright).

 Whee, here's a shortcut to make your life easier.

 This icon is just a friendly reminder to do something.

 And this icon is a friendly reminder *not* to do something... or else.

 This icon calls attention to information you should "take note" of.

Where To Next?

If you're just getting started, flip the page and start reading the first chapter.

If you've got a special problem or question, use the table of contents or the index to find out where that topic is covered and then turn to that page.

Part I
Zen, Quicken, and The Big Picture

By Rich Tennant

"THE IMAGE IS GETTING CLEARER NOW... I CAN ALMOST SEE IT... YES! THERE IT IS-THE GLITCH IS IN A FAULTY CELL REFERENCE IN THE FOOTBALL POOL SPREADSHEET."

In this part...

When you go to a movie theater, there are some prerequisites for making the show truly enjoyable. And I'm not referring to the presence of Sharon Stone or Arnold Schwarzenegger. Purchasing a bucket of popcorn is essential, for example. One should think strategically both about seating and about soda size. And one may even have items, of a, well, personal nature to take care of — like visiting the little boys' or girls' room.

I mention all this for one simple reason. To make getting started with Quicken as easy and fun as possible, there are some prerequisites, too. And this first part of *Quicken 4 For Windows For Dummies* — "Zen, Quicken, and the Big Picture" — talks about these sorts of things.

Chapter 1
Setting Up Shop

In This Chapter

▶ Starting Quicken for the first time

▶ Setting up your bank accounts and credit card accounts if you're a first-time user

▶ Retrieving existing Quicken data files

*I*f you haven't ever used Quicken, begin here. The next section tells you how to start the program for the first time.

You also learn how you go about setting up Quicken accounts to track banking activities — specifically, the money that goes into and out of a checking or savings account.

If you have already begun to use Quicken, don't waste any time reading this chapter unless you want the review. You already know the stuff it covers.

By the way, I assume that you know a little bit about Windows. No, you don't have to be some sort of expert. Shoot, you don't even have to be all that proficient. You do need to know how to start Windows and Windows applications (such as Quicken). It'll also help immensely if you know how to choose commands from menus and how to enter stuff into windows and dialog boxes.

If you don't know how to do these kinds of things, flip to Appendix B. It provides a very quick and rather dirty overview of how you work in Windows. Read this stuff, or at least skim it, and then come back to this chapter.

Starting Quicken for the First Time

The very first time you start Quicken, you'll see a window named Quicken New User Setup, as shown in Figure 1-1. To start the new user setup, you click the Next button. Quicken steps you through a couple of tutorials. (Or, at least, it gives you the option of seeing a couple of tutorials — one on Windows and one on Quicken.) I'm not going to describe what happens during the tutorial. Having me provide a tutorial on a tutorial is overkill. Mostly you just click and watch.

If later you change your mind

You don't have to look at the Windows or Quicken tutorial right now. To skip the tutorials, just click the No button when Quicken asks, "Would you like to see a tutorial now?" To see the tutorial later on, just choose the Help menu's Tutorials command. When Quicken displays the choice of tutorials, choose either Introduction Windows or To Quicken.

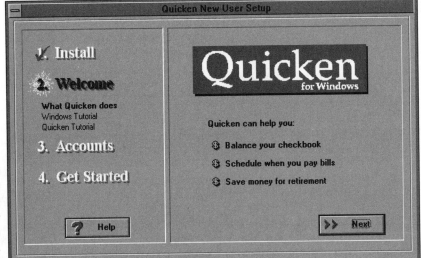

Figure 1-1:
The Quicken
New User
Setup
window.

Setting Up Your First Accounts

Once you get done with the whole tutorial thing, Quicken redisplays the Quicken New User Setup window and tells you it's about to set up some new accounts for you. Mostly, this is just a matter of you reading the instructions on screen and then filling in the text box provided. Read and type, read and type. That's all there is to it. To get started on all this stuff, click the Next button. Quicken displays another bit of prose that says you need your checkbook and most recent bank statements. Quicken is right, so you better go find those things. Don't worry. I'll wait for you:

OK. Assuming you're now back with your checkbook and most recent bank statement, click Next and then follow these steps:

1. **When Quicken asks whether you have a checking account, click the Yes button.**

   I guess I'm assuming that you've got a checking account. That's reasonable, right? You probably wouldn't get a checkbook-on-a-computer program if you don't have a checking account.

2. **Tell Quicken which name you want to use for the account.**

   You do this by typing a name into the Account Name text box. When you finish naming the account, click the Next button. By the way, you can be as general or as specific as you want. I like to give my accounts incredibly clever, wildly precise names such as Checking. A cool feature you'll notice is that Quicken displays a little message box, called a Qcard, which tells you what you should have entered in the selected text box. If you like the Qcards, great. If you don't, click the Control Menu icon in the Qcard message box.

3. **Tell Quicken whether you've got the last bank statement.**

   This is pretty simple. If you do, click the Yes button. If you don't, click the No button. (If you click No, Quicken doesn't do any more setup stuff for the checking account.)

4. **Provide the ending bank statement date — if you have the bank statement.**

   If you indicate that you do have the bank statement handy, Quicken asks for the ending statement date. This will be the date you start using Quicken. Enter the date in MM/DD/YY fashion. "Geez, Steve," you're now saying to yourself, "What's MM/DD/YY fashion?" OK. Here's an example. If things are really going to be different starting January 1, 1995, enter **1/1/95.** When you are done entering the date, click the Next button.

5. **Provide the ending bank statement balance — if you have the bank statement.**

   This is whatever shows on your bank statement. It's also the amount of money in your account on the date you will begin your financial record-keeping. If you had four dollars and sixteen cents in your checking account, and type **4.16** into the Ending Balance text box. When you're done entering the bank statement balance, click Next. Quicken displays a message in the Quicken New User Setup dialog box that tells you what you've just done — for example, "You've just set up an account named checking with a starting balance of $4.16 on 1/1/95."

6. **Set up a savings account.**

   Once you've set up your first checking account — a process I've described in the preceding steps — Quicken asks whether you want to set up a savings account. If you click Yes, indicating that you do indeed, Quicken asks you all the same questions as it asks for a checking account. You just fill in the text boxes and click the Next button. If this seems too complicated or unwieldy, by the way, you can easily start out with just a checking account.

7. Set up a credit card account.

When you get done setting up a savings account, Quicken asks whether you want to set up a credit card account. This will be a big surprise to you, but if you click Yes, Quicken asks you all the same questions as it asks for a checking account or savings account: "Type in a name for this account"; "What's the ending balance on the statement?"; and "What is the date of the statement?" Again, you just fill in the text boxes and click the Next button a couple of times.

8. Indicate whether you want to use the business categories list or the home categories list.

When Quicken asks whether you want to use its business categories list, click the Yes button if you will use Quicken for business record-keeping. (In this case, Quicken creates a list of categories that include both business and home categories.) Otherwise, click No. (In this case, Quicken creates a list of categories that include only home categories.)

9. Click Done.

Why? Because you are done. Quicken displays the Quicken application window with something called the Quicken Homebase showing (see Figure 1-2).

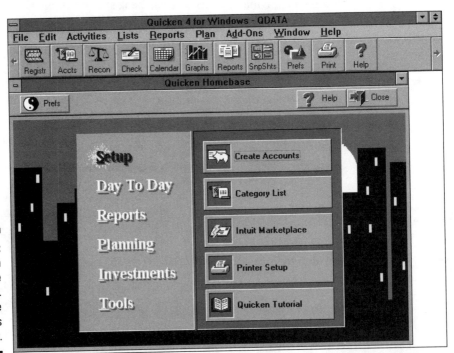

Figure 1-2:
The Quicken Homebase window. You're in the big leagues now.

Homebase in a nutshell

If you're really interested in this Homebase thing, let me give you a couple of pointers. Basically, the Homebase is just another menu system. Rather than organizing Quicken's commands into the usual Windows menus like File, Edit, and so on, it organizes Quicken commands into categories of tasks, like Setup tasks, Day to Day tasks, and so on. To see a list of the tasks within a category, you click on the category name. To start a task — which is the same thing as choosing a command — you click on the task name.

About the Homebase

For the most recent version of Quicken, the folks at Intuit created a new interface element called the Homebase. The idea is that this Homebase is where it all happens. It's the financial version of mission control. I'm not all that excited about it, though. I think the regular Windows menus and commands are just as easy. They also have the advantage that if you've worked with another Windows application before, you already know how to use them.

So, I'm not going to describe the Homebase way of doing things here. In fact, I'm going to suggest something totally outrageous. I'm going to suggest you simply close the Homebase window and forget you ever saw it. If you follow my advice, Quicken removes the Homebase window. And you'll never see it again.

If you want to use the Homebase, by the way, you need to choose the Activities Homebase command. Quicken places a checkmark next to the command name. Every time you start Quicken, it displays the Homebase window.

About the iconbar

The iconbar is not a place where icons go to "tie one on." The iconbar is a set of command icons located at the top of the Quicken application window (see Figure 1-2). You can easily choose a common Quicken command by clicking one of these icons with the mouse.

I refer to the iconbar icons by their names in the pages that follow. (I also refer to an icon in the paragraph — which is why I brought up the icon business here.) If you want to see a list of the iconbar icons along with descriptions of what they do, flip open the front cover of this book.

Getting to the Account Register

Once you get past the Homebase confusion and understand the iconbar —
knowledge you've hopefully garnered in the past twenty or thirty seconds —
you're pretty much on your way with Quicken. To see the account register
window you'll spend most of your time working with, click the Registr icon.
Quicken displays the account register (Checking: Bank) window shown in
Figure 1-3. That thing in the lower right corner of the screen is a Qcard. In the
chapters that follow, you'll basically learn how to use this account register to
keep track of all your financial affairs.

Setting up Quicken if you've used Quicken before

Let's say that you're not new in town. Suppose that you're a Quicken veteran.
An old hand. A long-time friend. Well, anyway, you get the idea.

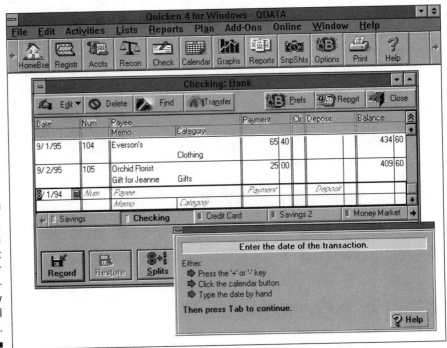

Figure 1-3:
The Quicken
account
register
window —
this is really
where it all
happens.

Can you use the existing Quicken files you've been working on? Sure you can, as long as you've been using Quicken for DOS versions 5.0, 6.0, 7.0, or Quicken for Windows versions 1.0, 2.0, or 3.0. In fact, if the Quicken installation program can find a version of old Quicken files on your desk, it'll ask you if it should move them to the new Quicken directory. If you're asked this question, answer "Yes" by clicking the Move button.

If Quicken doesn't find the old files, you need to specifically open the files.

Using the File Open command

Use the File menu's Open command to select and open your existing Quicken files.

Here's how you do this:

1. Choose the File⇨Open command.

Press Alt+F, O, for example. Figure 1-4 shows the Open Quicken File dialog box that appears after you choose the command. Quicken uses this dialog box to ask the burning question: "Hey, buddy, what file you wanna open?"

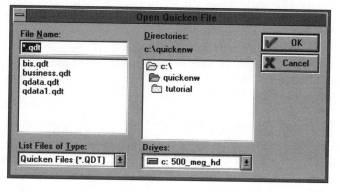

Figure 1-4:
The Open
Quicken File
dialog box.

2. Tell Quicken which drive the files are stored on.

If the correct drive isn't the one already shown in the Drives text box in the Open Quicken File dialog box, tell Quicken which is the correct drive. Click the down arrow at the end of the Drives box. When you do, Quicken drops down a list of the disk drives your computer has. (This is why, as a point of fact, the little Drives box is called a drop-down list box. Get it?) When the list of disk drives appears, click the one where you've stored your Quicken files. Quicken closes the drop-down list box and displays your selection in the Drives box.

3. Tell Quicken in which directory you've stored your existing Quicken files.

If the active directory shown in the Directories box in the Open Quicken File dialog box isn't where the existing Quicken files are located, you need to tell Quicken where you store the files. If you've been working with Quicken for DOS, your files are probably stored in the Quicken directory which will be in the main, or root, directory on your C drive. To tell Quicken to look in the root directory, click the first line of the Directories list box — the one that shows the following:

```
C:\
```

Quicken displays a list of all the directories in the main directory or root directory. Use the PgDn key or the mouse to scroll through the list until you see the name of the directory in which your Quicken data files are stored — probably QUICKEN. Then click this directory to select it.

4. Select the file from the File Name list box.

After you tell Quicken on which disk and in which directory you stored your data files, the Quicken files in that location appear in the File Name list box. Just click the file you want. If the list is long, click the first file in the list and then use the PgDn and PgUp keys or mouse to scroll through the list. Quicken data files, by the way, use the QDT file extension.

5. Choose OK.

After you find the file, choose OK by clicking the OK button. Quicken opens the file and displays the active account in the Register document window. (Quicken will display its Reminder window to show any unprinted checks or scheduled transactions.)

What if you can't find the Quicken file?

Uh-oh. This is a problem. But don't worry. You're not out of luck. What you need to do is to look through each of the directories on the disk. Or, if you've got more than one hard disk, look through each of the directories on each of the hard drives.

Bummer, huh? Maybe this is a reasonable place to bring up a point. If you're a new user, it's really best to just go with whatever an application (such as Quicken) suggests. If Quicken suggests that you use the QUICKENW directory — this is the suggestion for Windows versions of Quicken, by the way — just do it. If Quicken suggests that you use the drive C, just do it. If Quicken suggests that you take all your money, put it in a coffee can, and bury the can in your backyard. . . . Whoa, wait a minute. Bad idea.

Maybe there's a better rule. Hmmm. . . . How about this? While you shouldn't follow suggestions blindly and without thinking, you also shouldn't ignore Quicken's suggestions unless you've got a good reason. And "Just because . . . ," "I don't know," and "For the heck of it" aren't very good reasons.

Command shortcuts

If you look closely at any menu, including the File menu, you will notice that a key combination follows many menu names. After the File menu's Open command, for example, you can see Ctrl+O. Key combinations such as Ctrl+O represent com-mand shortcuts. By simultaneously pressing the two keys, you choose the command. Pressing Ctrl+O, for example, is equivalent to choosing the Open command from the File menu.

Starting Quicken for the Second Time

The second time you start Quicken — and every subsequent time, too — things work pretty much the same way as the first time. The only real difference is that if you installed Quicken in the usual way, it'll display the Quicken Reminders window (see Figure 1-5). What this window does is, in effect, show you half-completed transactions you still need to do something with — such as checks you entered but still need to print.

Figure 1-5: The Quicken Reminders window shows you half-completed transactions you still need to do something with.

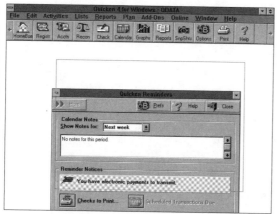

You don't need to pay any attention to the Quicken Reminders window right now. I'll talk about how you use it later in the book. You can remove the Quicken Reminders window by clicking its Close button.

Chapter 2
Introduction to the Big Picture

· ·

· ·

*B*efore you spend a bunch of time and money on Quicken, you must understand the big picture. You need to know what Quicken can do. You need to know what you actually want to do. And, as a practical matter, you need to tell Quicken what you want it to do.

Boiling Quicken Down to Its Essence

When you boil Quicken down to its essence, it does four things:

1. **It lets you track your tax deductions.**

   This makes preparing your personal or business tax return easier for you or your poor accountant, Cratchit.

2. **It lets you monitor your income and outgo either on-screen or by using printed reports.**

   Usually this stuff is great fodder for discussions about the family finances.

3. **It lets you print checks.**

   This device is mostly a timesaver, but it can also be useful for people who are neat-freaks.

4. **It lets you track the things you own (such as bank accounts, investments, and real estate) and the debts you owe (such as home mortgage principal, car loan balances, and credit card balances).**

You can do some of these things or all of these things with Quicken.

Tracking tax deductions

To track your tax deductions, make a list of the deductions you want to track. To do so, pull out last year's tax return. Note which lines you filled in. This tactic works because there's a darn good chance that the tax deductions you claimed last year will also be the tax deductions you'll claim in the future.

Just a little bit later in the chapter you'll learn about Quicken's categories, which are used to track your tax deductions.

Monitoring spending

At our house we (Sue, my wife, and me, your humble author) use Quicken to monitor our spending on the mundane little necessities of life: groceries, clothing, baby food, cable television, and, well . . . you get the picture. (Yeah, I do watch too much TV.)

To keep track of how much we spend on various items, we also use Quicken's categories. (Is the suspense building?)

If there is a spending category you want to monitor, it's really easier to decide up front what it is.

Your list of spending categories, by the way, shouldn't be an exhaustive list of super-fine pigeon-holes like "Friday-night Mexican food," "Fast food for lunch," and so on. To track your spending or eating out, one category named something like "Meals" or "Grub" usually is easiest.

In fact, I'm going to go out on a limb. You can probably get away with half a dozen categories or less:

- Household Items (food, toiletries, cleaning supplies)
- Car
- Rent (or mortgage payments)
- Entertainment and Vacation
- Clothing
- Work Expenses

If you want to, of course, you can expand this list. Heck, you can include dozens and dozens of categories. My experience, though, is that you'll probably only use a handful of categories.

Do you want to print checks?

You can use Quicken to print checks. And this little trick provides a couple of benefits: it's really fast if you have a lot of checks to print, and your printed checks look very neat and darn professional.

To print checks you need to do just two things. First, look through the check supply information that comes with Quicken and pick a check form that suits your style. Then order the form. (The check forms that come with remittance advices — or check stubs —work well for businesses.)

You'll notice that the preprinted check forms aren't cheap. If you're using Quicken at home with personal-style checks (like those that go in your wallet), using computer checks may not be cost effective. Even if you're using Quicken for a business where you are used to buying those outrageously expensive business-style checks, you'll still find computer checks a bit more expensive.

I'm pretty much a cheapskate, so I don't use printed checks at home or in my business. I should admit, however, that I also don't write very many checks.

By the way, I've "checked" around. Although you can order Quicken check forms from other sources (like your local office supplies store), they're about the same price from Intuit (the maker of Quicken).

Tracking bank accounts, credit cards, and other stuff

You must decide which bank accounts and credit cards you want to track. In most cases, you want to track each bank account you use and any credit card on which you carry a balance.

You may also want to track other assets and liabilities. *Assets* are just things you own: investments, cars, a house, and so on. *Liabilities* are things you owe: margin loans from your broker, car loans, a mortgage, and so on.

Shoot, I suppose you could even track the things your neighbor owns — or perhaps just those things you especially covet. I'm not sure that this is a very good idea, though. (Maybe a healthier approach is to track just those things which your neighbor owns, but you've borrowed.)

Setting Up Additional Accounts

When you start Quicken for the first time, you set up a checking account, a savings account, and a credit card account. If you want to track any additional accounts — for example, an additional savings account — you must set them up, too.

Setting up an additional bank account

To set up a bank account, give the account a name and then its balance as of a set date. Here's how:

1. Choose the Accts icon button.

You can also choose Account from the Lists menu. Quicken displays the Account List window, as shown in Figure 2-1.

2. Choose the New button in the Account List window.

Quicken displays the Create New Account dialog box (see Figure 2-2).

3. Unmark the Guide Me check box.

You don't need Quicken's guidance. You have me.

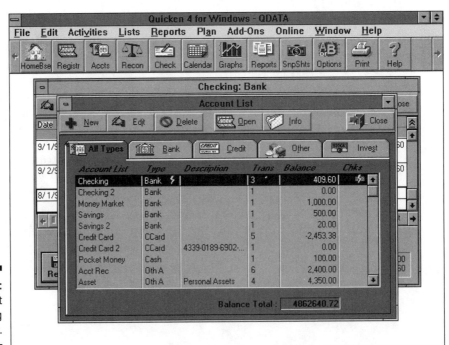

Figure 2-1:
The Account
List dialog
box.

Figure 2-2:
The Create
New
Account
dialog box.

4. **Choose the type of account.**

   Tell Quicken which type of account you want to set up by clicking one of the account buttons. (I'm assuming that at this point you're just doing bank accounts. I'll discuss why and when you use the remaining account types later in the book.) Quicken displays Create Account dialog box (see Figure 2-3).

   Wondering about those other accounts? If the suspense is just killing you, you can look ahead. Chapter 10 describes how to set up and use Credit Card accounts. Chapter 14 describes how to set up and use a Cash account. Chapter 11 describes how to set up and use Liability accounts. Chapters 12 and 13 describe how to set up and use Investment accounts. And, finally, Chapter 16 describes how to set up and use Assets accounts.

5. **Name the account.**

   Move the cursor to the Account Name text box and enter a name.

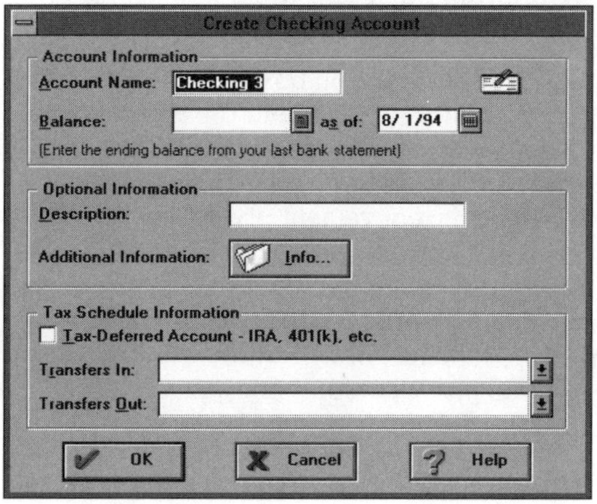

Figure 2-3:
The Create
Checking
Account
dialog box.

6. Enter the bank account balance.

Move the cursor to the Balance text box and enter the balance using the number keys. (The folks at Intuit, by the way, really want you to use the balance from your bank statement. If you have terrible financial records — for example, you haven't reconciled your account since Ronald Reagan left office — this idea is probably good advice. If you have neat, accurate financial records, go ahead and use your check register balance.)

If you use the bank statement balance as your starting balance, enter all the transactions that cleared after the bank statement balance date. This should make sense, right? If a check or deposit isn't reflected in the bank statement figure, you must enter it later.

7. Enter the account balance date.

Enter the date you'll start keeping records for the bank account with Quicken. Move the cursor to the As Of text box and type the month number, a slash, the day number, a slash, and the year number. If you start on January 1, 1994, for example, type **1/1/94**. Or, if this is way too complicated for you, click the down arrow at the end of the As Of text box so that Quicken displays a pop-up calendar. Then click the date. Use the << and >> buttons to move back and forth a month at a time.

8. Indicate whether this account is tax deferred.

You need to indicate whether an account's interest income is tax deferred. You do this by marking the Tax Deferred Account check box. Just for the record, it's highly unlikely that this is the case with a simple bank account.

9. Enter the account description.

Move the cursor to the Description text box and type whatever you want to use to describe the account. Your favorite color, the name of your first boyfriend or girlfriend, or anything else you want. Heck, you may even want to follow the pack and type a description of the account here. (Some people get really crazy and enter the account number, for example.)

10. Collect a bit more information if you want.

See that command button labeled "Info…" If you click it, Quicken displays another dialog box. This other dialog box provides spaces for you to record a bunch of other information about the bank account you're setting up: the name of the bank, your account number, the name of the person you deal with at the bank, and so on. You can fill in this stuff if you want to and would like a reasonably convenient place to store this information.

11. Choose OK.

Quicken redisplays the Account List dialog box — just like the one I showed in Figure 2-1. This time, however, the window will list an additional account — the one you just created.

12. **Close the Account List dialog box if you don't need it any longer.**

    You can do so by double-clicking the dialog box's control menu. Or you can activate the control menu and choose Close. (To activate the dialog box's control menu, click the "hyphen" in the upper-left corner of the window.)

Hey, Quicken, I want to use that account!

In Quicken, you work with one account at a time. The logic is quite simple: in Quicken you record income and expense for a particular account — a specific checking account, savings account, and so on.

You use the Account List dialog box (see Figure 2-1) to tell Quicken which account you want to work with.

To display the Account List dialog box, choose the Accts icon button, or choose the Account command from the Lists menu. (If you're experiencing a sense of *déjà vu* right now, it's probably because I've already told you about these commands earlier in the chapter.)

After you display the Account List dialog box, highlight the account you want by using the up- and down-arrow keys or by clicking the mouse. Then press Enter or choose Open. Quicken selects the account and displays either the register window or the Write Checks window. (Chapter 4 describes how to enter checking account transactions.)

Let me see if there's anything else I should tell you at this point. Oh yes, I know. If the Account List dialog box gets in your way after you display it, you can remove it from the application window by clicking the Close button.

Whipping Your Category Lists into Shape

When you set up Quicken, you told it to use either the predefined business categories or both the home and business categories.

The predefined categories lists may be just want you want. Then again, they may not. Table 2-1 shows the home categories list, and Table 2-2 shows the business categories list. If you told Quicken to use both the home and business categories, your actual category list combines the categories shown in Table 2-1 and those shown in Table 2-2.

Take a minute to look through both lists. If you find categories you don't need, cross them off the list in the book. You'll be able to delete them in a minute or so on your computer. If you need categories you don't see, add them at the bottom of the list. You'll be able to add them in about two minutes or so.

Remember that determining whether you need or don't need a category is pretty simple:

- ✔ To track a certain income or spending item for income tax purposes, you need a Quicken category.

- ✔ To track a certain income or spending item because you're just interested in how much you really spend (for example, renting VCR tapes), you need a Quicken category.

- ✔ Because you also budget by categories, you need a category for any income or spending item that you want to budget.

Table 2-1	The Predefined Home Categories
Categories	*Descriptions*
Income Categories	
Bonus	Bonus Income
Canada Pen	Canadian Pension
Div Income	Dividend Income
Gift Received	Gift Received
Int Inc	Interest Income
Invest Inc	Investment Income
Old Age Pension	Old Age Pension
Other Inc	Other Income
Salary	Salary Income
Expense Categories	
Auto	Automobile Expenses
Fuel	Auto Fuel
Loan	Auto Loan Payment
Service	Auto Service
Bank Chrg	Bank Charge
Charity	Charitable Donations
Cash	Cash Contributions
Non-cash	Non-cash Contributions
Childcare	Childcare Expense
Christmas	Christmas Expenses

Categories	Descriptions
Clothing	Clothing
Dining	Dining Out
Dues	Dues
Education	Education
Entertain	Entertainment
Gifts	Gift Expenses
Groceries	Groceries
Home Rpair	Home Repair & Maintenance
Household	Household Miscellaneous Expense
Housing	Housing
Insurance	Insurance
Int Exp	Interest Expense
Invest Exp	Investment Expense
Medical	Medical Expense
Doctor	Doctor & Dental Visits
Medicine	Medicine & Drugs
Misc	Miscellaneous
Mort Int	Mortgage Interest Expense
Other Exp	Other Expenses
Recreation	Recreation Expense
RRSP	Reg Retirement Savings Plan
Subscriptions	Subscriptions
Supplies	Supplies
Tax	Taxes
Fed	Federal Tax
Medicare	Medicare Tax
Other	Miscellaneous Taxes
Prop	Property Tax
Soc Sec	Social Security Tax
State	State Tax

(continued)

Table 2-1 *(continued)*

Categories	Descriptions
Tax Spouse	Spouse's Taxes
Fed	Federal Tax
Medicare	Medicare Tax
Soc Sec	Social Security Tax
State	State Tax
UIC	Unemployment Insurance Commission
Utilities	Water, Gas, Electric
Gas & Electric	Gas and Electricity
Water	Water

Table 2-2   The Predefined Business Categories

Categories	Descriptions
Income Categories	
Other Inc	Other Income
Rent Income	Rent Income
Expense Categories	
Ads	Advertising
Bus. Insurance	Insurance (not health)
Bus. Utilities	Water, Gas & Electric
Business Tax	Taxes & Licenses
Car	Car & Truck
Commission	Commissions
Freight	Freight
Int Paid	Interest Paid
L&P Fees	Legal & Professional Fees
Meals & Entertn	Meals & Entertainment
Office	Office Expenses
Rent on Equip	Rent - Vehicle, Machinery, Equipment
Rent Paid	Rent Paid

Categories	Descriptions
Repairs	Repairs
Returns	Returns & Allowances
Supplies, Bus.	Supplies
Travel	Travel Expenses
Wages	Wages & Job Credits

Subcategories . . . yikes, what are they?

One of the things I'm trying to do with this book is make Quicken easier for you to use. A big part of this goal is telling you which features you can ignore if you're feeling a bit overwhelmed. Subcategories are among those things I think you can ignore.

"Subcategories," you say. "Yikes, what are they?"

Subcategories are categories within categories. If you look at the Taxes expense category in Table 2-1, for example, you'll notice a bunch of categories that follow the Tax category and are slightly indented: Fed (Federal Tax), Medicare (Medicare Tax), Other (Miscellaneous Taxes), Prop (Property Tax), Soc Sec (Social Security Tax), and State (State Tax).

When you use subcategories, you can tag a transaction that pays, for example, federal taxes; you can further break down this category into subcategories like federal income tax, Medicare tax, and Social Security tax. If you want to see a list of the ways you've spent your money, Quicken summarizes your spending both by category and, within a category, by subcategory. On a Quicken report, then, you can see this level of detail:

Taxes

Federal Tax	900
Medicare Tax	100
Soc Sec Tax	700
Total Taxes	1700

Subcategories are useful tools. There's no doubt about it. But they make working with Quicken a little more complicated and a little more difficult. As a practical matter, though, you usually don't need them. If you want to track a spending category, it really belongs on your list as a full-fledged category. For these reasons, I'm not going to get into subcategories here.

If you get excited about the topic of subcategories later on — after you have the hang of Quicken — you can peruse the Quicken documentation for more information.

If you do want to use Quicken's subcategories, don't delete the subcategories shown in Table 2-1. If you don't want to use the subcategories, go ahead and delete them.

Supercategories . . . double yikes!

Supercategories are a recent invention of the Intuit development people. (The supercategory feature appears only in the most recent versions of the DOS, Windows, and Macintosh products.) Supercategories combine categories into sets you can use in reports and in your budgeting. Sure. They're sort of cool. But you don't need to worry about them if you're just starting with Quicken.

Three tips on categorization

I have just three tips for categorizing:

1. **Cross off any category you won't use.**

   If you're Jewish or Muslim, for example, you may decide to delete the Christmas Gift category. If you're a Canadian, get rid of the United States tax categories. Extra, unneeded categories just clutter your list. (I think it's great if you can get down to just a handful of categories.)

2. **Don't be afraid to lump similar spending categories together.**

   Take your utilities expense, for example. If you pay water, natural gas, electricity, and sewer, why not use a single Utilities category? (If you pay different utility companies for your water, natural gas, electricity, and sewer, you'll still be able to see what you spent on just electricity, for example, even with a single, catch-all category for utilities.)

3. **Be sure to categorize anything that may be a tax deduction.**

   Categorize medical and dental expenses, state and local income taxes, real estate taxes, personal property taxes, home mortgage interest and points, investment interest, charitable contributions, casualty and theft losses, moving expenses, unreimbursed employee expenses, and all those vague miscellaneous deductions. (By the way, the foregoing is the complete list of itemized deductions at the time this book was being written.)

Ch-ch-changing a category list

OK, you should now be ready to fix any category list problems. Basically, you will do three things: add categories, remove categories, and change category names and descriptions.

Adding categories you'd love to use

Adding categories is a snap. Here's all you have to do:

1. **Choose the Category & Transfer command from the Lists menu.**

   Quicken displays the Category & Transfer List window (see Figure 2-4). This window lists the categories available and the accounts you've set up.

2. **Select the New button on the Category & Transfer List window.**

   Quicken, dutifully following your every command, displays the Set Up Category dialog box (see Figure 2-5). It probably won't surprise you to learn that you use this puppy to describe the new category.

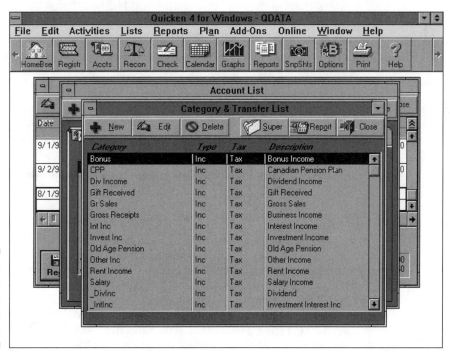

Figure 2-4:
The
Category &
Transfer List
window.

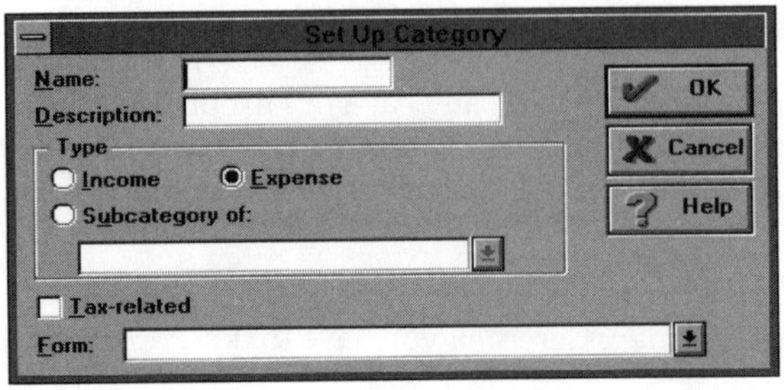

Figure 2-5:
The Set Up
Category
dialog box.

3. **Enter a short name for the category.**

   Move the cursor to the Name text box and enter a name. Although you can use up to 15 characters, use as short a name as possible to clearly identify the category. Why? Because you'll need to use this category name every time you want to tag a transaction to fall into the category.

4. **Enter a description for the category.**

   Move the cursor to the Description text box and then describe the category. (If you don't enter a description, Quicken uses the category name on reports that show the category.)

5. **Indicate whether the category is an income category or an expense category.**

   Select the appropriate Income, Expense, or Subcategory radio button — just click your furry little friend, the mouse. If you've totally blown off my admonition not to use subcategories just yet, use the dialog box's drop-down list to indicate into which income or expense category a new subcategory falls.

6. **Indicate whether the category tracks an amount you will use on an input line on next year's tax return. (By line, I mean the actual tax form line — such as line 7 on the 1040 form.)**

   Move the cursor to the Tax-related check box and then mark the check box if the category is tax-related, or unmark the check box if the category isn't tax-related. Just to clear up any confusion, vacationing in Hawaii isn't a tax deduction — even if the guy on Channel 22 promises it is.

7. **Choose OK.**

   Quicken adds the new category to the Category & Transfer List window shown in Figure 2-4 and then redisplays the window. Now that you understand the stuff in the Category & Transfer List window, note that it shows the category name, its type, the notation that a category is tax-related, and, golly darn, even its description.

Removing categories you loathe

Removing categories takes only a couple of keystrokes. With the Category & Transfer List window displayed, use the arrow keys or click the mouse to highlight the category you want to remove. Then select the Delete button. Quicken displays a message that asks you to confirm your decision. Assuming that you want to remove the selected category, choose OK. Otherwise, press Esc or click Cancel.

Changing category names and descriptions

You can change a category name, its type, its description, and its tax-related setting if you later discover you've made some mistake, such as misspelling a word in a description.

To do so, display the Category & Transfer List window. Use the arrow keys or click your mouse to highlight the category you want to change. Then click the category and choose the Edit button. Quicken, in a surprise move, displays a dialog box which is cleverly labeled Edit Category (see Figure 2-6). The dialog box's text boxes and option buttons describe the selected category's information: name, description, type, and tax-related setting.

Figure 2-6:
The Edit
Category
dialog box.

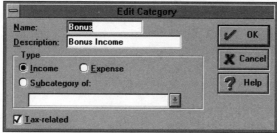

Make the changes you want by replacing text box contents or changing option button settings. Then choose OK to save your changes and return to the Category & Transfer List window.

Do You Need a Little Class?

Categories aren't the only way you can summarize your financial records. Quicken provides a second tool, called *classes*.

I have mixed feelings about classes, and I'll tell you why. I use them — with good success — to track the types of gross income that my business produces (writing, consulting, teaching, and so on) and the types of expenses my business incurs in these activities. (In fact, *Writing*, *Consulting*, and *Teaching* are the names of three of my classes.)

Classes present a couple of problems, however. First, you can't budget by classes. (Before you say, "Ah, Steve, I don't want to budget," please read the next chapter.) Second, you need to remember to tag transactions with their classes. (In comparison, Quicken will remind you to include a category.)

Because I really don't think you'll use it now, I'm not going to describe how you use classes. But if you get really comfortable with Quicken's categories and you want a way to organize your financial information across categories, consider using Quicken's classes. You can flip to the Quicken documentation to get this information.

Chapter 3
Maximum Fun, Maximum Profits

. . . .

In This Chapter

▶ Tips for personal budgets

▶ Tips for business budgets

▶ Setting up a budget manually

▶ Setting up a budget automatically

. . . .

I don't think a budget amounts to financial handcuffs and neither should you. A budget is really a plan that outlines the way people need to spend their money to achieve the maximum amount of fun or the way businesses need to spend their money to make the most profit.

Should You Even Bother?

A budget, as you probably know, is just a list of the ways you earn and spend your money. And if you've created a good, workable categories list, you're halfway to a good solid budget. (In fact, the only step left is to specify how much you earn in each income category and how much you spend in each expense category.)

Does everybody need a budget? No, of course not. Maybe at your house, you're already having a bunch of fun with your money. (You lucky dog!) Maybe in your business, you make your money so effortlessly that there's really no reason to plan your income and outgo. (And just what business are you in?)

For everyone else, though, a budget improves your chances of getting to wherever it is you want to go financially. In fact, I'll stop calling it a budget. The word has such negative connotations. I know — I'll call it *The Secret Plan.*

Serious Advice about Your Secret Plan

Before I walk you through the mechanics of outlining your secret plan, I want to give you a few tips.

Your personal secret plan

You can do certain things to make it more likely that your secret plan will work. Here are four things:

✔ *Plan your income and expenses as a family.*

When it comes to this sort of planning, two heads are invariably better than one. What's more, though I don't really want to get into marriage counseling here, a family's budget — oops, I mean secret plan — needs to reflect the priorities and feelings of everyone who has to live within the plan. Don't use a secret plan as a way to minimize what your spouse spends on clothing or on long-distance telephone charges talking to relatives in the old country. You need to resolve clothing and long-distance charges issues before you finalize your secret plan, anyway.

✔ *Include some cushion in your plan.*

In other words, don't budget to spend every last dollar (or if you're German, every last deutsche mark). If you plan from the start to spend every dollar you make, you'll undoubtedly have to fight the mother of all financial battles: paying for unexpected expenses when you don't have any money. (You know the sort of things I mean—car repairs, medical expenses, or that cocktail dress or tuxedo you absolutely *must* have for a special party.)

✔ *Regularly compare your actual income and outgo to your planned income and outgo.*

This is probably the most important part and also what Quicken will help you with the most. As long as you use Quicken to record what you receive and spend, you'll be able to print reports showing what you planned and what actually occurred.

✔ *Make adjustments as necessary.*

When there are problems with your secret plan — and there will be — you'll know that your plan isn't working. You can then make adjustments, by spending a little less calling the old country, for example.

Your business secret plan

These tips for personal secret plans also apply to businesses. But I've also got a special tip for small businesses using Quicken. (I'm going to write very quietly now so that no one else hears…).

Here's the secret tip: go to the library, ask for the Robert Morris & Associates Survey, and look up the ways that other businesses like yours spend money.

This is really cool. Robert Morris & Associates surveys bank lending officers, creates a summary of the information these bankers receive from their customers, and publishes the results. For example, you can look up what percentage of sales the average tavern spends on beer and peanuts.

Plan to take an hour or so at the library. It takes a while to get used to the way the Robert Morris & Associates information is displayed. There won't actually be a line on the tavern's page labeled "beer and peanuts," for example. It'll be called "cost of goods sold" or some similarly vague accounting term. (You've got to love those accountants, huh?)

Remember to make a few notes so that you can use the information you glean to better plan your own business financial affairs.

Two things that really goof up secret plans

Because we're talking about you-know-what, let me touch on a couple of things that really goof up your financial plans: windfalls and monster changes.

The problem with windfalls

Your boss smiles, calls you into his office, and then gives you the good news. You're getting a bonus: $5,000! *Yippee!* you think to yourself. Outside, of course, you maintain your dignity. You act grateful, but not gushy. Then you call your husband.

Here's what happens next. Bob (that's your husband's name) gets excited, congratulates you, and tells you he'll pick up a bottle of wine on the way home to celebrate.

On your drive home you mull over the possibilities and conclude that you can use the $5,000 as a big down payment for that new family van you've been looking at. (With the trade-in and the $5,000, your payments will be a manageable $200 a month.)

Bob, on his way home, stops to look at those golf clubs he's been coveting for about three years, charges $800 on his credit card, and then, feeling slightly guilty, buys you the $600 set. (Let's say that you're just starting to play golf.)

You may laugh at this scenario, but suppose that it really happened. Furthermore, pretend that you really do buy the van. At this point, you've spent $6,400 on a van and golf clubs, and you've signed up for what you're guessing will be another $200-a-month payment.

This turn of events doesn't sound all that bad now, does it?

Here's the problem. When you get your check, it's not going to be $5,000. You're probably going to pay roughly $400 of Social Security and Medicare taxes, maybe around $1,500 in federal income taxes, and then probably some state income taxes. (Gotta love your government!)

There may be other money taken out, too, for forced savings plans (like a 401K plan) or for charitable giving. After all is said and done, you'll get maybe half the bonus in cash — say $2,500.

Now you see the problem, of course. You've got $2,500 in cold, hard cash, but with Bob's help you've already spent $6,400 and signed up for $200-a-month payments.

In a nutshell, there are two big problems with windfalls. Problem one is that you never get the entire windfall — yet it's easy to spend like you will. Problem two is that windfalls, by their very nature, tend to get used for big purchases (often as down payments) that ratchet up your living expenses. Boats. New houses. Cars.

Regarding windfalls, my advice to you is simple:

- ✔ Don't spend a windfall until you actually hold the check in your hot little hand. (It's even better to wait, say, six months. That way Bob can really think about whether he needs those new golf clubs.)

- ✔ Don't spend a windfall on something that increases your monthly living expenses without first redoing your budget.

About monster income changes

If your income changes radically, it becomes *really* hard to plan.

Suppose that your income doubles. One day you're cruising along making $35,000 and the next day you're suddenly making $70,000. (Congratulations, by the way.)

I'll tell you what you'll discover, however, should you find yourself in this position. You'll find that $70,000 a year isn't as much money as you might think.

Go ahead. Laugh. But for one thing, if your income doubles, your income taxes almost certainly more than quadruple.

One of the great myths about income taxes is that the rich don't pay very much or that they pay the same percentage. Poppycock. If you make $30,000 a year and you're an average family, you probably pay about $1,500 in federal income taxes. If you make $200,000 a year, you'll pay about $45,000 a year. So if your salary increases by roughly seven times, your income taxes increase by about thirty times. I don't bring this fact up to get you agitated about whether it's right or fair to make the rich pay more; I bring it up so that you can better plan for any monster income changes you experience.

Another thing — and I know it sounds crazy — but you'll find it hard to spend $70,000 smartly when you've been making a lot less. And if you start making some big purchases such as houses and cars and speedboats, you'll not only burn through a lot of cash, you'll also ratchet up your monthly living expenses.

Monster income changes that go the other way are even more difficult. If you've been making, say, $70,000 a year and then see your salary drop to a darn respectable $35,000, it's going to hurt, too. And probably more than you think.

That old living-expenses ratcheting effect comes into play here, of course. Presumably, if you've been making $70,000 a year, you've been spending it — or most of it.

But there are some other reasons why it's very difficult — at least initially — to have a monster salary drop. You've probably chosen friends (nice people, like the Joneses), clothing stores, and hobbies that are in line with your income.

Another thing about a moster salary drop is sort of subtle. You probably denominate your purchases in amounts related to your income. Make $35,000 and you think in terms of $5 or $10 purchases. But make $70,000 a year and you think in terms of $10 or $20 purchases.

This observation all makes perfect sense. But if your income drops from $70,000 down to $35,000, you'll probably still find yourself thinking of those old $20 purchases.

So what to do? If you do experience a monster income change, redo your secret plan. Be particularly careful and thoughtful, though.

Zen and monster income changes

To conclude this secret plan business, I'll make a philosophical digression.

At the point you've provided yourself and your family with the creature comforts — a cozy place to live, adequate food, and comfortable clothes — more stuff won't make the difference that you think.

I don't mean to minimize the challenges of raising a family of four on, say, $14,000 a year. But, hey, I work with a fair number of wealthy people. What continually surprises me is that when you get right down to it, someone who makes $300,000 or $600,000 a year doesn't live a better life than someone who makes $30,000.

Sure, they spend more money. They buy more stuff. They buy more expensive stuff. But they don't live better. They don't have better marriages. Their kids don't love them more. They don't have better friends or more considerate neighbors.

But you already know all this. I know you do.

Setting Up a Secret Plan

OK, enough metaphysical stuff. Let's set up your budget — er, I mean, secret plan.

Getting to the Budget window

To get to the window in which you'll enter your budget, just choose the Budgeting command from the Plan menu. Quicken displays the Budget window shown in Figure 3-1.

There's nothing very complicated about the window. The income and expense categories — including the ones you've created — appear along the left edge of the screen. There are subtotals for any categories with subcategories (if you have these), for the total inflows, and for the total outflows.

Across the top of the screen, there's a row of command buttons that make your budgeting job easier. (I'll describe the more useful commands in a few paragraphs and provide brief descriptions of those that aren't quite as useful.)

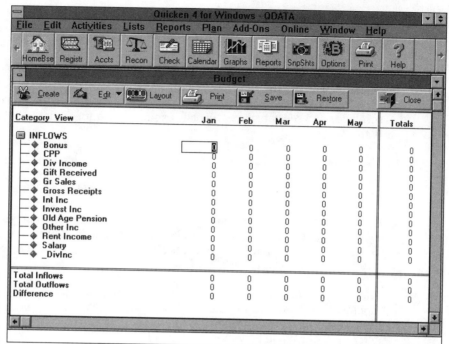

Figure 3-1:
The Budget
window.

Entering budgeted amounts the simple way

Here's the two-step way to enter budgeted amounts — not to be confused with the Texas Two-Step:

1. **Select the amount you want to budget.**

   Highlight the budgeted income or expense amount you want to enter either by using the arrow keys or by clicking the amount with the mouse. For example, to select the January Salary budget field, click it with the mouse. Or use the arrow keys to move the square and highlight the field. (You're doing this stuff so that you can enter the budgeted amount.)

2. **Enter the budgeted amount.**

   Type the amount you've budgeted. Suppose that you've already selected the January Salary budget field and now need to enter a value. Say that you take home $3,000 a month. To use this figure as the January Salary budget, type **3000**.

After you press Enter, Quicken updates any subtotals and grand totals that use the Salary Income amount, as shown in Figure 3-2. For example, look at the Total Inflows subtotal at the bottom of the screen. And look at the Totals column along the right edge of the window.

You need to scroll the screen to the right to see months near the middle and end of the year. Unless you're using a really short categories list, you need to scroll down to see categories (usually expense categories) that aren't at the top of the list.

The easiest way to scroll is by using the mouse to click and drag on the scroll bars. If you don't already know how to do this, you can experiment (probably the most fun), or you can flip to Appendix B, "Quick and Dirty Windows."

If you don't want to use the mouse or you just need to be different, you can use the old navigation keys, too. To scroll the screen right, just press the Tab key. To scroll the screen back, or left, press Shift+Tab. To scroll the screen up and down, use the PgUp and PgDn keys.

The Category View and Totals columns don't scroll. You know what else? The months, Total Inflows, and Total Outflows rows don't scroll either. Quicken leaves these elements frozen in the window so that you can tell which column and row is which and how things are going.

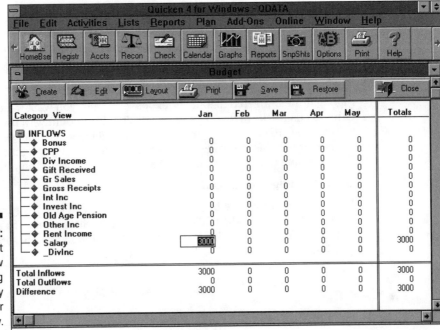

Figure 3-2:
The Budget window showing salary income for January.

Category View	Jan	Feb	Mar	Apr	May	Totals
INFLOWS						
Bonus	0	0	0	0	0	0
CPP	0	0	0	0	0	0
Div Income	0	0	0	0	0	0
Gift Received	0	0	0	0	0	0
Gr Sales	0	0	0	0	0	0
Gross Receipts	0	0	0	0	0	0
Int Inc	0	0	0	0	0	0
Invest Inc	0	0	0	0	0	0
Old Age Pension	0	0	0	0	0	0
Other Inc	0	0	0	0	0	0
Rent Income	0	0	0	0	0	0
Salary	3000	0	0	0	0	3000
_DivInc	0	0	0	0	0	0
Total Inflows	3000	0	0	0	0	3000
Total Outflows	0	0	0	0	0	0
Difference	3000	0	0	0	0	3000

Entering budgeted amounts the fast way

It just figures, doesn't it? There's the simple way and there's the fast way, and "never the 'twain shall meet."

If monthly budgeted amounts are the same over the year

Enter the first month's figures (as I described earlier). After you've done this step, choose the Edit button and then choose Fill Columns. If you choose Yes in the window that appears, Quicken takes your January budget numbers and copies them into February, March, April, and through the rest of the year.

What if you make a mistake? What if you fill some row with a bunch of goofy numbers? No problem. Move the selection cursor to that row and choose the Clear Row command from the Edit menu (the one that appears when you clidk the Edit button).

If budgeted amounts are the same as last year

If you used Quicken for record-keeping in the prior year, you can copy the actual amounts from the previous year and use these as part or all of the current year's budget.

To do so, choose the Create button. Quicken displays the Automatically Create Budget dialog box, as shown in Figure 3-3. You can then tell Quicken what it should copy from last year.

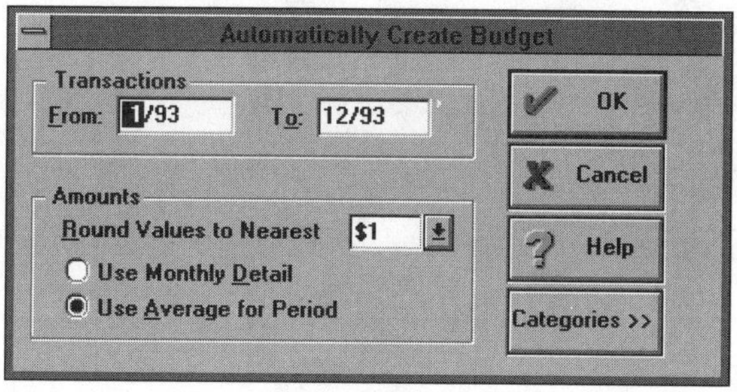

Figure 3-3:
The
AutoCreate
Budget
dialog box.

Here's how to use this dialog box:

1. **Indicate which months you want to copy.**

   Use the From and To text boxes to indicate from which months in the previous year actual category totals should be copied. If you want to copy the entire previous year and it's now 1995, for example, specify these entries as **1/94** and **12/94**.

2. Indicate whether the actual category totals should be rounded.

Want to round the actual category totals? No problem. Just use the Round Values to Nearest drop-down list box to indicate how much rounding you want: to the nearest $1, to the nearest $10, or to the nearest $100.

3. Use category averages (optional).

To use the average actual spending in a category for the months identified in the From and To text boxes, indicate that you want to use averages for the period. To do so, mark the Use Average for Period option button. If you leave the Use Monthly Detail option button marked, Quicken doesn't calculate and use averages; it just uses the actual monthly amounts from the previous year as the budgeted monthly amounts for the current year.

4. Limit the categories automatically budgeted (optional).

To tell Quicken you want only some of your categories automatically budgeted, choose the Categories button. Quicken adds a list of categories to the dialog box (see Figure 3-4). Indicate which categories should be automatically budgeted by marking them. To mark or unmark a category, click it. To mark all the categories, choose Mark All. To unmark all the categories, choose Clear All.

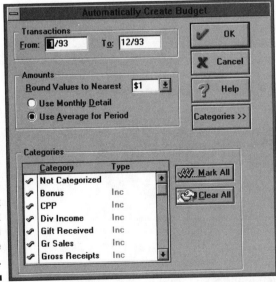

Figure 3-4:
The expanded Automatically Create Budget dialog box after you choose Categories.

5. Choose OK.

Quicken uses the information entered on the Automatically Create Budget dialog box and the previous year's actual category totals to completely fill in the Budget window.

If a single category's monthly budget is the same over the year

Hey, you're on a roll now. So let's say that a single category's monthly budget is the same over the year.

To do so, enter the first month's budget figure as described earlier. Choose the Edit button and choose the Fill Row Right command. If you choose Yes, Quicken takes the budget number for the highlighted category and copies it into the following months — probably February, March, April, and so on, through the rest of the year.

You can use Fill Row Right to copy budget amounts forward from months besides January. For example, if your rent runs $500 a month from January through June and then $600 from July through December, enter **500** into the January Rent field and use the Fill Row Right command to fill the rest of the year. Then enter **600** into the July Rent field. If you choose the Fill Row Right again, Quicken copies 600 forward to August, September, October, November, and December.

Budgeting biweekly amounts

Sometimes it doesn't make much sense to budget amounts on a monthly basis because you actually receive or spend on a biweekly basis. What if you're paid every two weeks? Or what if your bowling league meets every other Thursday? See the dilemma? You won't really know how many two-week periods there are in a month unless you look at a calendar and start counting with your fingers.

Lucky for you, Quicken provides a handy tool for budgeting those sorts of biweekly amounts: the Two-Week Command, which appears on the Edit menu. To use this command, select the category you want to budget biweekly and then choose the command. Quicken displays the Set Up Two-Week Budget dialog box. Coincidentally, this dialog box appears in Figure 3-5.

Figure 3-5:
The Set Up
Two-Week
Budget
dialog box.

Enter the biweekly amount in the Amount text box. Enter the first date you'll receive or spend the amount in the Every Two Weeks Starting text box and then choose OK.

When you finish entering your budget

After you enter your secret plan, either the simple way or the fast way (if you're the adventurous type), just choose Save to save your work.

I should mention, too, that you can simply choose Close if you don't want to save your work (in case you've been noodling around). If you want to revert to the previously saved version of the budget, choose Restore.

I'll talk more about using the budget in later chapters (like Chapter 6, for example). If you want to print a hard copy (computerese for paper) of the budget, choose Print and press Enter. If you have a printing question, go to Chapter 5.

You're not going to use the budget for a while. But don't worry. In Chapter 5, I explain how to print reports, including a report that compares your actual spending with, ugh, your budget. Stay tuned. Same time. Same place. Same Bat channel.

What about the Layout command button?

If you look closely at the Budget window, you can see that I haven't described one of the command buttons: the venerable Layout. Here's the lowdown on the Layout button:

When you choose the Layout button, Quicken displays the Layout Budgets dialog box. Because I thought you just might be interested in what this baby looks like, I included it as Figure 3-6. See? The bulleted list that follows describes what the mysterious buttons and boxes do.

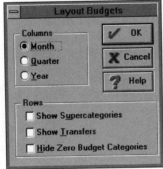

Figure 3-6:
The Layout
Budgets
dialog box.

- *Month.* Tells Quicken you want to budget by the month. You don't need to use this radio button unless you've used one of the other Column's buttons; Quicken budgets by the month unless you tell it to do otherwise. Just click the button or press Alt+M.

- *Quarter.* Tells Quicken you want to budget by the quarter. Just click the button or press Alt+Q.

- *Year.* Tells Quicken you really are a big picture person (or business) and that you'll be budgeting by the year. (If you flip-flop between months, quarters, and years, Quicken automatically converts the budget figures for you.) To work with the big picture, just click the button, or press Alt+Y.

- **Show *Supercategories*.** Tells Quicken either you do want to budget by supercategory or you don't want to budget by subcategory. You can turn the check box off and on by clicking or by pressing Alt+U.

- *Show Transfers.* Tells Quicken whether you want to budget account transfers. The only problem here is that you probably don't know what account transfers are. (Yet!) I'll talk about account transfers in the next chapter.

- *Hide Zero Budget Categories.* Hides all the budget categories that show zero.

Wanna budget with a spreadsheet?

Using the Edit menu's Copy To Clipboard command, you can copy the budget information shown in the Budget window to the clipboard. After the info is there, you can start a Windows spreadsheet program such as Excel and use its Edit Paste command to paste the budgeting stuff stored on the clipboard into the spreadsheet. If you're familiar with a Windows spreadsheet, such as Excel, go ahead and try it. You might like it.

Part II
The Absolute Basics

The 5th Wave   By Rich Tennant

PORTRAIT OF A
CYBERHOLIC

CYBERHOLICS SPEND HOURS BALANCING
THEIR CHECKBOOKS ON A COMPUTER,
WHEN THEY COULD DO IT IN MINUTES
WITH A PEN AND CALCULATOR.

In this part...

OK, you're ready for the show to start. Which is good. This next part — "The Absolute Basics" — covers all the nitty gritty details of using Quicken to keep your personal and business financial records.

If you're just starting to use the Quicken program or you've just come from Part I, you'll find the stuff covered here dang important — dare I say, essential — to using Quicken even in the most basic way.

Chapter 4
Checkbook on a Computer

*T*his is it. The big time. You're finally going to do those everyday Quicken things: entering checks, deposits, and transfers. Along the way, you'll also learn about some of the neat tools that Quicken provides for making these tasks easier, more precise, and faster.

Finding Your Checkbook

To enter checkbook transactions, use the register window (see Figure 4-1). (If you don't see the register window, choose the Registr icon from the iconbar.)

If you've set up more than one account — say you've set up both a checking account and a savings account — you may need to tell Quicken which account you want to work with. Geez Louise, how can you tell if Quicken gets confused? Easy. The register window will show the wrong account. To correct this problem, click the button naming the account near the bottom of the register; click Checking to show the checking account, Savings to show the savings account, and so on.

The starting balance you specified as part of setting up the account will be the first account listed. In Figure 4-1, for example, the starting balance is $4.16. Bummer.

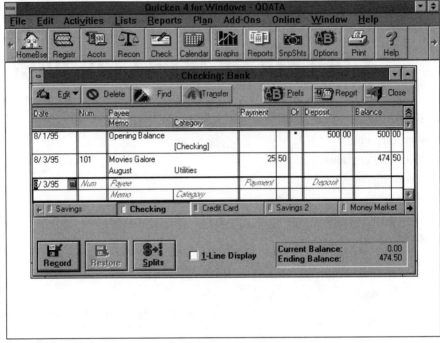

Figure 4-1:
The Quicken
application
window
showing the
register
window.

The account name appears at the top of the register window.

As you move the selection cursor through the register window's fields, Quicken displays *Qcards* — little message boxes that tell you what goes where. These little reminders are helpful but can get a little tiresome in much the same way a backseat driver gets tiresome. I turned them off because I reached my breaking point. When you reach your breaking point, choose the Show Qcards command from the Help menu. This tells Quicken, "Geez, stop nagging me, will ya?" If you want help later on, you can turn the Qcards back on by using the same command.

Recording Checks

First things first: you can enter checks using either the register window (see Figure 4-1) or the Write Checks window, described in Chapter 5.

You use the register window for the checks you don't want to print with Quicken; you use the Write Checks window to enter the checks you do want to print using Quicken. (This isn't an ironclad rule, but it does make things easier for you, so it's the rule we'll follow.)

Entering a check into the register

OK, back to the chase. Entering a check in the register window is a simple matter of describing who you wrote it to and how much you paid. Let's say, for the sake of illustration, that you paid $25.50 to the cable television company for your monthly cable service. Here's how you enter this check:

1. Enter the check date.

Move the cursor to the Date field in the next empty row of the register (if it isn't already there) and type the date using the MM/DD format. January 1, 1995, for example, gets entered as **1/1**. You usually won't have to enter the year because Quicken retrieves the current year number from the little clock inside your computer.

You can adjust the date in a Date field using the + and - keys. The + key adds one day to the current date; the - key subtracts one date from the current date.

2. Enter the check number.

Move the cursor (or tab) to the Num field and type the check number. Alternatively, move the cursor to the Num field and press Alt+down arrow so that Quicken displays a list box of entries, such as ATM, Deposits, EFT, Next Chk #, Print, and Transfer. You can select the Next Chk # if you want. In this case, Quicken fills in the number with its guess as to the new check number — one more than the old check number. If this guess is right, of course, you can just leave it in place. If it isn't right, type over Quicken's guess with the correct number or use the + or - keys to increase or decrease the check number.

3. Enter the payee.

Move the cursor to the Payee field. So enter the name of the person or business you're paying. If the cable company name is "Movies Galore," for example, type **Movies Galore**. (In the future, however, you probably will be able to select payee names from the list box.)

4. Enter the check amount.

Move the cursor to the Payment field and enter the check amount — **$25.50** in this example. You don't have to type the dollar sign, but you do have to type the period to indicate the decimal place and cents.

5. Enter a memo description.

Move the cursor to the Memo field and describe the specific reason you're paying the check. You may identify the cable payment as the February payment, for example. Businesses should use this field to identify the invoice paid — usually by entering the actual invoice number you're paying.

6. Enter the category.

Move the cursor to the Category field. Quicken displays a drop-down list box of category names from your Category & Transfer List. You can select one of these categories using the arrow keys or the mouse. Or if you're the independent type, just type the name yourself. A payment to your cable company may be categorized as "Utilities," for example.

If you go with the typing approach and you're not a super fast typist, Quicken will probably be able to guess which category you're entering before you enter it. If you start typing **Ut**, for example, Quicken will fill in the rest of the category name "ilities" for you ("Ut" + "ilities" = "Utilities"). This is called *QuickFill,* and I'll talk about it later in the chapter in a bit more detail.

7. Select Record.

Click the Record button at the bottom of the register window. This option tells Quicken you want to record the transaction into your register. Quicken beeps in acknowledgment, calculates the new account balance, and moves the cursor to the next slot, or row, in the register.

Figure 4-2 shows the cable television check recorded into the register. You can't see it in the figure, but the amount in the Balance field after the $25.50 check shows in red. This *red ink* indicates that you've overdrawn your account. I don't need to tell you what that means. Overdraft charges. Yuck.

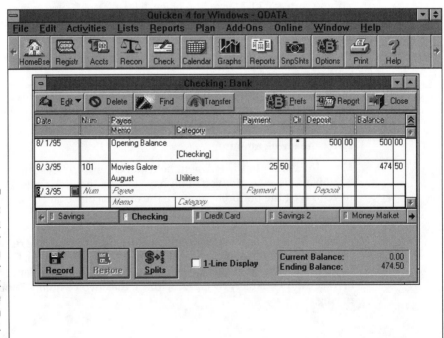

Figure 4-2:
The check register after you record your first check to the cable television company.

Packing more checks into the register

Normally, Quicken displays several rows of information about each check you've entered. It also displays several rows of information about each of the other types of transactions you've entered, too. If you want to pack more checks into a visible portion of the register, mark the <u>1</u>-Line Display check box, which appears at the bottom of the register window. When you do this, Quicken displays in a single line format all of the information in the register except the Memo field.

What if you need to change a check after you've already entered it? Say, you make a terrible mistake, such as recording a 52.50 check as 25.20. Can you fix it? Sure. Just use the arrow keys or click the mouse to highlight the check transaction you want to change. Use the Tab and Shift+Tab keys to move the cursor to the field you want to change. (You can also click the field with the mouse.) Then make your fix. Select the Re<u>c</u>ord button when you finish or press Enter.

A kooky (and clever) little thing named QuickFill

Here's kind of a funny quirk about Quicken. If Quicken can guess what you're typing into a field, it will fill in the rest of the field for you. I already mentioned how this works when you type category names. But it gets even better than that.

The second time you use a payee name, for example, Quicken knows that it's the second time. Quicken also figures that, "Hey, there's probably stuff from the last Movies Galore transaction that'll be the same for this transaction." So guess what Quicken does if you press Tab to accept the payee name Quicken supplies after you've typed the first few letters of the name? It uses the last transaction's information to fill in all the current transaction's fields.

This isn't as dumb as it sounds at first. In fact, it's a real time-saver. Suppose that you did write a $25.50 check to Movies Galore for your February cable television bill. When you type **Movies Galore** to record the next month's cable television check, the amount will probably be the same. The complete payee name will certainly be the same, and the category will also be the same. So Quicken fills in all these fields, too.

QuickFill doesn't do everything for you, however. You still need to make sure that the date and check number are correct. If Quicken "quickfills" a field with the wrong information, just replace the wrong information with what's right.

Memorized transactions

Quicken provides another feature — memorized transactions — which is almost obsolete now that the QuickFill feature exists. Just because you may have heard about this tool, however, I'll quick-as-a-bunny-rabbit describe how it works.

A *memorized transaction* is simply one that you've stored on a special list. (To store the transaction, you highlight it in the register and then choose the <u>E</u>dit menu's <u>M</u>emorize Transaction command.)

To later use or abuse one of the memorized transactions, you display a list of the previously memorized transactions by choosing the <u>L</u>ist menu's <u>M</u>emorized Transactions command. When Quicken displays the list, just select the one you want to reuse.

A memorized transactions list is a handy tool. But if you're feeling a little overwhelmed, don't spin your wheels trying to get up to speed on the feature. QuickFill will almost always do the job for you because — get this — it automatically grabs memorized transactions from the list for you.

Recording Deposits

You know what? Recording a deposit works almost the exact same way as recording a check. The only difference is that you enter the deposit amount in the Deposit field, rather than enter the check amount in the Payment field.

Entering a deposit into the register

Suppose that you receive a $100 birthday gift from your elderly aunt, Enid. Here's how you would record this deposit into the register:

1. **Enter the deposit date.**

   Move the cursor to the Date field of the next empty row of the register (if it isn't already there) and type the date. Use the MM/DD format. January 3, 1995, for example, gets entered as **1/3**. As with check dates, you only have to enter the year if the current year number, which Quicken retrieves from the little clock inside your computer, is wrong.

   You can adjust the date in a Date field in Quicken using the + and – keys. The + key adds one day to the current date; the – key subtracts one date from the current date.

2. **Enter the deposit number if the bank supplies one.**

   Are you the meticulous type? Then go ahead and move the cursor to the Num field and press Alt+down-arrow key. In the drop-down list box that Quicken displays, select Deposit.

3. Enter the name of the person from whom you received the deposit.

In this case, move the cursor to the Payee field and enter **Aunt Enid**. (I don't mean to sound presumptuous, but, well, the next time Aunt Enid sends you birthday money, you'll be able to choose her name from the Payee drop-down list box.)

4. Enter the deposit amount.

Move the cursor to the Deposit field and enter **100**. Don't type the dollar sign — or any other punctuation. (If Aunt Enid sweats money and sometimes passes out $1,000 gifts, for example, you would record the deposit as 1000 — not 1,000 or $1,000.)

5. (Optional) Enter a memo description.

Move the cursor to the Memo field and describe something like the reason for the deposit. Aunt Enid's money may be described as "Birthday Gift." If you're a business depositing a customer's check, though, use this entry to identify the invoice the customer is paying.

6. Enter the category.

You know how this works by now. Move the cursor to the Category field and select the appropriate category. Alternatively, if you like living on the edge, try typing in the category name. Aunt Enid's check may be described as "Gift Received." (This is an income category on the standard home category list.) A customer receipt may be described as "Sales."

To add a category, display the Category & Transfer List dialog box. (You can do this by choosing the Cat List icon from the iconbar.) Then choose the New button on the dialog box that Quicken displays to add a new category. Refer to Chapter 2 if you have questions about how this works.

7. Select Record.

This command tells Quicken that you want to record the transaction in your register. Quicken beeps in protest but then adds the transaction.

Figure 4-3 shows the check register after Aunt Enid's thoughtful gift. Your account's no longer overdrawn — so you've got that going for you. Maybe before you go any further, you should call Aunt Enid to thank her.

Changing a deposit you've already entered

Big surprise here, but this works just like changing a check. First, use the arrow keys or click the mouse to highlight the deposit. Use the Tab and Shift+Tab keys to move the cursor to the field you want to change. (You can also click the field with the mouse.) Then make your fix and select Record.

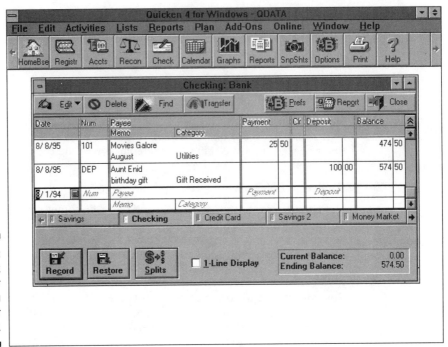

Figure 4-3:
The check
register
after you
record your
first deposit.

Recording Account Transfers

Account transfers occur when you move money from one account — such as
your savings account — to another account — such as your checking account.
But jeepers, why am I telling you this? If you've got one of those combined
savings and checking accounts, you probably do this sort of thing all the time.

Oh, now I remember why I brought this up — Quicken makes quick work of
account transfers as long as you've already got *both* accounts set up.

If you don't have the second account set up, you'll need to do this first. If you
don't know how, flip back to Chapter 2.

Entering an account transfer

Buckle up. I'll speed through the steps for recording an account transfer. For
the most part, recording an account transfer works the same way as recording
a check or deposit.

Suppose that you want to record the transfer of $50 from your checking account
to your savings account. Maybe you want to set aside a little money — little,
presumably, being a key adjective — to purchase a gift for generous Aunt Enid.

Here's what you need to do:

1. **Enter the transfer date.**

   Move the cursor to the Date field. Then enter the date that you move the money from one account to another.

2. **Flag the transaction as a transfer.**

   Move the cursor to the Num field and press Alt+Down arrow. When Quicken displays a drop-down list box, select the EFT entry. Why? My guess is that this stands for *Electronic Funds Transfer.*

3. **Enter a description of the transaction.**

   Use the Description field to describe the transfer — for example, "For Aunt Enid's Next Gift." You know how this works by now, don't you? You just move the cursor to the field. Then you pound away at the keyboard. Bang. Bang. Bang.

4. **Enter the transfer amount.**

   Amounts transferred out of an account get entered in the Payment field. Amounts transferred into an account get entered in the Deposit field. So move the cursor to the right field ("right" as in "right" and "wrong" not "right and left"); then enter the transfer amount.

5. **(Optional) Enter a memo description.**

   Enter more information about the transaction (if it's needed) in the Memo field. Perhaps a gift idea for Aunt Enid?

6. **Indicate the other account.**

   Enter the category as the name of the account to which or from which money is being transferred. (This is actually the only tricky part.) Move the cursor to the Category field and click the down arrow. When Quicken drops down a list box of categories, scroll to the very bottom of the list and then select the other account.

7. **Select Record.**

   This command tells Quicken that you want to record the transfer transaction into your register.

Figure 4-4 shows the check register after transferring money from your checking account to your savings account so that you'll have money to purchase something nice for Aunt Enid's next birthday. Maybe that new Def Leppard compact disc.

Take a look at the Category field. Notice that Quicken uses brackets ([ ]) symbols to identify the Category field entry as an account and not as an income or expense category.

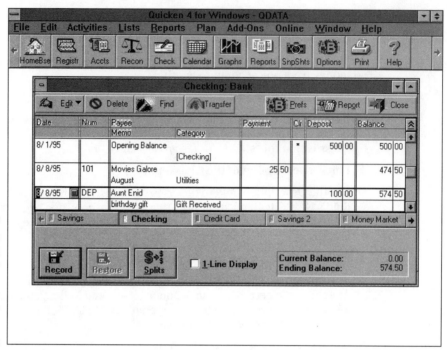

About the other half of the transfer

Here's the cool thing about transfer transactions. Quicken automatically records the other half of the transfer for you. Figure 4-4 shows the $50 reduction in the checking account because of the transfer. Quicken uses this information to record a $50 increase in the savings account. Automatically. Biddabam. Biddaboom.

To see the other half of a transfer transaction, highlight the transfer transaction using the arrow keys or the mouse. Then activate the Edit menu and choose the Go To Transfer command. Quicken displays the other account in a new register window (see Figure 4-5).

Changing a transfer you've already entered

Predictably, this works just like changing a check or a deposit. First, you highlight the transfer by using the arrow keys or by clicking the mouse. Then you use the Tab and Shift+Tab keys to move the cursor to the field that you want to change. Make your fix and then select Record and go to lunch.

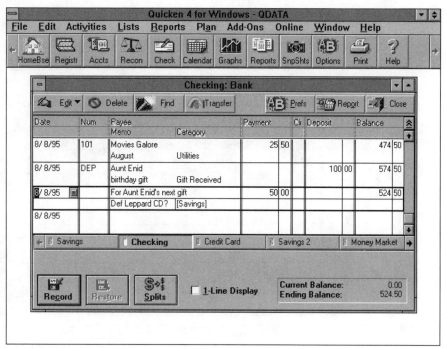

Figure 4-5:
The new
register
window.

Splitting Hairs

Here's a sort of Quicken riddle for you. Suppose that you've got a check that pays more than one kind of expense. You trot down to the grocery store, for example, and pick up $10 of junk food and junk beverages (which should be categorized as a "Groceries" expense) and $10 of 10W-40 motor oil (which should be categorized as an "Auto" expense). How do you categorize a transaction like this? Well, I'll tell you. You use a *split category*.

Here's how a split category works. When you're ready to categorize the check, you choose the Splits command button, which appears at the bottom of the register window. Quicken displays the Splits window (see Figure 4-6).

Steps for splitting a check

If you're a clever sort, you probably already know how the Splits window works. Let's go through the steps anyway. Suppose that you want to categorize a $20 check that includes $10 for groceries and $10 for car motor oil.

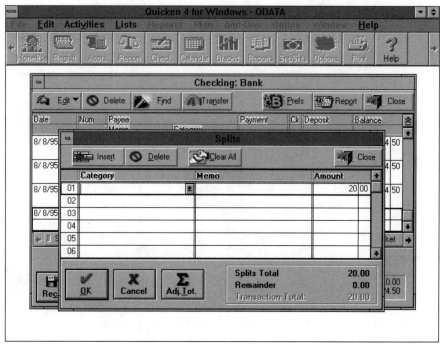

Figure 4-6:
The Splits
window.

To categorize a check in the Splits window, do the following:

1. Enter the first category name in the first category field.

Move the cursor to the category field (if it isn't already there). Activate the drop-down list box by pressing Alt+Down arrow or by clicking the down arrow, and then choosing the category name.

(Despite what a dietitian may say, let's call the pork rinds, beer, and pretzels "Groceries.")

2. Enter a memo description for the first categorized portion of the check.

Move the cursor to the first Memo field and then type whatever you want. (Maybe a description of the food you bought.)

3. Enter the amount spent for the first category.

Move the cursor to the first Amount field and then type, well, the amount. If the first category is what we're calling "Groceries," and you spent $10 on this, you type **10**. (I hear that in Germany they consider beer to be food.)

4. Repeat steps 1, 2, and 3 for each spending category.

If you spent another $10 on car motor oil, for example, move the cursor to the second Category field and enter the category you use to summarize spending on "Auto." Move the cursor to the second Memo field and enter a memo description of the expenditure, such as **10W-40 motor oil**. Move the cursor to the second Amount field and enter the amount of the expenditure, such as **10**.

Figure 4-7 shows a completed Splits window. You can have up to 30 pieces of a split transaction. Use the scroll bar and PgUp and PgDn keys to scroll through the list of split amounts.

5. **Verify that there isn't any uncategorized spending shown in the Splits window.**

   If you find "extra" spending, either add the needed category or delete the split transaction line that's uncategorized. To delete a split transaction line, move the cursor to one of the fields in the line, scream "Hi-Ya" loudly, and choose Delete. (I learned the "Hi-Ya" business in Tae Kwon Do. The only other thing I learned, by the way, was that those chest protectors don't really protect middle-aged men during full-contact sparring. So I quit.) If you want to insert a new line, move the selection cursor to the line above which you want to make your insertion and then choose Insert. If you're fed up and want to start over from scratch, choose the Clear All command. (Quicken erases all the Split Transaction lines if you do this.)

6. **Choose OK.**

   After you complete the Splits window— that is, you've completely and correctly categorized all the little pieces of the transaction — click OK. Quicken closes the Splits window. If you didn't enter an amount in the Payment column of the register before opening the Splitsdialog box, Quicken will display a dialog box that asks whether the transaction is a payment or a deposit. You click an option button to make your choice known. To let you know that the transaction is one that you've split, however, the Category field shows the word Split when you select the split transaction. Take a peek at Figure 4-8 to see this for yourself.

Editing and deleting split categories

You can delete or change any individual line of a split category. To do this, you first display the Splits dialog box by selecting the transaction and then clicking the Splits button or clicking the checkmark button which appears in the register window's Category field once you record the transaction. Once Quicken dutifully displays the Splits dialog box, you can edit any of the fields by clicking them and then typing over their contents. You can delete any line of the split category by clicking on one of the fields in the line and clicking the Delete button at the top of the Splits window. (If you want to delete all the lines of the split category so you can start over, click the Clear All button instead.)

If you want to unsplit the transaction so you can assign it to a single category, you need to use a little trick. Click the X button which appears in the register window's Category field once you record the transaction.

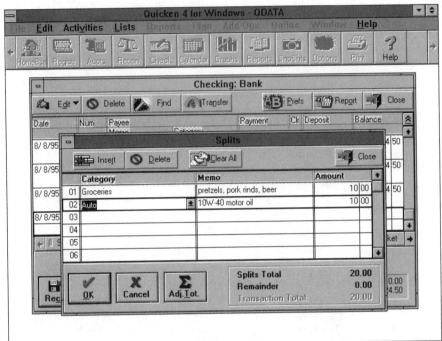

Figure 4-7:
The completed Splits window.

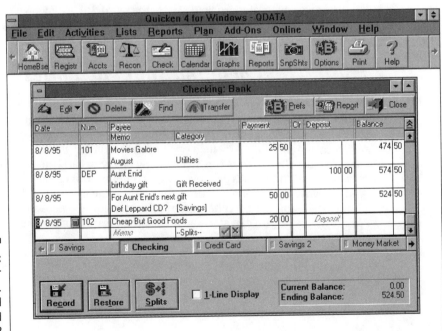

Figure 4-8:
The register window.
Can you find
the word
Splits?

Splitting hairs

Quicken assumes that any transaction amount you enter in the register window should agree with the total of the individual split transaction amounts entered in the Splits window.

If you're not sure what the split transaction amounts total is, your best bet is to NOT — I repeat, *NOT*— enter the amount on the register window. Instead, enter the individual split transaction amounts in the Splits window. When you leave the Splits window, Quicken totals your individual split amounts and then prompts you to see if the total is a payment or a deposit. Then it plugs this total into either the Payment or the Deposit field. If the total is a deposit, it plugs it into the Deposit field. If the total is a payment, it plugs it into the Payment field.

If you've already entered either a payment amount or a deposit amount but you're not sure

that the split transaction amounts agree with what you entered, you can tell Quicken to adjust the Payment or Deposit amount on the register window to whatever the individual split transaction amounts total. To do this, select the Splits window's Adj. Tot. button. In this case, Quicken adds up the split transaction lines and then plugs the total into the register. (This might best be called the "I don't care if it is a round hole, I want to pound this square peg into it" approach.)

By the way, Quicken shows any difference between the amount shown in the register window and the individual split transaction amounts. It shows this difference as the last split transaction line. So you'll be able to tell whether the individual splits agree with the payment or deposit amount shown in the register.

Steps for splitting deposits and transfers

Wondering if you can split deposits and transfers? Well, you can. The steps for doing so work just like the steps for splitting categories for a check transaction. The basic trick — if you can call it a trick — is just to use the Splits dialog box to list each of the category names and amounts.

One other point I should make here is that you can mix and match categories and transfers in the Splits window. Some of the splits, for example, can be categories and some can be transfer accounts. It would be quite common to do this in a business setting (see Chapter 15, for example).

Deleting and Voiding Transactions

You can delete and void register transactions using the Edit menu's Delete Transaction and Void Transaction commands. If you've looked at the Edit menu, of course, you've probably already guessed as much.

Sort of a voiding bug . . .

When you mark a transaction as void, Quicken does three things. It sticks the word VOID at the very start of the Payee field, it marks the transaction as cleared, and it erases the amount in the Payment or Deposit field. So far, so good. But if you happen to later fill in the Payment or Deposit field, Quicken will use that payment or deposit amount to adjust the account balance — even though Quicken still shows the transaction as void. I keep thinking the folks at Intuit will fix this, but they haven't — at least not yet. The bottom line is that you need to make sure that you don't edit transactions after you've voided them. Otherwise, it's all too easy to foul up your account balance. I won't tell you about how I happened to learn this. . . .

Using either command is a snap. Just highlight the transaction you want to delete or void by using the arrow keys or by clicking the mouse. Then choose the command. And that's that.

Use the Void Transaction command anytime you void a check. Quicken leaves voided transactions in the register but marks them as void and erases the Payment or Deposit amount. So by using the Void Transaction command, you keep a record of voided, or canceled, transactions.

Use the Delete Transaction command if you want to remove the transaction from your register.

The Big Register Phenomenon

If you start entering a bunch of checks, deposits, and transfers into your registers, you'll shortly find yourself with registers that contain hundreds and even thousands of transactions. You can still work with one of these big registers using the tools and techniques I've talked about in the preceding paragraphs. Nevertheless, let me give you some more help for dealing with... (drum roll, please)... the big register phenomenon.

Moving through a big register

You can use the PgDn and PgUp keys to page up and down through your register, a screenful of transactions at a time. Some people call this scrolling. You can call it whatever you want.

You can use the Home key to move to the first transaction in a register. Just move the cursor to the first (or Date) field in the selected transaction and press Ctrl+Home.

You can use the End key to move to the last transaction in a register. Bet you can guess how this works. Move the cursor to the last (or Category) field in the selected transaction and press Ctrl+End.

Of course, you can use the vertical scroll bar along the right edge of the register window, too. Click the arrows at either end of the vertical scroll bar to select the next or previous transaction. Click either above or below the square scroll bar marker to page back and forth through the register. Or, if you've no qualms about dragging the mouse around, you can drag the scroll bar marker up and down the scroll bar.

Finding that darn transaction

Want to find that one check, deposit, or transfer? No problem. The Edit menu's Find command provides a handy way for doing just this. Here's what you do:

1. **Choose Find command from the Edit menu or choose the Find button in the register window.**

   Quicken, with restrained but obvious enthusiasm, displays the Quicken Find dialog box (see Figure 4-9). You'll use this dialog box to describe the transaction you want to find in as much detail as possible.

2. **Enter the piece of text or number that identifies the transaction you want to locate.**

   Move the cursor to the Find text box. Then type the text or number. By the way, the case of the text doesn't matter. If you type **aunt,** for example, Quicken will find "AUNT" or "Aunt."

3. **Specify which pieces, or fields, of the register transaction you want Quicken to look at.**

   Move the cursor to the Search drop-down list box, drop down the list box, and then select the field Quicken should look at during the search: Amount, Cleared Status (the Clr field), Memo, Date, Category/Class (whatever is in the Category field), Check Number, (what's in the Num field), or Payee. Or get truly crazy and pick the All Fields list entry so that Quicken looks both high and low.

4. **Tell Quicken whether you're using a shotgun or a rifle.**

   You need to specify how closely what you stuck in the Find text box needs to match whatever you selected in the Search drop-down list box. To do this, drop down the Match If drop-down list box. Then select the appropriate matching rule:

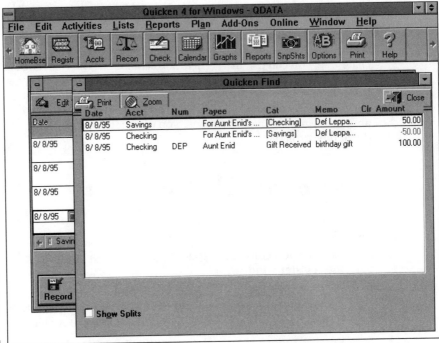

Figure 4-9:
The Find
dialog box.

- *Contains.* Select this rule if the field or fields you're searching just need to use a piece of text. If you enter **Aunt** into the Find text box and use this matching rule to search Payee fields, Quicken will find transactions that use the following payee names: Aunt Enid, Aunt Enid and Uncle Ob, Uncle Joob and Aunt Edna, and — well, you get the idea.

- *Exact.* Select this rule if the field you're searching needs to exactly match your Find text box entry. If you enter the Find text box entry as **Aunt,** for example, and you're searching Payee fields, Quicken looks for transactions where the Payee field shows *Aunt* — and nothing more or nothing less.

- *Starts With.* Select this rule if the field you're searching for just needs to start with what you entered in the Find text box. For example, you enter **Aunt** in the Find text box and you're searching the Payee fields. Quicken looks for transactions where the Payee field starts with the word *Aunt* — such as Aunt Enid or Aunt Enid and Uncle Ob. (Uncle Joob and Aunt Edna wouldn't cut the mustard in this case, though.)

- *Ends With.* Select this rule if the field you're searching for just needs to end with what you entered in the Find text box.

- *Greater.* Select this rule if the field you're searching for needs to hold a value that exceeds the number you entered in the Find text box. This makes sense, right?

- *Greater or Equal.* Select this rule if the field you're searching for needs to hold a value that either exceeds or equals the number you entered in the Find text box.

- *Less.* Select this rule if the field you're searching for needs to hold a value that is less than the number you entered in the Find text box.

- *Less or Equal.* Select this rule if the field you're searching for needs to hold a value that is less than or equal to the number you entered in the Find text box.

5. **Tell Quicken whether you want it to search forward or backward from the selected transaction.**

   Mark the Search Backwards check box if you want to look backwards starting from the selected transaction.

6. **Let the search begin.**

You click either the Find or Find All button to begin the search. If you click Find, Quicken looks through the register and, if it can find one like you describe, it highlights the transaction. If you're thinking, "Well, that sounds straight forward enough," you're right. It is.

If you click Find All, Quicken looks through the register and builds a list of all the transactions like the one you describe. Then, it displays the list in an expanded version of the Find dialog box — which, incidentally, looks much more like a window at this point (see Figure 4-10).

Quicken supplies a couple of other commands that are similar to Find. The Edit menu's Find/Replace command lets you both locate and modify transactions that look like the one you describe. (For example, you might say you want to locate any transaction showing Aunt Enid as the payee so you can replace payee fields showing "Aunt Enid" with "Great Aunt Enid.")The Find/Replace command works in a fashion very similar to the Find command except you need to describe what you want to modify in the found transactions. Once you complete the initial dialog box that Quicken displays when you choose the command, Quicken displays a window listing the transactions it's found. (This window looks like the one shown in Figure 4.10.) You mark — by clicking — the transactions you want to modify and then select the Replace button.

There's also a special version of Find/Replace called Recategorize. This command appears on the Activities menu. What it lets you do is locate all the transactions that use a specific category and then replace this category with some other category. Again, once you complete the initial dialog box that Quicken displays when you choose the command, Quicken displays a window listing the transactions it's found. You mark — by clicking — the transactions you want to modify and then choose the Replace button.

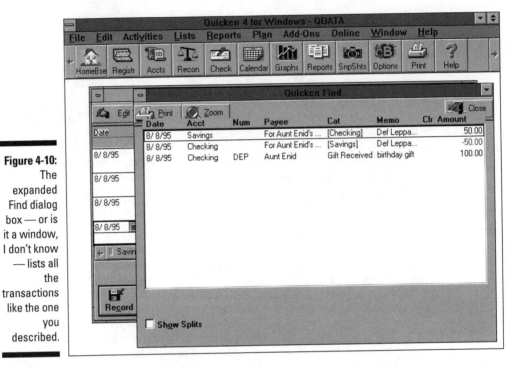

Figure 4-10:
The
expanded
Find dialog
box — or is
it a window,
I don't know
— lists all
the
transactions
like the one
you
described.

Pop-up Calendars and Calculators

Can I tell you just a couple more things? (If not, skip this section. If so, read on...). Quicken provides a pop-up calendar anytime you move the selection cursor to a date field. To get to the calendar, you just click the down arrow that appears at the right end of the date field. Quicken displays a calendar for the current month (see Figure 4-11). All you have to do is click the day you want as the date. (If you want to see a calendar for a different month, click the << and >> buttons.)

Figure 4-11:
The pop-up
calendar.

Quicken also provides a pop-up calculator anytime you move the selection cursor to an amount field. To get to the calculator, you just click the down arrow that appears at the right end of the amount field. Quicken displays a calculator like the one shown in Figure 4-12. This baby works like a regular, handheld calculator. You just type out the math you want to perform. Quicken displays the calculation result in the amount field.

Figure 4-12:
The pop-up
calculator

Do the calculator keys make sense? Here's how they work. Use the / (slash) key for division. Use the * (asterisk) for multiplication. Use the - (hyphen) and the + (plus) keys for subtraction and addition. Use the . (period) to indicate the decimal point. Use the % key to indicate that the number you just typed is a percentage and should be converted to a decimal value. Use = (the equal sign) to calculate the amount and remove the pop-up calculator. You can use the Backspace key to remove, or clear, the last digit you entered. You can use the C key to clear the amount text box, and you can use the CE key to clear the last number entered into the calculator.

Chapter 5
Printing 101

· ·

In This Chapter

▶ Collecting the information needed to print a check

▶ Fixing your mistakes before printing the check

▶ Printing a check

▶ Fixing check form alignment problems

▶ Recovering from a mistake after you've printed out the check

▶ Printing a register

· ·

I bet you can't guess what this chapter describes. Gee, you guessed it — how to print checks and reports.

Printing Checks

Printing checks in Quicken is, well, quick. All you need to do is collect the information you want printed on the check form, press a couple of keys, and enter the number you want Quicken to use to identify the checks. Sounds simple enough, doesn't it? It is, as you'll read in the paragraphs that follow.

Collecting the check information

When you want to write a check, you collect the information needed for the actual check form and the information needed to record the printed check into your register. If you've worked with the Quicken register or read Chapter 4, you'll find this all rather familiar.

Make sure that the active account is the one on which you want to write checks. You can confirm this by looking at the register window's title bar. This title bar identifies both the type of document window (a register, for example) and the account showing in the window. If the account in the register window isn't the one you want, click the Accounts button at the bottom of the register window. Quicken then displays a register window with this account's information.

One other thing. If you've done this before, you'll have several document windows on the Quicken desktop, or application window. You can close the unneeded windows if you want. To do this, display a window's control menu by double-clicking the thing that looks like a hyphen inside a square in the window's upper left corner. (If you have questions about how this all works, refer to Appendix B.)

To collect the information needed to print a check, take these steps:

1. **Display the Write Checks window.**

   Choose the Check icon from the iconbar, or choose the <u>W</u>rite Checks command from the Acti<u>v</u>ities menu. Figure 5-1 shows the Write Checks: Checking window. Get ready for some excitement.

2. **Enter the check date.**

   First use the mouse or Tab keys to move the cursor to the Date field. Then enter the date you'll print the check (probably today's date). Remember to enter the date in a MM/DD/YY format — April 8, 1995 is entered as **4/8/95.** You don't need to enter the year if the year number that Quicken retrieves from your computer's internal system clock is correct. If you want, you can use your new friend, the pop-up calendar. You can also adjust the date by a day using the + and – keys.

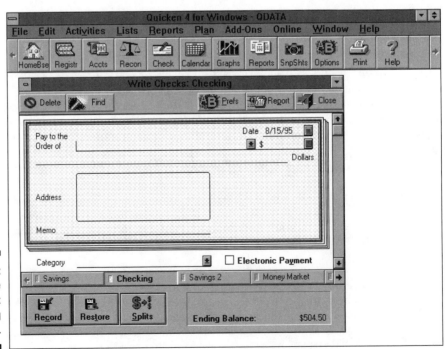

Figure 5-1:
The Write
Checks:
Checking
window.

3. Enter the name of the person or business you're paying.

Move the cursor to the Pay To The Order Of field and type away. For example, to write a check to me, type **Steve Nelson**. (Feel free to do this, by the way. If you send me a check, I'll even cash it as a sort of public service.) Or if you've written a check to the payee before, activate the Pay To The Order Of drop-down list box. When Quicken displays a list of the payees you've already used, just highlight one by using the mouse or the arrow keys.

4. Enter the amount of the check.

Move the cursor to the $ text box and type the amount. (If you are sending a check to me, be sure to make the amount nominal — for sure, not more than $10 or $20. . . .) When you move the cursor down to the next field, Quicken writes the amount out in words on the line under the payee name and before Dollars.

5. Enter the payee's address.

If you plan to mail the check in a window envelope, move the cursor to the Address field. Then enter the name and address of the person or business you're paying.

Here's a little address-entry trick: You can copy the payee name from the Pay To The Order Of text box to the first line of the Address field. To do so, move the cursor to the first line of the address field by pressing the Tab key. Then press the ' (apostrophe) key.

6. (Optional) Enter a memo description of the check.

Move the cursor to the Memo field and enter a description for why you are sending your money to this person or business, such as an account number or an invoice number. Or if you're sending someone a check because you didn't have time to go out and buy a real gift, type **Happy Birthday** in the Memo field. It's the little things that make a difference.

7. Enter the category.

Move the cursor to the Category field and type the category name for the expense you're paying with the check. If you don't remember the category name, activate the Category drop-down list box by pressing Alt+Down arrow, or Ctrl+C. Then pick the category you want to use from the list. Figure 5-2 shows the completed window for a rent check payable to one of the nicer places in the fictional town of Pine Lake, the venerable Marlborough Apartments.

Pressing Alt+Down arrow displays just the Category drop-down list box, and pressing Ctrl+C opens the full-blown category and Transfer List Window.

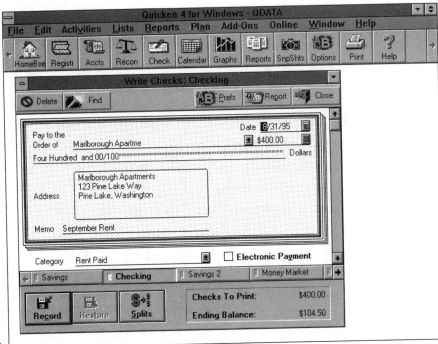

Figure 5-2:
A completed
check.

You can assign a check to more than a single category by using the Splits window. Using the Splits window with the Write Checks window works the same way as using the Splits window with the Register window. (I described using the Splits window with the Register window in the last chapter.) OK. So why do I bring this up? You may want to do this when a check pays more than one type of expense or is transferred to more than one account. For example, if you're writing a check to pay your mortgage, with part of the check paying the actual mortgage and part of the check going into an escrow account for property taxes, you can use the Splits window to describe the transaction's individual components. To split a check amount so that it's assigned to multiple spending categories, choose the Splits button at the bottom of the Write Checks window. Or Ctrl+S. Either way, Quicken displays the Splits window for you to use to indicate the categories and categorized amounts that make up the check total. If you have questions about how split transactions work, refer to Chapter 4.

8. Select Record.

Quicken records the check. It displays the current account balance, the ending account balance, and even adds a Checks to Print total at the lower right corner of the window. Shoot, it even scrolls the completed check off the screen and replaces it with a new, blank check that you can use to pay your next bill. It doesn't get much better than this, does it?

What if you make a mistake entering a check?

Don't worry; be happy. It's easy to fix the mistakes you make if you haven't yet printed the check. Use the PgUp or PgDn keys to scroll back and forth through the checks you've entered using the Write Checks window. This way you can display any check that you used the Write Check window to write (but have not yet printed).

When you find the incorrect check, you can fix the mistake in two ways. If you incorrectly entered some bit of check information, move the cursor to the field with the incorrect data and just type over the data.

Or if you're really mad or frustrated, you can delete the entire check by pressing Ctrl+D or by choosing the Delete Transaction command from the Edit menu. (I should 'fess up here and suggest that you do this if you accidentally entered a check to me, for example.)

Don't use this method to delete a check that you've already printed. To *void* a check that you've already printed, you must go into the register window. To display the register window, you can choose the registr icon from the iconbar. Then find the check in the register window, highlight the check, and void it by pressing Ctrl+V or selecting the Void Transaction command from the Edit menu. You should also write something like **VOID** in large letters across the face of the check.

Printing a check you've entered

For some reason, when I get to this part of the discussion, my pulse quickens. I don't mean this as a pun. It just seems that there's something terribly serious about actually writing a check for real money. I get the same feeling whenever I mail someone cash — even if the amount is nominal.

I think the best way to lower my heart rate (and yours if you're like me) is to just print the darn check. So let's do it:

1. **Load the checks into your printer.**

   This process works the same way as when you load any paper into your printer. If you have questions about how this works, refer to your printer documentation. (Sorry, I can't help more on this, but there are a million different printers out there, and I can't guess which one you have.)

2. **Choose the Print icon on the iconbar.**

   As long as the Write Checks window is the active window, Quicken displays the Select Checks to Print dialog box, as shown in Figure 5-3. At the top of the dialog box Quicken shows how many checks to print and the total dollar amount for those checks.

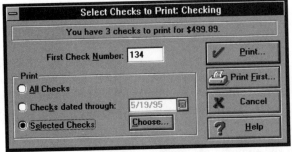

Figure 5-3:
The Select
Checks to
Print:
Checking
dialog box.

3. Enter the first check number.

Move the cursor to the First Check Number box and enter the number printed on the first check form you'll print. Figure 5-3 shows 134, for example, so the first check form is numbered 134. To quickly increase or decrease the check numbers, use the + and - keys from the keypad.

4. Indicate which checks Quicken should print.

Mark the All Checks options button under Print if you want Quicken to print all the checks you've entered by using the Write Checks window, which is the usual case. (Mark the Checks Dated Through option button under Print if you want to print all the checks through a certain date and then type that date in the text box.) Or if you want to pick and choose which checks to print, mark the Selected Checks option button.

5. If you selected which checks to print by marking the Print, Selected Checks option button, select the checks to print.

Select the Choose button. Quicken, with some annoyance, displays the Select Checks to Print window, as shown in Figure 5-4. Initially, Quicken marks all the checks dated on or earlier than the current date by placing a check mark in the Print column. If you don't want to print a check, either leave the Print field for that check clear (unchecked) or click the field to remove the check mark. In Figure 5-4, only the rent check is marked Print. When only the checks you want to print are marked to be printed or "in the Print field.", click the Close button to continue with this crazy little thing called *check printing*. Quicken, happy with your progress, redisplays the Select Checks to Print dialog box (refer to Figure 5-3).

6. Click the Print button or press Alt+P.

This command tells Quicken that you're ready, willing, and able to begin check printing. Quicken displays the Print Checks dialog box. Figure 5-5 shows this puppy.

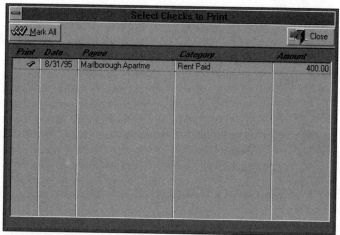

Figure 5-4:
The Select Checks to Print window.

Figure 5-5:
The Print Checks dialog box.

7. Indicate which Quicken check form you're using.

Move the cursor to the Checks Style drop-down list box, click the arrow so that the list drops down, and then choose the check form you purchased: standard, voucher, or wallet checks.

8. Tell Quicken if you're printing a partial page.

If you're printing a partial page of forms on a laser printer, indicate the number of check forms on the partial page using the Checks on First Page option buttons. Select the Th<u>r</u>ee option button if there are three checks, the T<u>w</u>o option button if there are two checks, or the <u>O</u>ne option button if there is one check.

9. Indicate if you want extra copies of the check form.

To do so, enter the number of copies you want in the Additional Copies text box. (This text box shows only if you are set up for certain check styles.)

If you use Quicken for business to keep accounts payable files, it's a good idea to make copies of checks to attach to the invoices that the checks pay. Then if a vendor calls later, starts hassling you, and asks which check paid an invoice, you can easily check your accounts payable files to quickly answer that question and cover your derriere.

10. Let the games begin.

Select OK to print your checks. If you're using a partial starting page of forms, your printer may prompt you to manually feed the first page of forms. When it finishes, Quicken asks if it printed your checks correctly. Figure 5-6 shows an example check made payable to Marlborough Apartments. At last, you get that landlord off your back.

Basically, it's just like one you would fill out manually. The only difference is that your computer has written the check for you.

11. Review the check or checks Quicken printed.

If it printed the checks correctly, answer the Did Checks Print OK? message box by clicking OK. (In this case, Quicken, apparently thinking you'll now want to do nothing but print checks, redisplays the Write Checks window.) If Quicken didn't print a check correctly, type the number of the first incorrectly printed check in the text box and then click OK. In this case, repeat the steps for check printing. Note, though, that you only need to reprint the first bad check and the checks that follow it. You don't need to reprint good checks that precede the first bad check. Figure 5-7 shows the message box.

12. Sign the printed checks.

Then — and I guess you probably don't need my help here — put the checks in the mail.

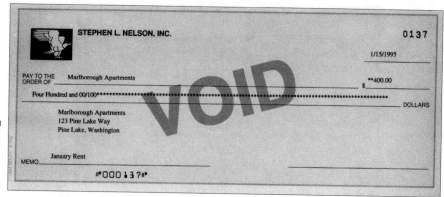

Figure 5-6:
An example
check.

A few words about check printing

Check printing is kind of complicated, isn't it?

For the record, I'm with you on this one. I really wish it wasn't so much work. But you'll find that printing checks does get easier after the first few times.

Pretty soon, you'll be running instead of walking through the steps. Pretty soon, you'll just skate around things like check-form alignment problems. Pretty soon, in fact, you'll know all this stuff and never have to read "pretty soon" again.

What if I discover a mistake after I've printed the check?

This problem isn't as big as you might think.

If you've already mailed the check, there's not a whole lot you can do. You can try to get the check back (if the person you paid hasn't cashed it) and replace it with one that's correct. (Good luck on this one.)

If the person has cashed the check, there's no way to get the check back. If you overpaid the person by writing the check for more than you should have, you need to get the person to pay you the overpayment amount. If you underpaid the person, you need to write another check for the amount of the underpayment.

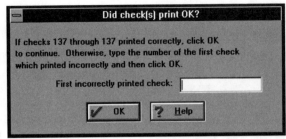

Figure 5-7:
The Did
check(s)
print OK?
message
box.

Did check(s) print OK?

If checks 137 through 137 printed correctly, click OK to continue. Otherwise, type the number of the first check which printed incorrectly and then click OK.

First incorrectly printed check: [   ]

✓ OK   ? Help

If you printed the check but haven't mailed it, void the printed check. This operation is in two-parts. First, write the word VOID in large letters across the face of the check form. (Use a ball point if you're using multipart forms so that the second and third parts also show as VOID.) Second, display the register, highlight the check, and then choose the Void Transaction command from the Edit menu, or Ctrl+V. (This option marks the check as one that's been voided in the system so Quicken does not use it in calculating your account balance.)

Printing a Check Register

You can print a check register or a register for any other account, too. Select the Registr icon from the iconbar to display the register window; then choose the Print icon from the iconbar. (Boy, that iconbar comes in handy, doesn't it?)

When you do this, Quicken displays the Print Register dialog box, as shown in Figure 5-8. To print a register, you follow these magic steps:

1. (Optional) Limit the range of dates.

To print a register of something other than the current year-to-date transactions, use the Print Transactions From and To text boxes. This is pretty dang obvious, isn't it? You just move the cursor to the From and To text boxes and enter the range of months the register should include.

2. (Optional) Enter a register title.

If you're the sort who likes to add your own special titles to things, move the cursor to the Title text box. Then enter the report title or description you want Quicken to print at the top of each and every page of the register.

Oh where, oh where, do the unprinted checks go?

Unprinted checks — those you've entered using the Write Checks window but haven't yet printed — are stored in the register. To identify them as unprinted checks, Quicken sets their check numbers as **Print**. What's more, when you tell Quicken to print the unprinted checks, what it really does is print the checks in your register that have **Print** in the check number text box. All this is of little practical value in most instances, but it results in several interesting possibilities. For example, you can enter the checks you want to print directly into the register — all you need to do is enter the check number as **Print**. (Note that you can't enter an address anywhere in the register, so this process isn't practical if you want addresses printed on your checks.) Another thing you can do is cause a check you've printed once to print again by changing its check number from, say 007, to **Print**. There aren't many good reasons you would want to do this. The only one I can think of is that you accidentally printed a check on plain paper and want to reprint it on a real check form.

3. **(Optional) Tell Quicken to use a single line per transaction.**

   To print each check and deposit transaction on a single line, move the cursor to the Print One Transaction Per Line check box. Then press the spacebar or click the check box to mark it.

4. **(Optional) Tell Quicken to print split transaction information.**

   To print the Split Transaction information — categories, memos, and amounts — move the cursor to the Print Transaction Splits check box. Then press the spacebar or click the check box to mark it.

5. **Tell Quicken to print transactions in check number order.**

   To print check and deposit transactions in check number order instead of transaction date order, move the cursor to the Sort By Number check box. Then press the spacebar or click the check box to mark it. (If you do this, your deposits will probably be listed before your checks because deposits usually don't have numbers.)

6. **Select Print.**

   Quicken displays the Print Report dialog box. (See Figure 5-10.) You don't have to fool around with this dialog box. If you want to print a register, pronto, just select Print. (Yes, again.) Then again, if you're the sort of person who likes to fool around with this kind of stuff, carry on with the rest of these steps.

   If you want to see the effect the different register-printing text boxes and check boxes have, just experiment. You can't hurt anything or anybody.

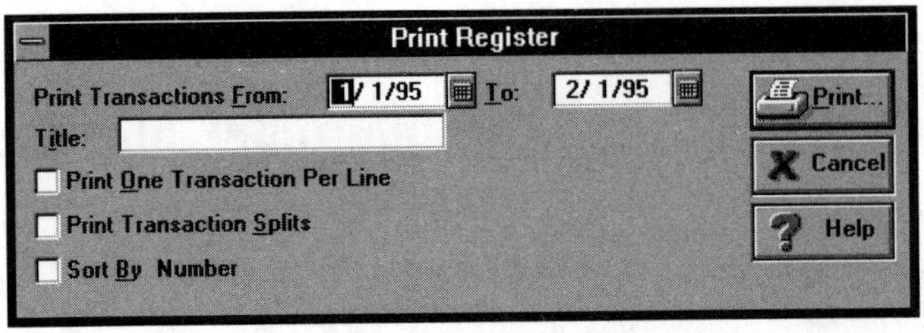

Figure 5-8:
The Print
Register
dialog box.

7. (Optional) Print the report to disk if you want.

To print the report to disk as a text file, mark one of the following Print To option buttons:

- ASCII Disk File if you want to create a text file, such as when you want to import the register into a word processing program

- Tab-delimited Disk File, such as when you want to import the register into a database program (Oooh . . . fancy. . .)

- 123 (.PRN) Disk File, such as when you want to import the register into Lotus 1-2-3

If you do indicate you want a disk file, when you select the Print command button to start the ol' printing process, Quicken displays the Create Disk File dialog box as shown in Figure 5-10. This dialog box asks for the filename Quicken should create as part of printing the file to disk and the location where you want the file stored. Just enter the filename you want into the — you guessed it — the Filename text box. (Use a valid DOS filename, of course.) Use the Directories and Drives list boxes to indicate where you want the file stored. Or don't do anything and Quicken creates the file in the active Quicken directory — probably C:\QUICKENW. And what do you do with the disk file? You're on your own here. . . .

8. (Optional) Color your world.

If you've got a color printer and want your register printed in color, mark the Print In Color check box on the Print Report dialog box. You can do this by clicking the check box.

9. (Optional) Trade speed for quality.

Or you can mark the Print In Draft Mode check box to tell Quicken it should print faster and spend less time worrying about the quality of the printing job it does. In other words, you can use this check box to trade print speed for print quality. Life is full of trade-offs, isn't it?

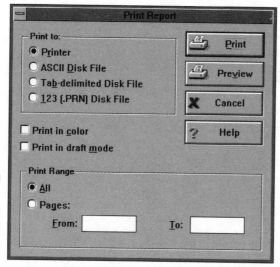

Figure 5-9:
The Print
Report
dialog box.

10. **(Optional) Tell Quicken which pages to print.**

    Use the Print Range option buttons and text boxes to limit the pages
    Quicken prints. How? Mark the Pages option button; then enter the range
    of page numbers you want printed. That's simple enough, right?

11. **Select Print.**

    Now select Print one last time. Quicken finally prints the register. If you're still
    with me, take a look at Figure 5-11. It shows a printer register. (This happens if
    you marked the Printer option button on the Print Report dialog box.

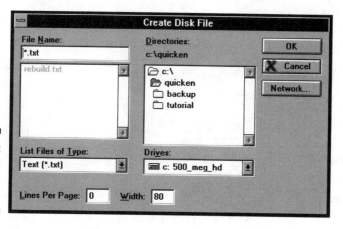

Figure 5-10:
The Create
Disk File
dialog box.

Check Register

Page 1

Checking
5/19/1995

Date	Num	Transaction	Payment	C	Deposit	Balance
1/1 1995	memo: cat:	Opening Balance [Checking]		x	4.16	4.16
1/1 1995	101 memo: cat:	Movies Galore February Utilities	25.50			-21.34
1/3 1995	DEP memo: cat:	Aunt Enid birthday gift Gift Received			100.00	78.66
1/5 1995	TXFR memo: cat:	For Aunt Enid's next gift Def Leppard CD? [Savings]	50.00			28.66
1/15 1995	137 memo: cat:	Marlborough Apartments January Rent Rent Paid	400.00			-371.34
1/15 1995	Print memo: cat:	Junebug's Antiques Household	75.00			-446.34
1/15 1995	Print memo: cat:	Puget Power Utilities	24.89			-471.23
2/1 1995	DEP memo: cat:	Salt Mine, Ltd Salary			1,000.00	528.77

Figure 5-11:
A real, live
check regi-
ster. At last.

The 5th Wave   By Rich Tennant

"I THINK I'VE FOUND YOUR FILE, MARGARET! IT FEELS LIKE
A SPREADSHEET! RIGHT?! RIGHT?!"

Chapter 6
Reports, Charts, and Other Cool Tools

. . . .

In This Chapter

▶ Printing Quicken reports

▶ Using the Reports menu commands

▶ QuickZooming report totals

▶ Sharing information with a spreadsheet

▶ Editing and rearranging report information

▶ Creating a chart

▶ Using QuickReports and SnapShots

. . . .

Quicken lets you summarize, slice, and dice register and account information in a variety of ways. This chapter describes how to use reports and produce graphs easily. This stuff is much easier to understand if you know how to print a register first. I described this trick at the end of Chapter 5.

Creating and Printing Reports

After you learn how to print checks and registers, all other printing in Quicken is easy, easy, easy.

Just the facts (of printing), ma'am

The transactions you enter in the register window and the checks you enter in the Write Checks window determine the information in a report. To print a report, then, just choose the Reports menu and tell Quicken which report you want to print (see Figure 6-1).

Home   ▶
Investment   ▶
Business   ▶
Other   ▶
Memorized Reports...
Graphs   ▶
Memorized Graphs...
Snapshots...
Reconciliation...

Figure 6-1:
The Reports
menu.

Quicken produces a bunch of different reports. To make sense of what might otherwise become mass confusion, Quicken arranges all of its reports into four groups: Home reports, Business reports, Other reports, and Investment reports. (These sort of sound like PBS documentaries, don't they? "Tonight, Joob Taylor explores the secrets of baby-sitting in the *Home Report*.")

To see the reports in one of these groups, select the report group from the Reports menu. If you read the fast-paced and exciting Appendix B, "Quick and Dirty Windows," you know that those little triangles to the right of menu command names tell you that another menu follows.

Figure 6-2 shows the Home group of reports. Pretty exciting stuff so far, don't you think?

To print a Home report (or any other report, for that matter), select the report from the appropriate menu. For example, to print the Home Cash Flow report, select the Home command from the Reports menu and then select the Cash Flow command from the Home reports menu.

Quicken displays the Create Report dialog box. This dialog box asks you to confirm your report selection and identify the range of dates the report should cover, as shown in Figure 6-3. You don't have to specify either piece of information.

If you don't enter a new range of dates, Quicken assumes that you want to include transactions from the start of the current calendar year through the present date.

Cash Flow...
Monthly Budget...
Itemized Categories...
Tax Summary...
Net Worth...
Tax Schedule...
Missing Checks...
Comparison...

Figure 6-2:
The Home
group of
reports.

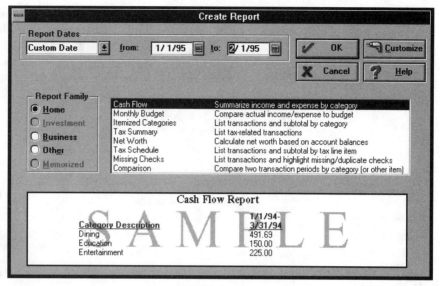

Note that a report that shows account balances — such as the Home Net Worth report, the Business Balance sheet, or the Investment Portfolio report — doesn't need a range of dates because these reports show account balances as of a specific date. In these cases, if you don't enter a date, Quicken assumes that you want account balances for the current system date from your computer's internal clock.

If you select the wrong report, you can indicate which report you want by using the Report Family option buttons and then selecting the correct report from the list box. The Report Family option buttons that Quicken supplies match the commands listed in the Reports menu. Quicken also lists the same reports in the list box to the right of the option buttons that it does in the Report submenus. For example, if you mark the Home option button, the list box shows the same reports as the Home Report menu. Wild.

The bottom chunk of the Create Report dialog box shows roughly what the report you're creating looks like. When it looks right, click OK. Quicken then copies an on-screen version of the report to a new document window. Figure 6-4 shows an on-screen version of the Home Cash Flow report. (The information shown in this report, by the way, is based on the transactions collected in Chapters 4 and 5.)

You can't see the entire on-screen version of a report unless your report is very small (or your screen is monstrously large). Use the PgUp and PgDn keys to scroll up and down and the Tab and Shift+Tab keys to move left and right. Or if you're a mouse lover, you can click and drag various pieces of the scroll bars.

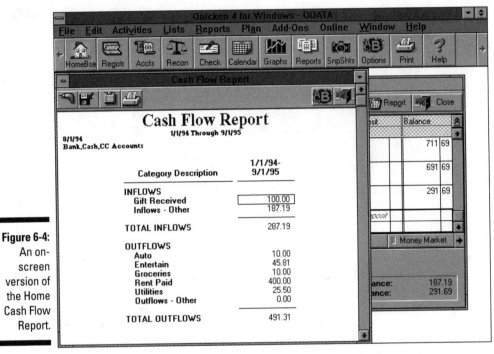

Figure 6-4:
An on-screen version of the Home Cash Flow Report.

To print your report, choose the Print icon from the iconbar or click the Print button (the cute picture of a laser printer) in the report window. Either way, Quicken displays the Print Report dialog box (see Figure 6-5).

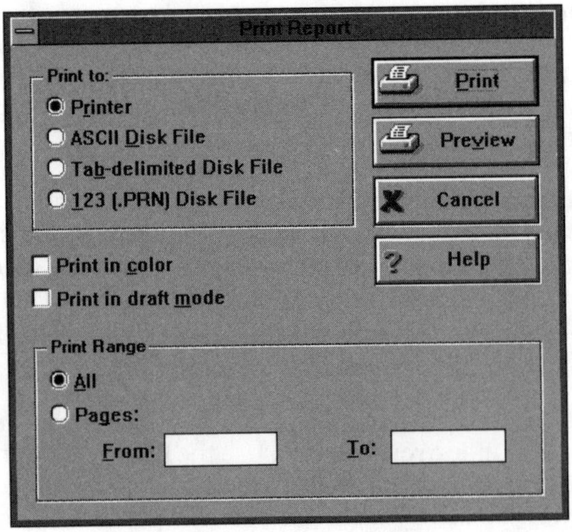

Figure 6-5:
The Print Report dialog box.

To accept the given specifications — which will almost always be fine — just click the Print button. You'll never guess what happens next: Quicken prints the report!

When you're ready — but not before — remove the on-screen version of the report by closing the report document window. (You do so by double-clicking the window's control menu icon and choosing Close, pressing Alt+F4, or pressing Esc.)

What about the other Print Report dialog box settings?

I almost forgot. The Print To option buttons let you tell Quicken where it should send the report it produces: to the printer or to a disk file. The check boxes let you control aspects of printing, and the Print Range option buttons and text boxes let you print a specific portion of the report.

I described how these things work in Chapter 5, so I won't repeat the discussion. If you want the scoop, refer to the section about printing a check register.

Reviewing standard reports

Most of the time, you want to select one of the reports listed in the Home, Business, or Investment reports menu.

Tables 6-1, 6-2, and 6-3 describe Quicken's Home, Investment, and Business reports. (Some of these babies won't make sense unless you understand how to collect the information that goes into the report, as described in Chapters 12, 13, and Part IV.)

Table 6-1	Quicken's Home Reports
Report	*Description*
Cash Flow	Summarizes the money that flows into and out of an account by income and expense categories and by transfers. Cash is king, dude, so this report only includes transactions recorded in your bank, cash, and credit card accounts.
Monthly Budget	Summarizes income and expense categories and compares actual category totals to budgeted category amounts. This report only includes transactions recorded in your bank, cash, and credit card accounts. (For this report to make any sense, of course, you need to have a budget set up.)
Itemized Categories	Summarizes income and expense category totals. This report includes transactions from all of your accounts.

(continued)

Table 6-1 *(continued)*

Report	Description
Tax Summary	Summarizes income and expense category totals for those categories marked as tax related. Like the Itemized Categories report, this report includes transactions from all of your accounts.
Net Worth	Lists all accounts, their balances, and the difference between the sum of the asset accounts and the sum of the liabilities accounts, which the report identifies as your net worth.
Tax Schedule	Summarizes income and expense category totals for those categories marked as tax related and assigned to specific tax schedule lines. This report includes transactions from all accounts. (If you export Quicken information to a tax preparation package like TurboTax, this report gets passed on to the package.)
Missing Checks	Lists all the checks you've written and flags any gaps in the check number sequence. (This report helps you identify missing checks.)
Comparison	Lets you compare category totals from two periods. You can use this report to compare January's activity with February's activity, for example. Remember: because you are comparing two periods, you need to enter two transaction date ranges.

Table 6-2   Quicken's Investment Reports

Report	Description
Portfolio Value	Lists the current value of all securities in your investment accounts.
Investment Performance	A power-user report. This report calculates the internal rates of report delivered by each of the individual investments in your portfolio.
Capital Gains	Lists all the unrealized gains on individual investments you hold. (*Unrealized* means that the investment is worth more than what you paid for it, but because you still own the investment, your gain is unrealized. When you sell the investment, you realize the gain.)
Investment Income	Summarizes income and expense categories for transactions recorded in your investment accounts.
Investment Transactions	Lists transactions recorded for all your investment accounts.

Table 6-3	Quicken's Business Reports
Report	*Description*
P&L Statement	Summarizes income and expense category totals. This report includes transactions from all your accounts. It also helps you answer the business question, "Am I getting fairly compensated for the hassle and the risk?"
P & L Comparison	Lets you compare profit and loss by category for two periods. You can use this report to compare January's profit with February's profit.
Cash Flow	Summarizes the money received by and paid out of an account by income and expense categories and by transfers. This report only includes transactions recorded in your bank, cash, and credit card accounts.
A/P by Vendor	Summarizes unprinted checks by payee for all your bank accounts. (*A/P* stands for *accounts payable.*)
A/R by Customer	Summarizes uncleared transactions for all other assets accounts. (*A/R* stands for *accounts receivable.*)
Job/Project	Summarizes income and expense category totals with each class's information displayed in a separate column. You must be using an advanced Quicken feature called *classes* for this report to make any sense.
Payroll	Summarizes income and expense categories which begin with the word *payroll.* If you've done things right, you can use this report to prepare quarterly and annual payroll tax reports. (See Chapter 15 for the rest of the story.)
Balance Sheet	Lists all accounts, their balances, and the difference between the sum of your asset accounts and the sum of your liabilities accounts, which the report identifies as your equity. Almost identical to the Home Net Worth report.
Missing Checks	Lists all the checks you've written and flags any gaps in the check number sequence. This report helps you identify missing checks and is identical to the Home Missing Checks report.
Comparison	Lets you compare category totals from two periods. You can use this report to compare January's activity with February's activity, for example. (Because you are comparing two periods, you must enter two transaction date ranges.) Identical to the Home Comparison report.

Those other reports

When you want to extract some financial tidbit, you can usually get what you want from one of the reports listed on the Home, Investment, or Business reports menus.

However, I should tell you something else: Quicken is remarkably sophisticated in its reporting. It supplies several additional reports: Transaction, Summary, Comparison, Budget, and Account Balances.

To access these reports, select the Other command from the Reports menu or select Other Report Family from the Create Report dialog box. Typically, you select one of these report commands when you specify exactly what you want to appear in the report and how you want the report organized. You do so by using the Customize button.

I'm not going to describe how the Customize button works. I feel kind of bad about this because there are probably a few people out there who, late one night, will decide they want to know how to filter, sort, and customize. Of course, there are also people who will decide late some night that they want to know how to replace the transmission on a 1971 Triumph Spitfire. And I'm not describing that here, either.

If you still want to learn how the Transaction, Summary, Comparison, Budget, and Account Balances reports work — or how the Customize button works — just noodle around. You can't hurt anything.

If you do play around with these items, you can save any custom report specifications that you create. To do so, click the Memorize button at the top of the report window. Quicken displays a dialog box that asks you to supply a name for your customized report. (You can also provide a default report date range.) After you name the customized report, Quicken lists it whenever you choose the Memorized command from the Reports menu.

At the printing dog-and-pony show

There are some neat things you can do with the reports you've created. I won't spend a bunch of time talking about these things, but I do want to give you a quick rundown of some of the most valuable tricks.

Got a question about a number? Just zoom it

If you don't understand where a number in a report came from, point to it with the mouse. As you point to numbers, Quicken changes the mouse pointer to a magnifying glass marked with a Z. Double-click the mouse, and Quicken displays a list of all the transactions that make up that number.

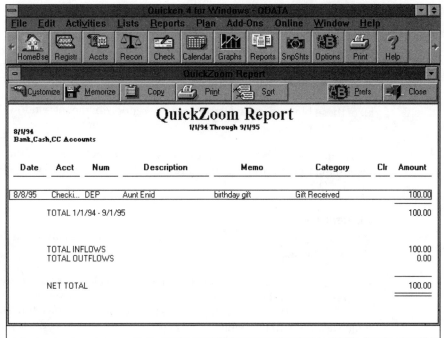

Figure 6-6:
The
QuickZoom
report.

This feature, called *QuickZoom*, is extremely handy for understanding the figures that appear on your reports. If you double-click the Gift Received number in the report (see Figure 6-4), for example, Quicken displays the QuickZoom report shown in Figure 6-6.

Ah, yes. You remember Aunt Enid's thoughtful gift. You've got to send her that thank-you note.

Sharing report data with spreadsheets

If you use a Windows spreadsheet such as Microsoft Excel, 1-2-3 for Windows, or Quattro Pro for Windows, you can copy the stuff that shows in a report window to the Clipboard. Highlight the information and then click the Copy button on the toolbar. This copies the selection to the Windows Clipboard. Then you can start your spreadsheet program and choose its Edit Paste command to paste the stuff from the clipboard into your spreadsheet. This process really isn't very hard, so go ahead and try it. You might want to do this if you want to analyze the report data with a spreadsheet.

Editing and rearranging reports

As you may have noticed, when Quicken displays the report window, it also displays a row of buttons, including Customize, Memorize, Copy, Print, Sort, and Close. Earlier in the chapter, I talk about the Copy, Print, and Close buttons. So in the interest of fair play, I'll briefly discuss what the other buttons do. (Not all of these buttons are available in every report document window. I don't know why, really. Maybe it's just to keep you guessing.)

You really don't need to worry about these other buttons. Read through the discussion that follows only if you're feeling comfortable, relaxed, and truly mellow, OK?

Customizing

The Customize button works pretty much the same no matter which report shows in the document window.

When you click this button, Quicken displays a dialog box that lets you enter the report title and specify the range of dates the report should cover using text boxes. It also lets you choose from a variety of other options, too, such as which accounts to use, which transactions to use, and how the report's information should be arranged.

Memorizing

Let's say you get into this customization thing. If you do, you should know that you can save your customized reports by clicking the Memorize button. When you click Memorize, Quicken displays the dialog box shown in Figure 6-7. Mostly, Quicken displays this dialog box so you can give a name to your creation. If you want, you can also specify whether some special date range should always be used.

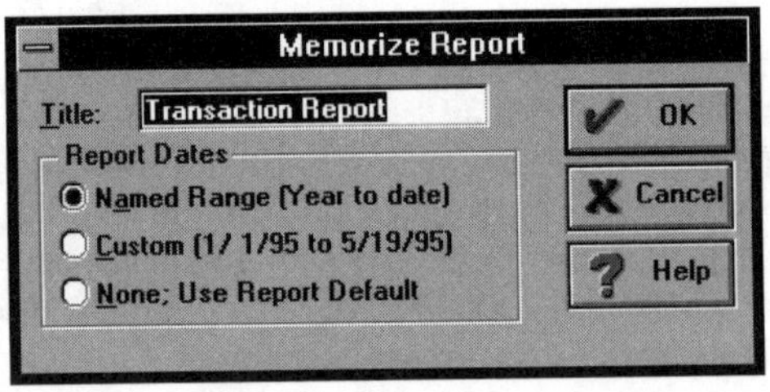

Figure 6-7:
The
Memorize
Report
dialog box.

By the way, once you create a memorized report, you can reproduce it by choosing the Memorized Reports command from the Reports name and then selecting the memorized report name.

Sorting

The Sort button displays a dialog box that looks suspiciously like the one shown in Figure 6-8. Using the dialog box's drop-down list box, you can tell Quicken how the report's transactions should be sorted: by check number, by date, by payee, or by some other field.

Figure 6-8:
The Select
Sort Criteria
dialog box.

What's the Prefs button do?

Most of the document windows that Quicken displays — the report window is just one example — also display a Prefs button. When you choose this button, Quicken displays a dialog box with a bunch of boxes and buttons that let you change the way the window looks or works.

If I were a really great writer — the John Grisham of computer books, for example — I might be able to whip up a riveting discussion of how the reports preferences dialog box options work. I'm going to do both you and my publisher a favor, however, by making a suggestion. Just play with these preferences settings if you're interested. You'll find it more fun and a better learning experience.

Charts Only Look Tricky

I love charts. I know that sounds goofy. But data graphics — as the snobs and academics call it — opens up wonderful opportunities for communicating. And Quicken's charts are really easy to use.

To produce a Quicken chart, choose the Graphs command from the Reports menu and select a graph. Or click the Graphs icon on the iconbar.

After you select one of these graph commands, Quicken displays a dialog box in which you describe how you want the chart to look. If you choose the Income and Expense graphs command or click the Graphs icon, for example, Quicken displays the Create Graph dialog box (see Figure 6-9).

Use the From and To text boxes to tell Quicken which days or months of account information you want summarized in the graph.

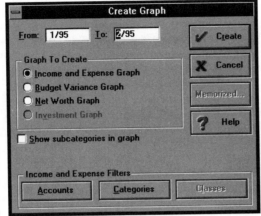

Figure 6-9:
The Create
Graph
dialog box.

Use the Graph To Create option buttons to confirm the graph choice. These option buttons mirror the Graphs menu commands. As you probably guessed, if you use the Graphs menu, Quicken marks the option button that names the Graph menu command you chose to get to the dialog box.

Use the Show Subcategories in Graph check box to tell Quicken — shoot, you can guess this — whether subcategories get graphed.

Finally, use the Accounts, Categories, and Classes buttons to tell Quicken that you want to pick and choose which accounts, categories, and classes you want included in the graph. If you choose a button, Quicken displays another dialog box that lists the things you pick and choose.

When you're ready to produce the graph, just command Quicken to do so. You can try saying "Quicken, I command thee to produce a graph." Unfortunately, this command doesn't work. So your best bet is to click the Create button.

Figure 6-10 shows a picture of a bar graph of monthly income and expense figures and a pie chart that breaks down your spending. They're kind of cool, but you'll have much more fun looking at your own data in a picture. By the way, you can use QuickZoom on a chart to see a report that describes the data being plotted.

The other graph types work basically the same way. The Budget Variance graph depicts your actual and planned spending and income in bar charts. The Net Worth graph shows your total assets, total liabilities, and net worth by month in a bar graph. The Investments graph displays a bar graph showing total portfolio and individual securities values by month. (If you're not working with Quicken's investments, of course, this last description sounds like gibberish. So you'll want to peruse Chapters 12 and 13 first.)

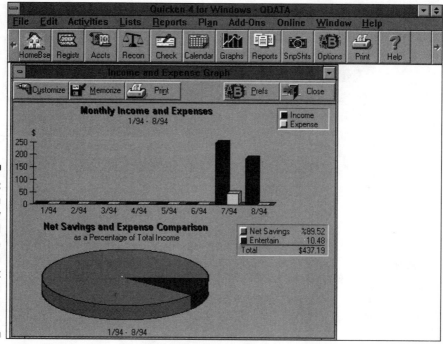

Figure 6-10:
A bar graph of monthly income and expense totals and a pie chart showing a spending breakdown.

You can memorize customized graphs the same way you memorize customized reports. Just click the Memorize button at the top of the Graph window. Then, when Quicken prompts you, give the graph a name. To later reuse the graph, choose the Memorized Graphs command from the Reports menu, select the memorized graph from the list that Quicken displays, and choose OK.

QuickReports and SnapShots: Last But Not Least

Before I forget, I need to tell you about two other variants of Quicken's reporting feature: QuickReports and SnapShots. Let's talk QuickReports first. Quicken supplies a quick-and-dirty report called, cleverly enough, a QuickReport. If you're working with the register, you can produce a quick report that summarizes the things like the checks written to a particular payee or the transactions assigned to a specific income or expense category. To produce a QuickReport, first move the cursor to the field you want to summarize in the report. Then click the Report button at the top of the register window. The report shown in Figure 6-11, for example, is a quick report summarizing all the transactions assigned to the Rent Paid category. (Only one transaction is shown.)

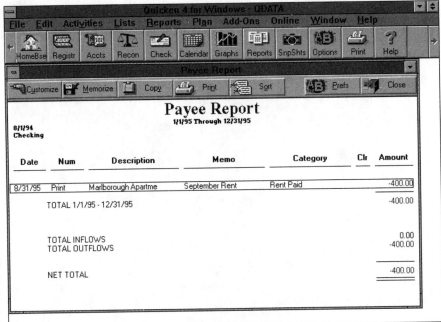

Figure 6-11:
Here's a
QuickReport.

Snapshots resemble QuickReports in that they're really easy to produce. All you do is choose the Snapshots command from the Reports menu or click the Snapshots icon. Either way, Quicken displays a clever little report that summarizes some interesting financial tidbits — such as your most expensive spending categories or the categories that are most out-of-line considering you budget. The snapshot reports are all really colorful because they use lots of graphics. So rather than showing you some bleak, black and white version of them here, how about if you just click on the Snapshots icon right now.

Chapter 7
A Matter of Balance

1 want to start this chapter with an important point: balancing a bank account in Quicken is easy and quick.

I'm not just trying to get you pumped up about an otherwise painfully boring topic. I don't think balancing a bank account is any more exciting than you do. (At the Nelson house, we never answer the "What should we do tonight?" question by saying, "Hey, let's balance an account.")

My point is this: because bank account balancing can be tedious and boring, use Quicken to speed up the drudgery.

Selecting the Account You Want to Balance

This step is easy. And you probably already know how to do it, too.

Choose the Accts icon from the iconbar or choose the Account command from the Lists menu. Quicken displays the Account List window (see Figure 7-1).

Next select the account that you want to balance. Use the arrow keys to highlight the account and then press Enter. Or, if you have a mouse, double-click the account. Quicken displays the register window, which lists information about the account.

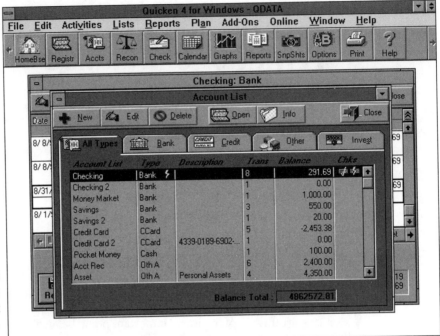

Figure 7-1:
The Account
List window.

Balancing a Bank Account

Like I said, balancing a bank account is remarkably easy. In fact, I'll go so far as to say that if you have any problems, they'll stem from . . . well, sloppy record-keeping that preceded your use of Quicken.

Enough of this blather; let's get started.

Telling Quicken, "Hey, man, I want to balance this account"

To tell Quicken that you want to *balance,* or *reconcile,* your account records with the bank's records, choose the Recon icon from the iconbar or choose the Reconcile command from the Activities menu. Quicken displays the Reconcile Bank Statement dialog box, as shown in Figure 7-2.

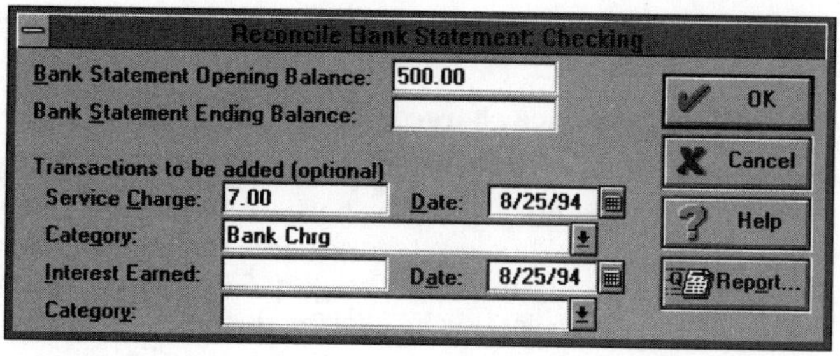

Figure 7-2:
The
Reconcile
Bank State-
ment dialog
box.

Reconcile Bank Statement: Checking

Bank Statement Opening Balance: 500.00
Bank Statement Ending Balance:

Transactions to be added (optional)
Service Charge: 7.00   Date: 8/25/94
Category: Bank Chrg
Interest Earned: Date: 8/25/94
Category:

OK
Cancel
Help
Report...

Giving Quicken the bank's information

As you probably know, in a reconciliation you compare your records of a bank account with the bank's records of the same account. You should be able to explain any difference between the two accounts — usually by pointing to checks that you've written but that haven't cleared. (Sometimes deposits fall into the same category; you've recorded a deposit and mailed it, but the bank hasn't yet credited your account.)

The first step, then, is to supply Quicken with the bank's account information. You get this information from your monthly statement. Supply Quicken with the figures it needs as follows:

1. **Verify the Bank Statement Opening Balance.**

   Quicken displays a figure in the Bank Statement Opening Balance text box. If this figure isn't correct, replace it with the correct figure. To do so, move the cursor to the text box and type over the given figure. (If this is the first time you've reconciled, Quicken gets this opening balance figure from your starting account balance. If you've reconciled before, Quicken uses the Bank Statement Ending Balance that you specified the last time you reconciled as the Bank Statement Opening Balance.)

2. **Enter the Bank Statement Ending Balance.**

   Move the cursor to the Bank Statement Ending Balance text box and enter the ending, or closing, balance shown on your bank statement.

3. **Enter the bank's service charge.**

   If your bank statement shows a service charge and you haven't already entered it, move the cursor to the Service Charge text box and enter the amount (for example, enter $4.56 as **4.56**).

4. **Enter a transaction date for the service charge transaction.**

   Quicken supplies the current system date from your computer's internal clock as the default service charge date. If this date isn't correct, enter the correct one.

Remember that you can adjust a date one day at a time by using the + and – keys.

5. **Assign the bank's service charge to a category.**

   Enter the expense category to which you assign bank service charges in the first Category text box — the one beneath the Service Charge text box. If you're using standard home categories, this category is Bank Chrg. If you want to select a category from the Category & Transfer List window, activate the drop-down list box by clicking the down arrow, highlighting the category by using the arrow keys, and pressing Enter.

6. **Enter the account's interest income.**

   If the account earned interest for the month and you haven't already entered this figure, enter an amount in the Interest Earned text box (for example, enter $.17 as **.17**).

7. **Enter a transaction date for the interest income transaction.**

   You already know how to enter dates. I won't bore you by explaining it again (but see step 4 if you're having trouble).

8. **Assign the interest to a category.**

   Enter the category to which the account's interest should be assigned in the second Category text box. If you're using the standard home category list, this category is probably Int Inc. To select a category from the Category & Transfer list, activate the drop-down list box by clicking the down arrow, highlighting the category, and pressing Enter.

9. **Tell Quicken that the reconciliation is complete.**

   To do so, just click OK.

Explaining the difference between your records and the bank's

Next, Quicken compares your register's account balance with the bank statement's ending account balance. Then it builds a list of checks and deposits that your register shows but that haven't yet *cleared* (haven't been recorded by the bank). Figure 7-3 shows the dialog box Quicken displays to provide you with this information.

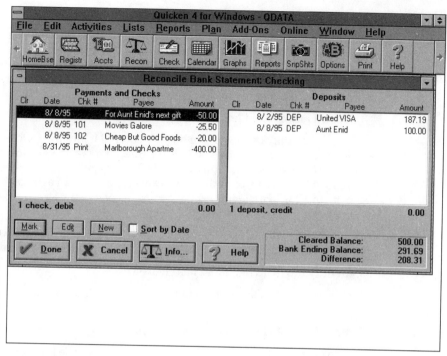

Figure 7-3:
The
Reconcile
Bank
Statement
window.

As Figure 7-3 shows, the Reconcile Bank Statment window is basically just two lists — one of account withdrawals and one of account deposits. The dialog box also displays some extra information at the bottom of the screen: the cleared balance (which is your account balance including only those transactions that you or Quicken have marked as cleared), the bank statement balance, the difference between these two figures, and the number of checks and deposits that you or Quicken have marked as cleared.

If you don't like the order in which withdrawals and deposits are arranged, you can change it. Mark the Sort by Date check box, and Quicken reorders the transactions by date.

Marking cleared checks and deposits

You need to tell Quicken which deposits and checks have cleared at the bank. (Refer to your bank statement for this information.)

1. Identify the first deposit that has cleared.

You know how to do so, I'm sure. Just leaf through the bank statement and find the first deposit listed.

2. Mark the first cleared deposit as cleared.

Scroll through the transactions listed in the Reconcile Bank Statment window, find the deposit, and then click it. You can also highlight the deposit using the arrow keys and then click the Mark button or press the spacebar. Quicken places a checkmark in front of the deposit to mark it as cleared and updates the cleared statement balance.

3. Record any cleared but missing deposits.

If you can't find a deposit, you haven't entered it into the Quicken register yet. I can only guess why you haven't entered it. Maybe you just forgot, for example. In any event, return to the Quicken register and then enter the deposit in the register in the usual way — but enter an asterisk in the C column. This mark identifies the deposit as one that's already cleared at the bank. To return to the Reconcile Bank Statment window, choose the Reconcile Bank Statement command from the Window menu.

4. Repeat steps 1, 2, and 3 for all deposits listed on the bank statement.

5. Identify the first check that has cleared.

No sweat, right? Just find the first check or withdrawal listed on the bank statement.

6. Mark the first cleared check as cleared.

Scroll through the transactions listed in the Reconcile Bank Statement window, find the first check, and then click it. You can also highlight it by using the arrow keys and then select Mark or press the spacebar. Quicken inserts a checkmark to label this transaction as cleared and updates the cleared statement balance.

7. Record any missing but cleared checks.

If you can't find a check or withdrawal — guess what? — you haven't entered it in the Quicken register yet. Display the Quicken register by clicking the Edit button. Then enter the check or withdrawal in the register. Be sure to enter an asterisk in the C column to identify this check or withdrawal as one that's already cleared at the bank. To return to the Reconcile Bank Account window, choose Close from the Register's control menu or click the Close button. Or reactivate the Reconcile Bank Statement window by clicking it if it's visible.

8. Repeat steps 5, 6, and 7 for withdrawals listed on the bank statement.

By the way, these steps don't take very long. It takes me about two minutes to reconcile my account each month. And I'm not joking or exaggerating. By two minutes, I really mean two minutes.

Does the difference equal zero?

After you mark all the cleared checks and deposits, the difference between the cleared balance for the account and the bank statement's ending balance should equal zero. Notice that I said "should," not "will." Figure 7-4 shows a Reconcile Bank Account window in which everything is hunky-dory and life is grand.

If the difference does equal zero, you're done. Just click the <u>D</u>one button to tell Quicken that you're finished. Quicken displays a congratulations message telling you how proud it is of you, and then it asks if you want to print a reconciliation report.

As part of the finishing-up process, Quicken changes all the asterisks to Xs. There's no great magic in this transformation. Quicken makes the change to identify the transactions that have already been reconciled.

Can't decide whether or not to print the Reconciliation report? Unless you're a business bookkeeper or accountant reconciling a bank account for someone else — your employer or a client, for example — you don't need to print the Reconciliation report. All printing does is prove that you reconciled the account. (Basically, this proof is the reason you should print the report if you *are* a bookkeeper or an accountant — the person for whom you're reconciling the account will know that you did your job and has a piece of paper to come back to later if there are questions.)

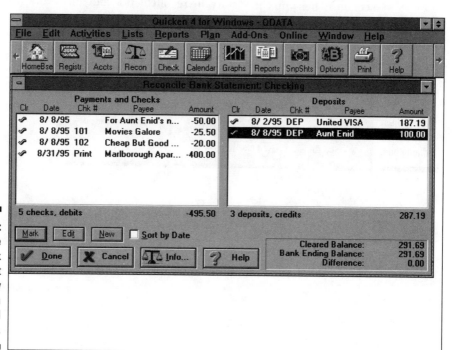

Figure 7-4:
A Reconcile
Bank
Account
window
showing a
balanced
account.

By the way, if you forget to print a reconciliation report, all is not lost. You can use the Reconciliation command in the Reports menu to print the report later.

If the difference doesn't equal zero, you've got a problem. If you select Done, Quicken provides some cursory explanations as to why your account doesn't balance via a dialog box like that shown in Figure 7-5. This box tells you that you can force the two amounts to agree by clicking the Adjust Balance button.

Forcing the two amounts to agree isn't a very good idea. To do so, Quicken adds a cleared transaction equal to the difference. (I'll talk about this transaction a little later in the chapter.)

If you press Esc with the Reconcile Bank Statment window open, Quicken asks whether you want to save the work or quit without saving it.

If you tell Quicken you want to save your work, Quicken leaves your reconciliation work basically half done. The transactions that you marked as cleared still show the asterisk in the C field. And you still have an explainable difference between the bank statement and your register. (You can also throw up your hands, give up, and tell Quicken you don't want to save your work. In this case, you'll need to start over next time.)

Either way, however, postponing a reconciliation and not choosing to adjust the bank account balance is usually the best approach. It allows you to locate and correct problems. (I'll give you some ideas about how to do so in the next section.) Then you can restart the reconciliation and finish your work. (You restart a reconciliation the same way that you originate one.)

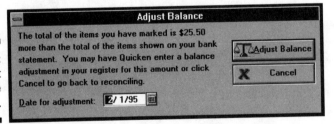

Figure 7-5:
The Adjust
Balance
dialog box.

Ten Things You Should Do If Your Account Doesn't Balance

Let me give you some suggestions for reconciling an account when you're having problems. If you're sitting in front of your computer wringing your hands, try the following tips.

Are you working with the right account?

Sounds dumb, doesn't it? If you have a bunch of different bank accounts, however, it's darn easy to end up in the wrong account. So go ahead and confirm, for example, that you're trying to reconcile your checking account at Mammoth International Bank using the Mammoth International checking account statement.

Look for transactions that the bank has recorded but you haven't

Go through your bank statement and make sure that you have recorded every transaction that your bank has recorded. Cash machine withdrawals, special fees or service charges (such as for checks or your safety deposit box), automatic withdrawals, direct deposits, and so on are easily overlooked.

If the difference is positive — that is, the bank thinks you have less money than you think you should — you may be missing a withdrawal transaction. If the difference is negative, you may be missing a deposit transaction.

Look for reversed transactions

Here's a tricky one. If you accidentally enter a transaction backwards — a deposit as a withdrawal or a withdrawal as a deposit — your account won't balance. And the error can be difficult to find. The Reconcile Bank Account dialog box shows all the correct transactions, but a transaction amount appears positive when it should be negative or negative when it should be positive. The check you wrote to Mrs. Travis for your son's piano lessons appears as a positive number instead of a negative number, for example.

Look for a transaction that's equal to half the difference

One handy way to find the transaction that you entered backwards — *if* there's only one — is to look for a transaction that's equal to half the irreconcilable difference. For example, if the difference is $200, you may have entered a $100 deposit as a withdrawal or a $100 withdrawal as a check.

I don't want to beat a dead horse, but the sign (that is, positive or negative) of the difference should help you find the problem. If the difference is positive — the bank thinks you have less money than your register indicates — you may have mistakenly entered a withdrawal as a deposit. If the difference is negative — the bank thinks you have more money than your register says — you may be missing a deposit transaction.

Look for a transaction that's equal to the difference

While I'm on the subject of explaining the difference by looking at individual transactions, let me make an obvious point. If the difference between the bank's records and yours equals one of the transactions listed in your register, you may have incorrectly marked the transaction as cleared or incorrectly left the transaction marked as uncleared.

I don't know. Maybe that was too obvious.

Check for transposed numbers

Transposed numbers occur when you flip-flop two digits in a number. For example, you enter $45.89 as $48.59.

These turkeys always cause accountants and bookkeepers headaches. If you look at the numbers, it's often difficult to detect an error because the digits are the same. For example, when comparing a check amount of $45.89 in your register with a check for $48.59 shown on your bank statement, both check amounts show the same digits: 4, 5, 8, and 9. They just show them in different orders.

Transposed numbers are tough to find, but here's a trick you can try. Divide the difference shown on the Reconcile Bank Account window by nine. If the result is an even number of dollars or cents, there's a good chance that there's a transposed number somewhere.

Have someone else look over your work

This idea may seem pretty obvious, but it amazes me how often a second pair of eyes can find something that you've been overlooking.

If you're using Quicken at home, ask your spouse. If you're using Quicken at work, ask the owner or one of your coworkers (preferably that one person who always seems to have way too much free time).

Be on the lookout for multiple errors

By the way, if you find an error using this laundry list and there's still a difference, it's a good idea to start checking at the top of the list again. You may, for example, discover-after you find a transposed number-that you entered another transaction backwards or incorrectly cleared or uncleared a transaction.

Try again next month (and maybe the month after that)

If the difference isn't huge in relation to the size of your bank account, you may want to wait until next month and attempt to reconcile your account again.

Before my carefree attitude puts you in a panic, consider the following example. You reconcile your account in January and the difference is $24.02. Then you reconcile the account in February and the difference is $24.02. Then you reconcile the account in March and, surprise, surprise, the difference is still $24.02.

What's going on here? Well, your starting account balance was probably off by $24.02. (The more months you try to reconcile your account and find that you're always mysteriously $24.02 off, the more likely it is that this type of error is to blame.)

After the second or third month, I think it's pretty reasonable to tell Quicken that it should enter an adjusting transaction for $24.02 so that your account balances. (In my opinion, this is the only circumstance that merits your adjusting an account to match the bank's figure.)

By the way, if you've successfully reconciled your account with Quicken before, your work may not be at fault. The mistake could be (drum roll, please) the bank's! And in this case, there's something else you should do. . . .

Get in your car, drive to the bank, and beg for help

As an alternative to the preceding idea — which supposes that the bank's statement is correct and that your records are incorrect — I propose this idea: Ask the bank to help you reconcile the account. Hint that you think the mistake is probably theirs. Smile a lot. And one other thing — be sure to ask about whatever product they're currently advertising in the lobby. (This behavior will encourage them to think that you're interested in that 180-month certificate of deposit, and they'll be extra nice to you.)

In general, the bank's record-keeping is usually pretty darn good. I've never had a problem as a business banking client or as an individual. (I've also been lucky enough to deal with big, well-run banks.)

Nevertheless, it's quite possible that your bank has made a mistake, so ask them to help you. Be sure to have them explain any transactions that you've learned about only by seeing these transactions on your bank statement.

Chapter 8
Housekeeping for Quicken

· ·

In This Chapter

▶ Formatting your floppy disks

▶ Backing up your Quicken data

▶ Knowing when and how often to back up your data

▶ Knowing what to do if you lose your Quicken data

▶ Creating and working with more than one set of Quicken data

▶ Turning off the Qcards

▶ Setting up a new file password

▶ Changing a file password

· ·

*O*K, chasing dust bunnies isn't something you need to worry about in Quicken, but you do have little housekeeping tasks to take care of. This chapter describes these chores and how to get them done right with minimal hassle.

Formatting Floppy Disks

You need someplace safe to store the financial information you collect with Quicken — someplace in addition to your computer's hard disk. No, I'm not talking about under your mattress, nor of that secret place in the attic. I'm talking about floppy disks. So, you, my friend, need to know how to format a floppy disk.

A floppy disk needs to be formatted before you can store information on it. You can buy formatted floppy disks. (The package says "Formatted Disks.") You also can buy unformatted floppy disks. The only trick is to make sure that you buy disks that match your drive in terms of density (low or high) and size (5¼ inches square or 3½ inches square).

Size is easy to determine: just get a ruler and measure one of the disks you're using. The disk is either 5¼ inches wide or 3½ inches wide. Simple, huh?

Density is a little trickier because you can use both low- and high-density disks in a high-density drive. If you don't know the density of your drive, I suggest that you find the paperwork you got when you (or whoever) bought the computer. The paperwork should tell you whether the drive is high density (by using the code HD or by giving you the amount of storage space that you have — 1.2MB on a 5¼-inch floppy or 1.44MB on a 3½-inch floppy). You also can scrounge around to see whether you've been using low-density or high-density floppy disks. High-density floppy disks often have the HD secret code on them. Low-density disks, however, use the DS/DD secret code or give the amount of storage space — 360K on a 5¼-inch floppy or 720K on a 3½-inch floppy.

Anyway, after you figure out the density and size thing, it's time to format the disk. Just follow these steps:

1. **Stuff a floppy disk of the right size and density into the correct floppy disk drive.**

2. **Start the File Manager application and then choose the Format Disk command from the Disk menu.**

   The File Manager displays a dialog box, like the one shown in Figure 8-1.

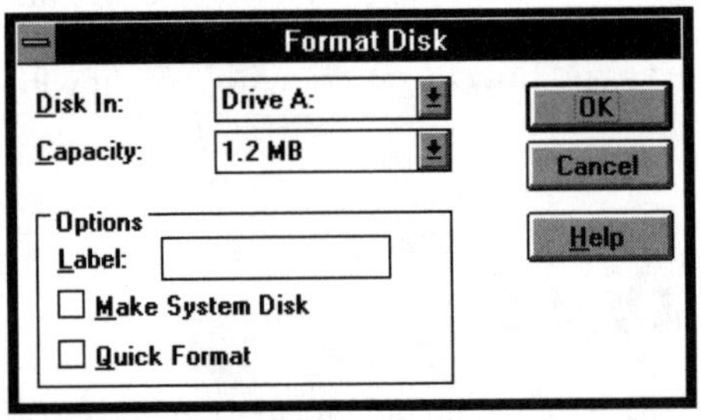

Figure 8-1:
The Format
Disk dialog
box in the
File
Manager
window.

3. **Use the Disk In drop-down list box to indicate which floppy disk drive you're using.**

4. **Use the Capacity drop-down list box to indicate the floppy disk density.**

5. **Then choose OK.**

   The File Manager displays a message box that asks you to confirm the formatting. (The File Manager asks this question because formatting erases everything on the disk.)

6. Choose Yes to confirm the formatting.

The File Manager goes off and formats the disk. Next, you see a message that tells you the format is complete and asks if you want to format another disk.

7. Select No to indicate "Heck no" and press Enter.

8. Exit the File Manager application by choosing Exit from the File menu.

There's more to this formatting business than I've described here. If you want more information and you're adventurous, flip open the Windows user guide that came with your computer and look up the Format command in the index. If you're not adventurous, you should probably be buying preformatted floppy disks.

Backing Up Is Hard to Do

You should back up the files that Quicken uses to store your financial records. But you need to know how to back up before you can back up. Got it? So let's get to it. . . .

Backing up the quick and dirty way

You're busy. You don't have time to fool around. You just want to do a passable job backing up. Sound like your situation? Then follow these steps:

1. Insert a blank, formatted floppy disk into your floppy drive.

If you have two floppy drives, the top one is the drive A, and the bottom one is the drive B. I'm going out on a limb here and assuming you're using the ol' drive A.

2. Verify that the file you want to back up is active.

Display the register window and make sure that it displays one of the accounts in the file you want to back up. (If you don't remember setting up multiple files, don't worry. You probably have only one file — the usual case.)

3. Start the backup operation.

Choose the Backup command from the File menu. Quicken displays the Select Backup Drive dialog box, as shown in Figure 8-2.

Figure 8-2:
The Select
Backup
Drive dialog
box.

4. Identify the backup floppy drive.

If necessary, activate the Backup Drive drop-down list box and select the letter of the floppy drive you stuffed a disk into. If you've followed my sage advice, this is drive A.

5. (Optional) Mark the Select From List option button only if the file you're currently working on isn't the file you want to back up.

(If you want to back up the current file you're working on, you can skip to step 7.)

OK, here's the deal. In Quicken, you can have more than one set of financial records, and each set of records gets stored in its own file. If you've been following along in this book, however, you probably have only one set of financial records so far. (In fact, I'd bet my neighbor's dog's life on it.) But if, by chance, you've used the New command on the File menu to create an entirely new file, you need to indicate which file you want to back up.

6. (Optional) Tell Quicken which file you want to back up — only if you have done step 5.

After you mark the Select From List option button and choose OK or press Enter, Quicken displays the Back Up Quicken File dialog box (shown in Figure 8-3) for you to select the file that should be backed up. Just select the file from the File Name list box. Figure 8-3 displays two files: QDATA.QDT, which you should have created, and BIZ.QDT, which I created to illustrate this step.

7. Choose OK.

You see a message on-screen that says, "Aye, Cap'n, I'm working just as fast as I can" (or something to that effect). Then you see a message that says the backup is finished. Don't worry. You'll never see a message that says, "She's starting to break up, Cap'n. She can't take warp 9 much longer." You will see a warning message if the file you want to back up is too large. In this case, you'll need to shrink it. (Later in the chapter, I describe how you do this.)

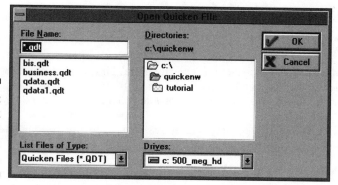

Figure 8-3:
The Back
Up Quicken
File dialog
box.

So when should you back up?

Sure, I can give you some tricky, technical examples of fancy backup strategies, but they have no point here. You want to know the basics, right? So here's what I do to back up my files. I back up every month after I reconcile. Then I stick the floppy disk in my briefcase, so if something terrible happens at home, I don't lose both my computer and the backup disk with the data.

I admit that there are a few problems with my strategy, however. For example, because I'm only backing up monthly, I may have to reenter as much as a month's worth of data if the computer crashes toward the end of the month. In my case, I wouldn't lose all that much work. However, if you're someone with real heavy transaction volumes — if you write hundreds of checks a month, for example — you may want to back up more frequently than this, such as once a week.

A second problem with my strategy is only remotely possible but is still worth mentioning. If something bad does happen to the Quicken files stored on my computer's hard disk *and* the files stored on the backup floppy disk, I'll be up the proverbial creek without a paddle. I should also note that a floppy disk is far more likely to fail than a hard drive. If this worse case scenario actually occurs, I'll need to start over from scratch from the beginning of the year. To prevent this scenario from happening, some people — who are religiously careful — make backups of their backups to reduce the chance of this mishap.

By the way, Quicken periodically prompts you to back up when you try to exit. (You'll see a message that, basically, says, "Friend, it would be a darn good idea for you to back up.") You can, of course, choose to ignore this message. Or you can take Quicken's advice and do the backup thing as described earlier.

You know what else? Here's a secret feature of Quicken: Quicken adds a subdirectory to the Quicken directory named Backup. And it'll stick a backup copy of your files in this directory every few days. (Sorry to be vague on this point, but it's hard to be specific and concrete when it comes to undocumented features.) More on this later.

Losing your Quicken data after you have backed up

What happens if you lose all your Quicken data? First of all, I encourage you to feel smug. Get a cup of coffee. Lean back in your chair. Gloat for a couple of minutes. You, my friend, will have no problem. You have followed instructions.

After you've sufficiently gloated, carefully do the following to reinstate your Quicken data on the computer:

1. **Get your backup floppy disk.**

   Find the backup disk you created and carefully insert it into one of your disk drives. (If you can't find the backup disk, forget what I said about feeling smug — stop gloating and skip to the next section.)

2. **Start Quicken.**

   You already know how to do this, right? By the way, if the disaster that caused you to lose your data also trashed other parts of your computer, you may need to reinstall Quicken. You may need to reinstall Windows. Shoot. I suppose it's possible you may even need to reinstall DOS.

3. **Choose the _R_estore command from the _F_ile menu.**

   Guess what? Quicken displays the Restore Quicken File dialog box. Figure 8-4 shows you what this box looks like.

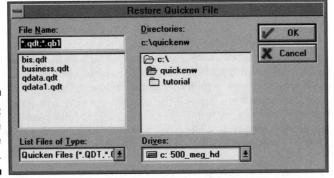

Figure 8-4:
The Restore
Quicken File
dialog box.

Quicken looks at the floppy disk in drive A and displays a list of the files stored on the floppy disk, as shown in Figure 8-4. (If you have only one Quicken file on the disk — the usual case — only one file is listed.) If your computer has another floppy disk in it and it's this other floppy disk that has the backup copy of the file, use the Drives drop-down list box to select the other floppy drive.

4. Select the file you want to restore and choose OK.

Use the arrow keys or the mouse to highlight the file you want to restore.

If the file you select is the one Quicken used last, the program displays a message asking if it's OK to overwrite, or replace, the open file with the file stored in the floppy disk.

When you restore a file, you replace the current, in-memory version of the file with the backup version stored on the floppy disk. Don't restore a file for fun. Don't restore a file for entertainment. Restore a file only if the current version is trashed and you want to start over by using the version stored on the backup floppy disk.

5. Choose OK.

Quicken replaces the file it's currently using with the one from the backup floppy disk. After it finishes, Quicken displays a message telling you that it has restored the file. You're almost done.

6. Update the accounts' registers as necessary.

Using the register windows for each of the accounts in a file, reenter each of the transactions you recorded since you created the backup. Be sure that you update your accounts because you've almost certainly entered transactions since the last time you backed up.

Just to be on the safe side, you should back up the file after you complete this process. I have heard that lightning never strikes the same place twice, but I'm not sure that the old saying is true. If you have hard disk problems or another recurring problem, whatever fouled up your file this time may rear its ugly head again — and soon.

Losing your Quicken data when you haven't backed up

What do you do if you haven't backed up your files in a while and you lose all the data in your Quicken files? OK. Stay calm. It's just possible that all is not lost. The first thing you can try is restoring from Quicken's backup directory. To do this, you follow the same file restoration steps I covered earlier with one minor exception. When you get to the Restore Quicken File dialog box, you will use Drives and Directories list boxes to indicate that you want to see the backup files in the BACKUP subdirectory of the QUICKENW directory. As long as you followed Quicken's default installation suggestions, you can probably do this by choosing the drive C from the Drives list box, then selecting the QUICKENW directory and next the BACKUP subdirectory from the Directories list box. At this point, you'll probably see a list of files with names similar to the file you lost. If the file you lost had the name QDATA, for example, you may see two files named QDATA1 and QDATA2. Select the newest file, which will be the one with the "1" suffix, as in QDATA1; then choose OK. Quicken will use the file to restore the current file. As alluded to earlier, this may just work. And if it does, you should feel very lucky. Very lucky indeed.

OK. So let's say that you've tried the approach described in the preceding paragraph. Let's say it didn't work. What next?

All you have to do is reenter all the transactions for the entire year. Yeah. I know. It's a bummer. This method isn't quick and it isn't pretty, but it works.

If you have copies of the registers, of course, you can use these as your information source to reenter the information in your files. If you don't have copies of the registers, you need to use your bank statements and any of the other paper financial records you have.

Files, Files, and More Files

As part of setting up Quicken, you create what Quicken calls a *file*, a place where all your accounts get stored (bank accounts, credit card accounts, investment accounts, and so on).

You can have more than one Quicken file at any time. In today's world, for example, it is wise to keep personal financial records separate from business financial records. You can use Quicken to create two files: a personal account and a business account. (In the old days, Quicken referred to these files as *account groups*. I mention this fact for the benefit of those readers who are history buffs and, therefore, love to fill their heads with interesting bits of technology trivia.)

Using multiple files does have a little drawback, however. You can't easily record, in one fell swoop, account transfer transactions between accounts in different files. You need to record the transaction twice — once in the *source account,* the file where the transaction originates, and again in the *destination account,* the file where the transaction is being transferred to.

If the two accounts involved in a transfer are in the same file, all you have to do is enter the account name in the Category text box. Quicken then records the transfer in the other account for you.

Setting up a new file

To set up a new file so that you can create accounts in it, just follow these steps:

1. Choose the New command from the File menu.

Quicken displays the Creating New File: Are You Sure? dialog box, as shown in Figure 8-5.

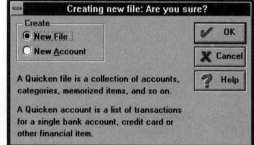

Figure 8-5:
The Creating
New File
dialog box.

2. Choose the New File option button and then Choose OK or press Enter.

Quicken displays the Create Quicken File dialog box, as shown in Figure 8-6.

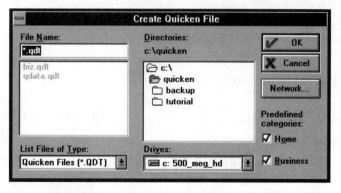

Figure 8-6:
The Create
Quicken File
dialog box.

3. Enter a name for the Quicken file.

With the cursor positioned on the File Name text box, type some meaning-ful combination of up to eight letters and numbers. You don't need to enter a file extension because Quicken supplies the correct file extension, QDT, for you.

> You can use the symbol characters on your keyboard, but this does get a little tricky. If you must use symbol characters in the filename, refer to the user documentation for Quicken.

4. **Use the default file location.**

   Accept Quicken's suggestion to store the file in the directory called QUICKENW because there is no good reason to put it in some other file location.

5. **Choose OK.**

   Quicken displays the Create New Account Type dialog box, as shown in Figure 8-7.

Figure 8-7: The Create New Account dialog box.

6. **Click one of the appropriate account buttons.**

   You need to set up at least one account for the new file, so unmark the Guide Me button and then click the appropriate account button.

7. **Describe the account.**

   Quicken displays the Create Account dialog box that you see in Figure 8-8. Fill out the text boxes to collect the starting account balance information for the new account. Because I have described how to fill out this dialog box in previous chapters, I won't go into detail here. If you need help in filling it out, refer to Chapter 2.

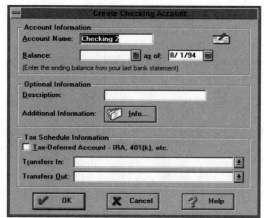

Figure 8-8:
The New
Account
Information
dialog box.

Flip-flopping between files

You can only work with one file at a time. So, after you create a second file, you need to know how to flip-flop between your files. If you're recording business stuff, for example, you want to be using the business file. However, a transaction comes in that clearly is meant for your personal file, and you want to enter it there immediately. Flip-flopping allows you to get from one file to another in no time.

Flip-flopping is easy: just choose the Open command from the File menu. Quicken displays the Open Quicken File dialog box. Pick the file you want from the File Name text box and then select OK. Zap! You are in the new file.

For people who just have to be in the know...

What Quicken refers to as a file is really a set of data and index files with the same filename, such as HOME, but different file extensions, such as QDI, QDT, QIF, QMT, and QNX. So when Quicken refers to the HOME file, it really is referring to the set of files that includes HOME.QDI, HOME.QDT, HOME.QIF, HOME.QMT, and HOME.QNX.

In most cases, you never need to know the distinction between the files in the set, but the knowledge may come in handy someday. For example, if you happen to stumble onto the Quicken directory, knowing about the set of HOME files keeps you from panicking when you see all the multiple copies of the HOME file. Or, on a more serious note, if you use a third-party backup utility, you need to know which of these files contain data that should be backed up.

When files get too big for their own good

You can enter a large number of transactions in a Quicken file; in fact, you can record as many as 65,535 transactions in a file and 30,000 transactions in a single account. Wowsers!

In spite of these huge numbers, there are some good reasons to work with smaller files, if you can. For example, you can fit only about 2,500 transactions on a double-density, 5¼-inch disk and 5,000 transactions on a double-density, 3½-inch disk. So working with files of a manageable size means you can more easily back them up on a floppy disk. Also, fewer transactions means Quicken runs faster because there's more memory available for Windows. (Windows likes lots of memory—the same way some people like lots of ice cream.)

If your files have gotten too big for their own good, you can knock them down to size by creating a new file with just the current year's transactions in it. This means you have a copy of the big file you won't use anymore, and a smaller, shrunken file with just the current year's transactions. This may sound like much ado about nothing, but it means you end up working with a smaller file. So, that probably means Quicken will run faster. (The memory thing comes into play again.) And smaller files should make backing up easier because you will probably be able to keep your files small enough to fit on a single double-density floppy disk.

Call me a Nervous Nellie — or a Nervous Nelson — but because shrinking a file involves wholesale change, I'd really feel more comfortable about helping you through this process if you first back up the file you're about to shrink. I don't think that there's anything to get anxious about, but just in case something does go wrong during the shrinking process, I know that you would like to have a backup copy of the file to fall back on.

To shrink a Quicken file, follow these steps:

1. **Choose the Year-End Copy command from the File menu.**

   Quicken displays a portrait of Barry Nelson, the first actor to portray James Bond. No, not really — I just wanted to see if you were awake. Actually, Quicken displays the Year-End Copy dialog box, as shown in Figure 8-9.

2. **Mark the Start New Year radio button.**

   You know how this works — just click the mouse.

3. **Choose OK.**

   Quicken displays the Start New Year dialog box, as shown in Figure 8-10.

4. **Enter a name in the Copy All Transactions To File text box.**

   Use a combination of up to eight letters and characters to name your new file. (If you have questions, get *DOS For Dummies* and read about DOS filename conventions.) At this point, the new file you're creating actually mirrors the original file — in other words, it's an exact copy.

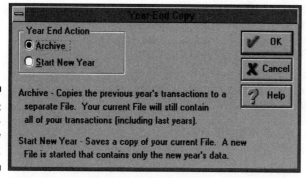

Figure 8-9:
The Year-
End Copy
dialog box.

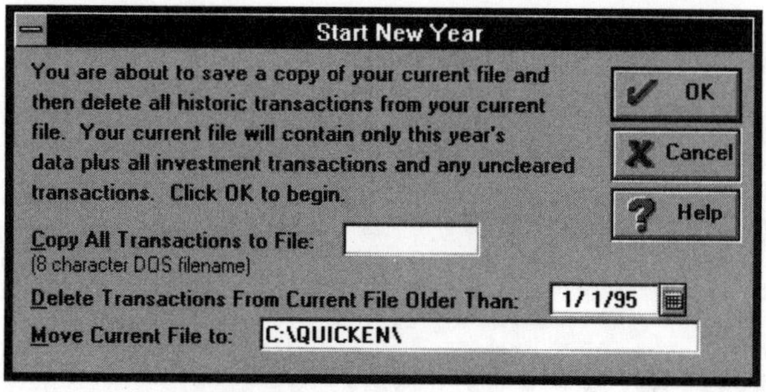

Figure 8-10:
The Start
New Year
dialog box.

5. Specify a cutoff date.

Using the Delete Transactions From Current File Older Than text box,
enter a cutoff date. All cleared transactions with a date that falls after this
cutoff date will automatically go in the new, smaller file. All transactions
with a date that falls before this cutoff date will be deleted from this new
file. I chose January 1, 1995, as the cutoff date in Figure 8-10 so that I could
create a new file for all 1995 transactions. (Note that Quicken doesn't delete
uncleared transactions and it doesn't delete investment transactions.)

6. (Optional) Move the current file.

You do this step only if you want to change the location of your new file
(which has become the current file) from the current Quicken directory to
another directory. Type the pathname of the new directory in the Move
Current File To text box. If this optional step sounds confusing or complicated, don't worry about it because you have no good reason to change
the directory right now anyway.

7. Choose OK.

Quicken creates a new file with the filename you gave it in the Start New
Year dialog box. This new file contains only the transactions that are dated
after the cutoff date. The original file still exists with its original name and
all transactions intact.

Quicken then displays the message box shown in Figure 8-11 that tells you the file was successfully copied. Mark the Use Old File option button if you want to use the original file that contains the original transactions. Mark the Use File For New Year option button if you want to use the new file you created. Select OK after you have made your choice.

If you want to see the old file again without going to this message box, you can select it from the dialog box of the File Open command. You should *not* enter any new transactions in the old file because these new transactions will change the old file's ending account balance without changing the new file's beginning account balance.

Figure 8-11:
The
message
box that
asks you
which file
you want to
use.

Using and Abusing Passwords

I have mixed feelings about passwords. Theoretically, they let you lock up your Quicken data so that your rebellious teenagers (if you're using Quicken at home) or the night janitors (if you're using Quicken in a business) can't come in, print checks, process automatic payments, and just generally mess things up.

Using passwords sounds pretty good, of course. But before you set up a password and then start relying on it to protect your information, let me remind you that a Quicken password only prevents someone from accessing your data with Quicken. Using a password does not prevent someone from fooling around with your computer itself. If the night janitors — or, heaven forbid, your teenagers — are the nefarious types, they can erase your files with DOS or scramble them with another program, such as a spreadsheet or word processor. And it's possible that they even can get in and manipulate the data with another checkbook or accounting program.

There's one other last little annoying problem with passwords, too. Darn it, you've got to remember them.

For these reasons, I think that passwords are best left to computer systems that use them on a global basis to control access to all programs and to computer systems that can track all users (you, your teenagers, the night janitors, and anyone else) by name. Your PC doesn't fall in this category.

Setting up a file password

You still want a password? OK, with much trepidation, I give you the following steps for setting up a password for a Quicken file:

1. **Select the file you want to protect with a password.**

   If the file you want to password-protect is not the active file, the Open command from the File menu and then either double-click the file you want or select it and click OK.

2. **Select the Passwords command from the File menu.**

   Quicken displays the — you guessed it — Passwords menu, which lists two commands: File and Transaction.

3. **Choose the File command**

   Quicken displays the Set Up Password dialog box, as shown in Figure 8-12.

Figure 8-12:
The Set Up
Password
dialog box.

4. **Enter the password you want to use.**

   You can use up to 16 characters. Quicken doesn't differentiate between lower- and uppercase characters, by the way, so Washington, wASHINGTON, and WASHINGTON are all the same from its point of view. Quicken doesn't display the actual characters you type; it displays asterisks instead. If you type **Dog**, for example, it displays ***. (Passwords require strict secrecy, you see.)

5. **Choose OK.**

   Quicken displays the Confirm Password dialog box, which looks very much like the Set Up Password dialog box. This dialog box is not here to confuse you but to confirm your choice of password.

6. **Enter the password you want to use again and choose OK.**

   Congratulations! You're done.

Assigning a password to a file does not prevent you from doing anything with the file that you would normally do. However, the next time you try to use this file — after you start Quicken or when you try to select the file by using the File menu's Open command — Quicken will ask you for the file's password. You need to supply the password to gain access to the file.

Changing a file password

After you set up a file password, you're not stuck with it forever. You either can change the password or remove it by using the File command on the Password menu.

If you've already set up a password, however, Quicken doesn't display the Set Up Password dialog box shown in Figure 8-12. Instead, Quicken displays a dialog box that asks for the current password you're now using and the new password you want to use in the future. Enter the current password in the Old Password text box and the new password in the New Password text box. Then press Enter. From now on, you need to use the new password to gain access to the file. If you don't want to use a password anymore, just leave the New Password text box blank.

So what are transaction passwords?

After you choose the Passwords command from the File menu, Quicken asks whether you want to create a file password or a transaction password. In general, you will be using a *file password* to protect the access into a Quicken file.

A *transaction password* works like a file password except that it requires the user to enter the transaction password if the date of the transaction the user is trying to enter is before a specified date. You specify the date, called cutoff date, when you set up the transaction password.

Maybe it's just me, but transaction passwords don't make a lot of sense. I guess the logic is that you use a transaction password to prevent some idiot from fouling up last year's or last month's transactions. It seems to me, though, that there are a couple of easier approaches. One is that you can create and safely store backup copies of the Quicken file for last year or last month. Another is to not have idiots fooling around with your Quicken files. Jeepers, if somebody can't understand an instruction like, "Use the current date," do you really want them mucking about in your books?

Chapter 9

Compound Interest Magic and Other Mysteries

*T*he folks at Intuit have added several nifty little calculators (most are dialog boxes called Planners) to recent versions of Quicken. I strongly encourage you to use these tools. At the very least, the calculators should make your work easier. And if you invest a little time, you should gain some enormously valuable perspectives on your financial affairs.

Using the Quicken Calculator

The Quicken calculator lets you perform simple arithmetic — like you do when you're entering transactions into a register or writing a check.

If you need to perform some basic arithmetic and the cursor is in an amount text box, you can start the calculator by choosing the Use Calculator command from the Activities menu. Quicken displays its calculator, as shown in Figure 9-1.

Getting started with the calculator

Use the calculator like you use any ten-key calculator. If you know how to work a calculator, skip the next discussion.

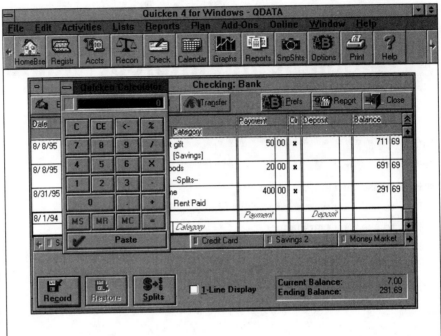

Figure 9-1:
The Quicken
calculator

Adding

To add, type the first number and + (the plus symbol), the second number and +, the third number and +, and so on. You get the idea.

When you want to indicate cents, use . (the period key) to show the decimal point.

The calculator displays the numbers as you enter them. When you press the plus symbol, the calculator adds the numbers and displays the result. To total all the numbers, press = (the equals sign).

To express a percentage as an equivalent decimal value, type the number, and then press % (the percentage key).

To clear the display, press C (the clear key). To clear the last number or operator entered, press CE (the clear entry key). To remove the last digit typed, press <- (the clear digit key).

Is the difference between CE and <- confusing? Here's a quick example: Type the number **123**. Pressing CE clears the entire calculator display, pressing <- clears just the 3 (the calculator displays the number 12).

Subtracting, multiplying, and dividing

You can subtract, multiply, and divide with the calculator, too. To subtract, use
- (the minus sign). To multiply, use ×. To divide, use / (the slash). Simple, huh?

Table 9-1 provides some examples.

Table 9-1	Quicken Calculator Examples
Calculator Keys Pressed	*Final Calculator Display*
25 - 5 =	20
25 * 5 =	125
25 / 5 =	5

Working with memory

The MS, MR, and MC keys work with the calculator's memory.

- ✔ MS stores the number on the calculator display in the memory.
- ✔ MR recalls the number stored in the memory.
- ✔ MC clears the memory.

Imagine that you've just calculated how much your spouse charged last month,
for example. To your horror, the calculator displays 914.89. Of course, you want
to store this number temporarily so that you and your spouse can discuss this
rampant disregard for your collective financial well-being.

Press MS to store the number in the calculator's memory (Quicken will put an
M in the little box below the calculator Control menu box, reminding you that a
number is stored in memory).

When you want to see the number stored in the memory, press MR.

If, on second thought, you remember that you ran up the credit card bill, press
MC to clear the memory.

The calculator's memory isn't supposed to provide ammunition for arguments
about family finances. In reality, the memory serves as a scratch pad, letting
you store numbers you want to use in later calculations.

Putting the calculator away

To remove the calculator from your view, close the Calculator window. You also can leave the calculator on the Quicken desktop. Just activate another Quicken document window.

If you want to paste the number shown on the Calculator display into some field, move the cursor to the field and then select the Calculator's Paste button.

For mouse users only

Got a mouse? You can select any of the calculator keys by clicking (press the mouse's left button).

To add the numbers 4 and 8, for example, you could either type **4+8=** or you could (using the mouse):

1. **Click the 4.**
2. **Click the +.**
3. **Click the 8.**
4. **Click the =.**

Noodling Around with Your Investments

My favorite Quicken calculator is the Investment Savings Planner. I guess I just like to forecast portfolio future values and other similar stuff.

Using the Investment Savings Planner

Let's say that you want to know how much you'll accumulate if you save $2,000 a year for 35 years, using a stock mutual fund you anticipate will earn 10 percent annually. Use the Investment Savings Planner to estimate how much you should ultimately accumulate:

1. **Display the Investment Savings Planner.**

   Choose the Financial Planners command from the Plan menu. Then choose Savings from the Financial Planners menu. Quicken displays the Investment Savings Planner dialog box (see Figure 9-2).

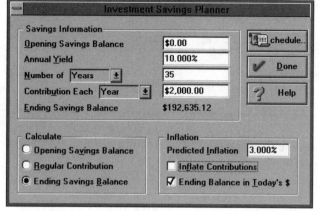

Figure 9-2:
The
Investment
Savings
Planner
dialog box.

2. **Enter what you've already accumulated as your Opening Savings Balance.**

   Move the cursor to the Opening Savings Balance text box; then enter the amount of your current investments. If this amount is zero, for example, type **0.**

3. **Enter the annual yield that you expect your investments to earn.**

   Move the cursor to the Annual Yield text box and type the percent. If you plan to invest in the stock market and expect your savings to match the market's usual return of about 10 percent, for example, type **10** (don't type .10).

4. **Indicate how long you plan to let your investments earn income.**

   Move the cursor to the Number Of drop-down list box and select the time period appropriate to your investments planning. (Usually, you will select Years, as Figure 9-2 shows.) Then move the cursor to the Number Of text box and indicate how long (enter the number of time periods) you want to maintain these investments.

5. **Enter the amount you plan to add to your investments every period.**

   Move the cursor to the Contribution Each drop-down list box and indicate how often you plan to add to the savings. Then move the cursor to the Contribution Each text box and enter the amount you plan to add. (Figure 9-2 shows how to plan a $2,000 annual contribution.)

6. **Enter the anticipated inflation rate.**

   Move the cursor to the Predicted Inflation text box and enter the inflation rate. By the way, from 1926 to 1992, the inflation rate has averaged just over 3 percent (see Figure 9-2).

A timing assumption you should know

The Investment Savings Planner assumes that you will add to your portfolio at the end of the period — what financial planners call an *ordinary annuity.*

7. **Indicate whether you plan to increase your annual contribution as a result of inflation.**

    Mark the In<u>f</u>late Contributions check box if you plan to annually increase — by the annual inflation rate — the amount you add to your investment portfolio. Don't mark the check box if you don't want to inflate the payments.

After you enter all the information, the <u>E</u>nding Savings Balance field shows how much you'll accumulate in present day, uninflated dollars: $192,635.12. Hmmm. Nice.

If you want to know the amount you'll accumulate in future-day, inflated dollars, unmark the Ending Balance In <u>T</u>oday's $ check box.

To get more information on the annual deposits, balances, and so on, select the <u>S</u>chedule button, which appears on the face of the Investment Savings Planner dialog box. Quicken whips up a quick little report showing the annual deposits and ending balance for each year you plan to add into the savings. Try it. You may like it.

How to become a millionaire

So you want to be a millionaire some day.

To learn how to realize this childhood dream, use the Calculate option buttons. With these buttons, you mark the financial variable (Opening Sa<u>v</u>ings Balance, <u>R</u>egular Contribution, or Ending Savings <u>B</u>alance) you want to calculate. For example, to determine the annual amount you need to contribute to your investment so that your portfolio reaches $1,000,000, here's what you do:

1. **Mark the Calculate <u>R</u>egular Contribution option button.**

2. **Mark the In<u>f</u>late Contributions check box.**

3. **Unmark the Ending Balance in <u>T</u>oday's $ check box.**

4. **Enter all the other input variables. Remember to set the <u>E</u>nding Savings Balance text box to 1000000 (the <u>E</u>nding Savings Balance field becomes a text box after you mark the Ending Balance in <u>T</u>oday's $ check box).**

The Investment Savings Planner computes how much you need to save annually to hit your $1,000,000 target.

Starting from scratch, it'll take 35 years of roughly $2,800-a-year payments to reach $1,000,000.00 (see Figure 9-3). (All those zeros look rather nice, don't they?) Note that this calculation assumes a 10 percent annual yield.

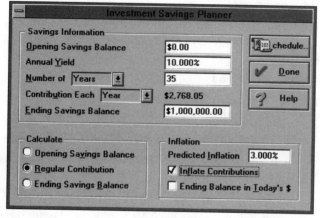

Figure 9-3:
The secret to your success: $2,800 a year for 35 years.

"Jeepers, creepers," you say. "This seems too darn good to be true, Steve."

Well, unfortunately, the calculation is a little misleading. With 3 percent inflation, your million bucks will *only* be worth $355,383 in current day dollars. (To confirm this present value calculation, mark the Ending Savings Balance option button and the Ending Balance in Today's $ check box.)

The Often Unbearable Burden of Debt

To help you better manage your debts, Quicken provides a neat Loan Planner that computes loan payments and balances.

Using the Loan Planner to calculate payments

Let's say that one afternoon, you're wondering what the mortgage payment is on one of those monstrous houses: tens of thousands of square feet, acres of grounds, cottages for the domestic help, and so on. You get the picture — something that's a really vulgar display of wealth.

To learn what you would pay on a 30-year, $10,000,000 mortgage if the money costs 7.5 percent, use the Loan Planner:

1. **Display the Loan Planner.**

   Choose the Financial Planners command from the Plan menu. Then choose the Loan command from the Financial Planner menu. Quicken displays the Loan Planner dialog box (see Figure 9-4 for a picture of this handy tool).

2. **Enter the loan amount.**

   Move the cursor to the Loan Amount text box and enter the amount of the loan. (If you're checking the lifestyle of the ostentatious and vulgar, enter **10,000,000.**)

3. **Enter the annual interest rate.**

   Move the cursor to the Annual Interest Rate text box and enter the interest rate percent. If a loan charges 7.5 percent interest, for example, enter a **7.5**.

4. **Enter the number of years you want to take to repay the loan.**

   Move the cursor to the Number Of Years text box and enter the number of years you'll make payments.

5. **Indicate how many loan payments you plan to make a year.**

   Move the cursor to the Periods Per Year text box and enter the number of loan payments you'll make in a year. If you want to make monthly payments, for example, enter **12**.

Quicken calculates the loan payment and displays the amount in the Payment Per Period field. Yikes! $69,921.45 a month.

I guess if you have to ask how much the mortgage payment is, you really can't afford it.

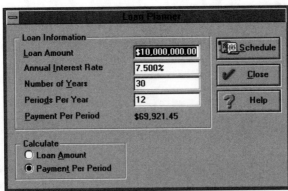

Figure 9-4:
The Loan
Planner
dialog box.

To get more information on the loan payments, interest and principal portions of payments, and outstanding loan balances, select the <u>S</u>chedule button, which appears on the face of the Loan Planner dialog box. Quicken whips up a quick loan amortization schedule showing all this stuff.

Calculating loan balances

To calculate the loan principal amount, click the Loan <u>A</u>mount option button under Calculate. Then enter all the other variables.

For example, those $70,000-a-month payments for the monster mansion seem a little ridiculous. So calculate how much you can borrow if you make $1,000-a-month payments over 30 years and the annual interest rate is 7.5 percent:

1. **Mark the Loan <u>A</u>mount radio button.**

2. **Enter 7.5 in the Annual <u>I</u>nterest Rate text box.**

3. **Enter 30 in the Number of <u>Y</u>ears text box.**

4. **Enter 12 in the Perio<u>d</u>s Per Year text box.**

5. **Enter 1000 in the Payment Per Period text box.**

The Loan Planner computes a Loan Amount of $143,017.63.

Why You Won't Read about the Refinance Planner Here

You won't read about the Refinance Planner here — but not because I'm lazy. (Believe it or not, I enjoy writing about things that help you make better financial decisions.) The Refinance Planner merely calculates the difference in mortgage payments if you make lower payments; then it tells you how long it would take with these lower payments to pay back the refinancing costs you incur.

For example, if you save $50 a month because you refinance and it costs $500 to refinance, the Refinance Planner tells you that it would take ten months of $50-a-month savings to recoup your $500.

You know what? Although you may want to know how long it would take to recoup the refinance costs, that information doesn't tell you whether it's a good idea to refinance.

Deciding whether to refinance is very, very complicated. You can't just look at your next few payments, like the Refinance Planner does. You also need to look at the total interest you would pay with the old mortgage and the new mortgage. And you need to factor in the time value of money.

I don't think there's any good reason to use the Refinance Planner; it just doesn't do what it purports to do.

So that I don't leave you hanging; however, let me give you two rules of thumb to help you make smarter refinancing decisions.

First, if you want to save interest costs, don't use refinancing as a way to stretch out your borrowing. That is, if you refinance, make sure that you make payments large enough to pay off the new mortgage by the same time you would have paid off the old mortgage. In other words, if you have 23 years left on your old mortgage, don't go out and get a 30-year mortgage. Find a lender who will let you pay off the new mortgage in 23 years.

Here's a second trick, if you can find a willing lender. Ask the lender to calculate the annual percentage rate (APR) on the new mortgage, assuming you'll pay off the mortgage by the same time you would have paid off the old mortgage. (An APR includes all the loan's costs — interest, points, miscellaneous fees, and so on — and calculates an implicit interest rate.) If the APR on the new loan is lower than the current loan's interest rate, you would probably save money by refinancing.

Let me issue one caveat. When you base your refinancing decision on the comparison between the new loan's APR and the current loan's interest rate, you're saying that you'll live in your current house until the mortgage is paid.

I hope this information helps. Like I said, mortgage refinancing decisions are tough if you truly want to save money.

Using the Retirement Planner

I think this is the book's most important section. No joke. Your financial future is much too consequential to go for easy laughs or cheap shots.

The dilemma in a nutshell

By the time the 30-something and 40-something crowd reaches retirement, Social Security coverage probably will be scaled back. As you may know, the current recipients are getting everything they paid in as well as most of what we pay in.

If you currently receive Social Security, please don't feel defensive or betrayed. I think your generation overcame challenges far more important (World War I, the Great Depression, World War II, the Cold War, the end of segregation, and so on) than the problem of inadequate Social Security funding we younguns face.

I know this sentiment sounds corny, but I think you've left the world a better place. I hope my generation does the same.

But the problem isn't just Social Security. More and more often, employer-provided pension plans are defined contribution plans, which add specific amounts to your pension (like 2 percent of your salary), rather than defined benefit plans, which promise specific pension amounts (like $1,000 a month). As a result, although you know that someone will throw a few grand into your account every so often, you don't know how much you'll have when you retire.

I urge you to think ahead about your financial requirements. Fortunately, Quicken's Retirement Planner can help you.

I'll get off my soapbox now. Thank you.

Making retirement planning calculations

Imagine that you've decided to jump into your employer's 401K thing (a type of deferred compensation system), which will allow you to plop about $3,000 into a retirement account that you think will earn about 9 percent annually.

Fortunately, you don't need to be a rocket scientist to figure this stuff out. You just use the Retirement Planner:

1. **Display the Retirement Planner.**

   Choose the Financial Planners command from the Plan menu. Then choose the Retirement Planner command from the Financial Planner menu. Quicken displays the Retirement Planner dialog box shown in Figure 9-5.

2. **Enter what you've already saved as your Current Savings.**

   Move the cursor to the Current Savings text box and enter your current retirement savings (for example, if you have some individual retirement account money or you've accumulated a balance in an employer-sponsored 401K account). Don't worry if you don't have anything saved — most people don't.

3. **Enter the annual yield that you expect your retirement savings to earn.**

   Move the cursor to the Annual Yield text box and type the percent. In the little example shown in Figure 9-5, I say the annual yield is 9 percent.

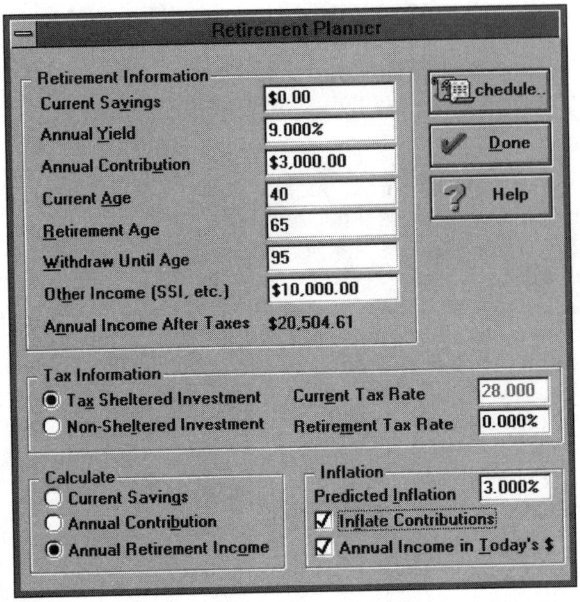

Figure 9-5:
The
Retirement
Planner
dialog box.

4. Enter the annual amount added to your retirement savings.

Move the cursor to the Annual Contribution text box and enter the amount that you or your employer will add to your retirement savings at the end of each year. In the example, I say that I plan to add $3,000 (refer to Figure 9-5).

5. Enter your current age.

Move the cursor to the Current Age text box and enter a number. You're on your own here, but let me suggest that this is a time to be honest.

6. Enter your retirement.

Move the cursor to the Retirement Age text box and enter a number. Again, purely a personal matter. (Figure 9-5 shows this age as 65, but you should retire when you want.)

More about timing

The Retirement Planner assumes that you or your employer will add to your retirement savings at the end of the year — what financial planners call an *ordinary annuity*. If you or your employer adds to your retirement savings at the beginning of the year, you earn an extra year of interest. As a result, your aftertax income will be more than Quicken shows.

7. Enter the age to which you want to continue withdrawals.

Move the cursor to the Withdraw Until Age field and enter a number. Let's not beat around the bush here. This number is how old you think you'll be when you die. I don't like the idea any better than you do. Let me say, though, that ideally you want to run out of steam — there, that's a safe metaphor — before you run out of money. So go ahead and make this age something pretty old — like 95 (sorry, Grandma).

8. Enter any other income you'll receive — such as Social Security.

Move the cursor to the Other Income (SSI, etc.) text box and type a value (Figure 9-5 shows $10,000). Note that this income is in current day, or uninflated, dollars.

9. Indicate whether you plan to save retirement money in a tax sheltered investment.

Mark the Tax Sheltered Investment option button if your retirement savings earns untaxed money. Mark the Non-Sheltered Investment option button if the money is taxed. Tax sheltered investments are things like individual retirement accounts, annuities, and employer-sponsored 401Ks and 403Bs (a 403B is kind of a profit-sharing plan for a non-profit agency). (As a practical matter, tax sheltered investments are the only way to ride. By deferring income taxes on your earnings, you earn interest on the money you otherwise would have paid as income taxes.)

10. Enter your current marginal tax rate, if needed.

If you're investing in taxable stuff, move the cursor to the Current Tax Rate text box. Then enter the combined federal and state income tax rate that you pay on your last dollars of income.

11. Enter your anticipated retirement tax rate.

Move the cursor to the Retirement Tax Rate text box, then . . . hey, wait a minute. Who knows what the rates will be next year, let alone when you're retired. I think you should enter **0**, but remember that the Annual Income After Taxes, is really your pretax income (just like your current salary is really your pretax income).

12. Enter the anticipated inflation rate.

Move the cursor to the Predicted Inflation text box and enter the inflation rate. By the way, from 1926 to 1992, the inflation rate has averaged just above 3 percent (see Figure 9-5).

13. Indicate whether the annual additions will increase.

Mark the Inflate Contributions check box if the additions will increase annually by the inflation rate. (Because your salary and 401K contributions will presumably inflate if there's inflation, Figure 9-5 shows the Inflate Contributions check box marked.)

After you enter all the information, take a peek at the Annual Income After Taxes field (Figure 9-5, for example, shows $20,504.61). Not bad. Not bad at all. If you want to see the aftertax income in future day, inflated dollars, unmark the Annual Income in Today's $ check box.

To get more information on the annual deposits, balances, income, and so on, select the Schedule button, which appears on the face of the Retirement Planner dialog box. Quicken whips up a quick little report showing the annual deposits, income, and ending retirement account balances for each year you plan to add to and withdraw from your retirement savings.

If you're now bummed out about retirement

First, don't feel depressed. At least you know *now* if your golden years seem a little tarnished. After all, you acquired Quicken to help you sort out your finances. Now you can use Quicken and your newly gained knowledge to help improve your financial lot.

Basically, retirement planning depends on just three things:

- ✔ The number of years that the retirement savings will accrue interest
- ✔ The real yield (that is, adjusted for inflation) you earn — in other words, the annual yield minus the predicted inflation
- ✔ The yearly payments

Anything you do to increase one of these variables will increase your retirement income.

If you invest, for example, in something that delivers higher real yields, such as the stock market, you should see a big difference (of course, you usually bear more risk). Or if you wait an extra year or two to retire, you wind up making more annual payments and earning more interest. Finally, if you boost the yearly payments (for example, by participating in an employer-sponsored 401K or 403B plan, where your employer matches a portion of your contribution), you'll see a huge change.

Noodle around with the variables. See what happens. You may be surprised.

Playing retirement roulette

Use the Calculate option buttons to determine a retirement income variable. You can calculate current savings, annual contribution, or, as described earlier, the annual aftertax income.

To calculate the yearly payment required to produce a specific level of retirement income, for example, mark the Annual Contribution option button. Then enter all the other variables — including the desired aftertax income. The Retirement Planner calculates how much you need to save to hit your target retirement income.

Planning for the Cost of College

Ouch. I have a couple of daughters, so I know how you feel. Man, oh man, do I know how you feel.

Using the College Planner

Let's say that you have a daughter who may attend college in 16 years. And you haven't started to save yet. If the local university costs $9,500 a year and you can earn 9 percent annually, how much should you save?

The College Planner works like the Retirement Planner:

1. **Display the College Planner.**

   Choose the Financial Planners command from the Plan menu. Then choose the College command from the Financial Planners menu. Quicken displays the College Planner dialog box shown in Figure 9-6.

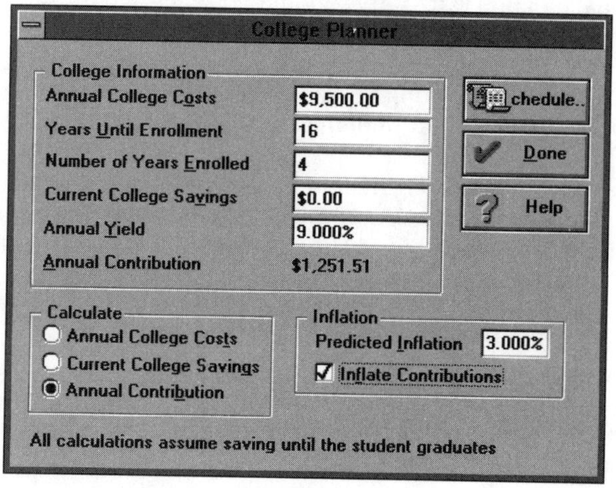

College Planner	

College Information

Annual College Costs	$9,500.00
Years Until Enrollment	16
Number of Years Enrolled	4
Current College Savings	$0.00
Annual Yield	9.000%
Annual Contribution	$1,251.51

Schedule..
Done
Help

Calculate
○ Annual College Costs
○ Current College Savings
● Annual Contribution

Inflation
Predicted Inflation 3.000%
☑ Inflate Contributions

All calculations assume saving until the student graduates

Figure 9-6:
The College
Planner
dialog box.

2. **Enter the annual college costs.**

Move the cursor to the Annual College Costs text box. Then enter the current annual costs at a school Junior may attend. Figure 9-6 shows this amount as $9,500.

3. **Enter the number of years until enrollment.**

Move the cursor to the Years Until Enrollment text box and enter a number. For example, if Junior will start college in 16 years, enter **16**.

4. **Enter the number of years enrolled.**

Move the cursor to the Number Of Years Enrolled text box and enter a number. Assuming Junior doesn't fool around, enter **4** or **5**.

5. **Enter the amount of the current college savings.**

Move the cursor to the Current College Savings field and enter an amount. Figure 9-6 shows this amount as $0.00.

6. **Enter the annual yield that you expect the college savings to earn.**

Move the cursor to the Annual Yield text box and type the percent. Figure 9-6 shows the yield as 9 percent.

7. **Enter the inflation rate anticipated in college tuition.**

Move the cursor to the Predicted Inflation text box and enter the inflation rate percent. Figure 9-6 shows this rate as 3 percent.

8. **Indicate whether you plan to increase your annual contribution as a result of inflation.**

Mark the Inflate Contributions check box if you plan to annually increase — by the annual inflation rate — the amount you save. Figure 9-6 shows this check box marked.

After you enter all the information, the Annual Contribution field shows how much you need to save each year until the child graduates from college.

Just to beat this thing to death, Figure 9-6 shows that the lucky student will attend four years at a college that currently costs $9,500 a year and that you expect to earn 9 percent annually and anticipate 3 percent annual inflation. Given these cold hard facts, you need to ante up $1,251.51 every year.

To get more information on the annual deposits, tuition, and balance, select the Schedule button, which appears on the face of the College Planner dialog box. Quicken whips up a quick little report showing the annual deposits, tuition, and ending college savings account balances for each year you'll add to, and Junior withdraws from, the college savings money.

If you're now bummed out about college costs

Look at the positive side: you now understand the size of the problem and the solution.

College planning depends on four things:

- ✔ College costs

- ✔ The number of years that the savings will earn interest

- ✔ The real yield (that is, adjusted for inflation) you earn — in other words, the annual yield minus the predicted inflation

- ✔ The yearly payments

I don't mean to sound like a simpleton, but there are three basic ways to successfully save for a college education:

- ✔ Reduce the costs (find a less expensive school)

- ✔ Invest in things that deliver higher real yields

- ✔ Boost the yearly payments

Use the Calculate option buttons to compute a specific financial variable. Mark which variable you want to calculate; then input the other values. The College Planner computes the flagged variable.

Estimating Your Income Taxes Expenses

The folks at Quicken added a very cool calculator to the most recent release of Quicken, a Tax Estimator. Okay — you two guys in the back row. Stop sniggering. I'm serious. I think it's really neat. Not because I like income tax planning and preparation. No, I think it's neat because this little tool makes it possible to estimate with a fair degree of accuracy one of the most complicated expenses of our little lives: federal income taxes.

Using the Tax Planner Calculator

The Tax Planner works pretty much like the other financial planning calculators. Here's the straight scoop:

1. **Display the Tax Planner.**

   Select the <u>T</u>ax Planner command from the Pl<u>a</u>n menu. Quicken displays the Tax Planner calculator shown in Figure 9-7.

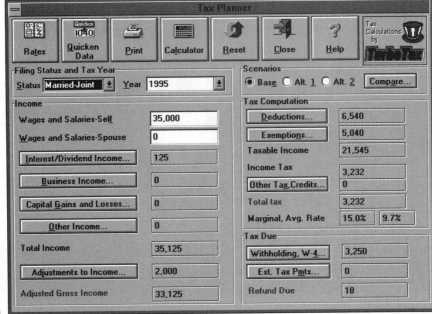

Figure 9-7:
The Tax
Planner
calculator.
Friends, it
doesn't get
much better
than this.

2. Indicate your filing status.

Move the cursor to the Filing Status field and click the down arrow. Then, when Quicken displays a list of possible filing statuses, pick the one you think you'll use this year: Single, Married filing separate, Married filing jointly, and so on.

3. Enter the wages and salaries you and your lovely or handsome spouse expect.

Move the cursor to the Wages and Salaries-Self field and type what you think you'll make this year. If your filing status isn't single, move the cursor to the Wages & Salaries-Spouse field and type what you think your spouse will make this year.

4. Indicate approximately how much other taxable income you'll have.

Quick as you can, click the Interest/Dividend Income, Business Income, Capital Gains and Losses, and Other Income buttons and fill in the pop-up worksheets that Quicken displays. (In each case, Quicken's pop-up worksheets prompt you for a handful of inputs.) If some income thingamajig doesn't apply, just leave it blank. Figure 9-8 shows the Interest/Dividend Income pop-up worksheet. This makes sense, right? You enter your taxable interest income into the first input field. You enter your taxable dividend income into the second field. When you're done, click OK. Quicken calculates the total and then plugs this value back into the Tax Planner calculator.

Figure 9-8:
The
Interest/
Dividend
Income pop-
up
worksheet.

Interest/Dividend Income - Schedule B		
Taxable Interest Income	125	✓ OK
Dividends	0	✗ Cancel
(Excluding Capital Gain Distributions and Nontaxable Distributions.)		
Total Interest and Dividends	125	? Help

5. Indicate whether you'll have any adjustments to your gross income.

This sounds too technical, I know. But there are really only a handful of these adjustments: IRA, SEP/IRA, and Keogh deductions; alimony; moving expenses; a couple of adjustments for self-employed types (half their self-employment tax and a chunk of their health insurance premiums); and any penalty on early withdrawals of savings. If you have one or more of these, click the Adjustments to Income button and fill in the appropriate blanks on the dialog box Quicken displays. When you're done, click OK.

6. Indicate the tax year.

Move the cursor to the Year field and click the down arrow. When Quicken displays a pop-up box listing 1994 and 1995, select one of the years.

7. Estimate your itemized deductions.

Click the Deductions button and then describe any itemized deductions you have by filling in the blanks on the dialog box Quicken displays. You'll also need to answer a handful of questions including, "Is taxpayer a dependent?" and "Are you or your spouse blind or over age 65?" You answer these questions by marking or unmarking check boxes. Once you enter all this information, click OK. Quicken calculates your standard deduction and then uses whatever is larger for your return: your standard deduction or your total itemized deductions.

For most people, there are only three itemized deductions that actually matter: mortgage interest, property taxes, and charitable deductions.

8. Indicate the number of personal exemptions you'll claim.

You know the drill by now, right? Click the Exemptions button and then use the dialog box that Quicken displays to indicate the number of personal exemptions you get. When you're done, click OK. The basic rule is that you get one exemption for everybody in your family (you, your spouse if you're filing jointly, and your dependents) as long as they live at your house. I should mention, however, that things get tricky if you've got shirt-tail relatives living at your house, your kids live away from home or are married, or some of the kids in the house have divorced parents. If you have questions because one of these situations sounds vaguely familiar, get the IRS return preparation instructions and read the part about who is and is not dependent.

9. **Indicate whether you owe any other taxes or have tax credits you can use to reduce your taxes.**

   Click the Other Tax (or) Credits button and fill in the blanks on the dialog box that Quicken displays. When you're done click OK. By the way, if you and your spouse get all your income from salaries and a handful of investments, you probably don't need to worry about this "other taxes and credits" business.

10. **Enter any estimated taxes or federal income withholding you've paid.**

    Click the Withholding, W-4 button and fill in the blanks on the dialog box that Quicken displays. When you're done click OK. If you make estimated tax payments — and you'll know if you do — click on the Est. Tax Pmts button and fill in the blanks on the dialog box that Quicken displays. All you are doing here is indicating how much you and your spouse have already had withheld and how much you'll have withheld from your future paychecks.

When you complete these ten steps, you'll be able to see not only what your total income taxes are, but also whether you'll need to increase your payments. (Look at the Remaining Tax Due field in the lower right corner of the screen to see whether it looks like you're coming up short.)

If you want to print the tax planner information, click the Print button. If you want to erase all your inputs and start over, click the Reset button. When you're done using the calculator, click the Close button.

Some More Tax Planner Tricks

I think the way I've described in the preceding paragraphs makes the most sense for the average Quicken user. There are a couple of other tricks the Tax Planner lets you try. First, rather than enter the data into text boxes (as I described here), you can tell the Tax Planner to grab taxable income and tax deduction information from your registers. This is pretty straightforward as long as you're diligently using tax-related categories to track these income and expense amounts and — this is important — you've indicated the tax schedule line on which category totals should be reported.

You can update the tax rates and tax brackets by clicking the Rates button and then filling a worksheet that Quicken provides. (If you're still using Quicken 4 for Windows in 1996, for example, you'll either need to do this or get new tax rate information from Quicken to use the Tax Planner calculator.) This worksheet pretty much mirrors the tax schedules provided by the Internal Revenue Service, so if you're familiar with these, updating the tax rates should be a breeze.

Part III
Home Finances

The 5th Wave — By Rich Tennant

YUNT INSTITUTE OF COMPUTING
SUMMER PERFORMANCE
SIDESHOW MELODY

"ALL RIGHT, NOW, WE NEED SOMEONE TO PLAY THE PART OF THE GEEK."

In this part...

Are you going to be using Quicken for personal financial stuff? If so, you should know there's more to the program than just the checkbook-on-a-computer business described in the preceding part. Quicken can help you manage and monitor things like credit cards, home mortgages, and investments. If this stuff sounds interesting, then keep reading.

Chapter 10
Credit Cards (and Debit Cards, Too)

. . . .

In This Chapter

▶ Tracking credit cards with Quicken

▶ Setting up a credit card account

▶ Selecting a credit card account so that you can use it

▶ Recording a credit card charge

▶ Changing charges you've already entered

▶ A most bodacious way to pay a credit card bill

▶ A less bodacious way to pay a credit card bill

▶ Reconciling a credit card balance

▶ Handling debit cards

▶ Deciding whether to use Intelli-Charge

. . . .

*Y*ou can use Quicken to track your credit cards in much the same way you use Quicken to keep a checkbook. The process works very much the same, but with a few wrinkles.

First, I'll discuss whether you should even bother.

To Bother or Not to Bother...

I don't use Quicken to track my credit card purchases because I always pay my credit card balance in full every month. (Don't feel bad if you don't do this — it's like a natural law that CPAs like me must do this.) Therefore, I don't have an open credit card balance to track. What's more, when I pay the monthly credit card bill, I easily can use the Splits windows to describe my spending categories: $3.53 on food for lunch, $52.64 for a car repair, and $217.54 for books (a personal weakness).

If you're in the same boat — meaning you use a credit card but you don't carry a balance — you don't need anything special to track your credit card purchases and, of course, you don't need to use Quicken to tell you your account balance because it's always zeroed out at the end of the month.

Of course, if you do carry a credit card balance — and most people do — you can set up a Quicken credit card account and use it for tracking credit card purchases. If you just need to keep track of how much you've charged during the month (even if you are going to pay the balance in full), you must also set up a credit card account and use it.

I should make one other point: in order to track not just what you charged by using spending categories, but also *where* you charged it by using the Payee field, you must set up a credit card account and use it.

My father-in-law uses a Quicken credit card account for this purpose. Although he doesn't carry a balance (or so he says), he does like to know how much he spends at International House of Pancakes, K Mart, and the truck stop. He could use the Splits window to record spending on things like breakfast, clothing, and gasoline when he pays his credit card balance at the end of the month. But, the Splits window does not have a field to record where he said, "Charge it."

Setting Up a Credit Card Account

If you want to track credit card spending and balances with Quicken, you must set up a special credit card account. (In comparison, you use bank accounts to track things like the money that flows into and out of a checking account).

If you set up a credit card account as part of setting up Quicken, you don't need to do it again. Skip ahead to the next section.

Adding a credit card account

To set up a credit card account, you follow roughly the same steps as you do for a bank account. Here's what you do:

1. **Choose the Accts icon from the iconbar.**

    Quicken displays the Account List window, as shown in Figure 10-1.

2. **Select the New command button on the Account List window.**

    Quicken displays the Create New Account dialog box, as shown in Figure 10-2.

3. **Unmark the Guide Me check box if it's marked.**

    You don't need the extra hand-holding the Quicken guide provides if you've been working with Quicken a bit.

4. **Mark the Credit Card Account option button.**

    This option tells Quicken you want to set up a credit card account. This last bit of data, I'm sure, is a big surprise.

    Quicken — always sensitive to your feelings — displays the Create Credit Card Account dialog box. Because I'm sensitive to your feelings too, I've included this dialog box as Figure 10-3.

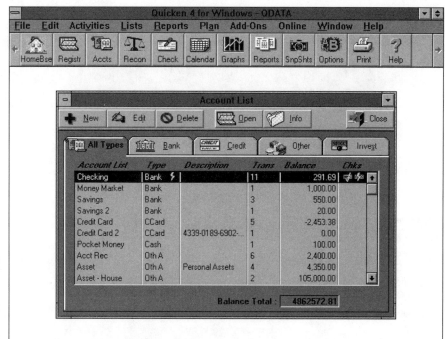

Figure 10-1:
The
Account List
window.

Figure 10-2:
The Create
New
Account
window.

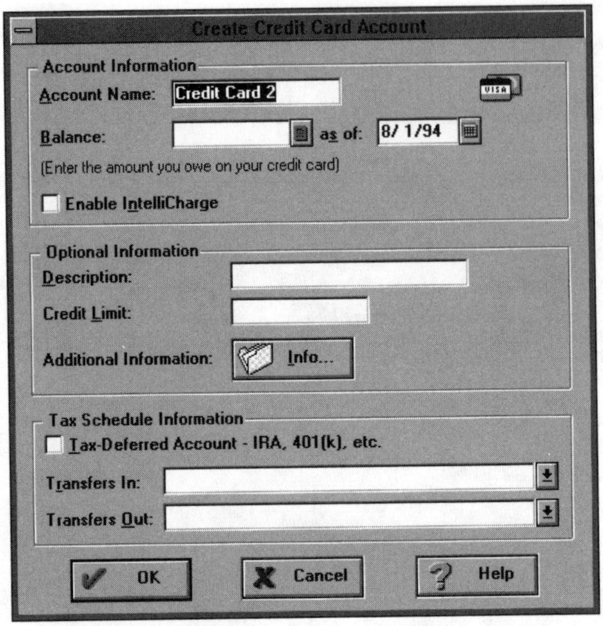

Figure 10-3:
The Create
Credit Card
Account
dialog box.

5. Name the account.

Why not do it, right? Move the cursor to the <u>A</u>ccount Name text box and enter a name.

6. Enter the balance you owed at the end of the last credit card billing period after making your payment.

Move the cursor to the <u>B</u>alance text box and enter the balance value using the number keys.

7. Enter the date on which you will start keeping records for the credit card account.

This should probably be the date you made your payment. Move the cursor to the A<u>s</u> Of text box and type a two-digit number for the month, a two-digit number for the day of the month, and a two-digit number for the year.

8. Indicate whether you'll use I<u>n</u>telliCharge.

If you are using Quicken's IntelliCharge feature (which allows you to get a list of your credit card charges on disk or by modem), indicate this by marking the I<u>n</u>telliCharge check box. (I'll ramble on about IntelliCharge later in the chapter.)

9. Enter a description for the account.

Move the cursor to the <u>D</u>escription text box and type a description of the account or some other important piece of account information, such as the credit card account number.

10. **Type in the amount of your credit limit (optional).**

If you want, indicate the amount of your credit card limit by moving the cursor to the Credit Limit text box and then type in whatever number the credit card company has arbitrarily decided is a reasonable balance for you to shoulder.

Ignore the Tax-Deferred Account check box. It doesn't apply to credit card accounts.

11. **Choose OK.**

Quicken redisplays the Account List window, as shown in Figure 10-1. But you know what? This time the window lists an additional account — the credit card account you just created.

Selecting a credit card account so that you can use it

To tell Quicken you want to work with an account, you use the Account List window — the same window you saw in Figure 10-1. Go figure!

Choose the Accts icon from the iconbar to display the dialog box. After you display the dialog box, select the account you want to use. You know how this works. You highlight the account you want by using the arrow keys or by clicking the account name with that long-tailed plastic rodent that sits on your desk. Then you select the Open button or press Enter. Quicken selects the account and displays the register window for that account so that you can begin recording transactions.

Entering Credit Card Transactions

After you select a credit card account, Quicken displays a special version of the register window, as shown in Figure 10-4.

A whirlwind tour of the Credit Card register

The Credit Card register works like the regular register window you use for a bank account. You enter transactions into the rows of the register. When you record a charge, Quicken updates the credit card balance and the remaining credit limit (if you entered the optional credit limit info when you set up the account).

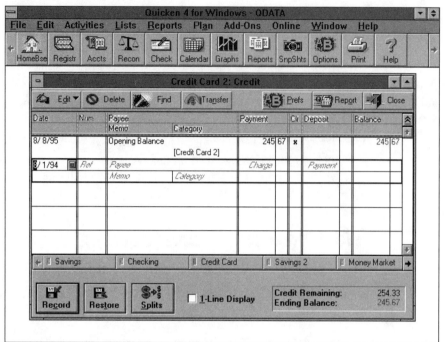

Figure 10-4:
The credit
card version
of the
Register
window.

You can use the same icons and commands as you do for your regular ol' bank account register. I talked about these in earlier chapters, so I won't regurgitate them here. Old news is no news.

Recording a credit card charge

Recording a credit card charge is similar to recording a check or bank account withdrawal. For the sake of illustration, suppose that you charged $30.47 for dinner at your favorite Mexican restaurant. Here's how you record this charge:

1. Enter the charge date.

Move the cursor to the Date field (if it isn't already there) and type the date using the MM/DD format. For example, enter July 4, 1995 as **7/4.** You usually don't have to type the year because Quicken retrieves the current year number from the little clock inside your computer. Or if you want, get crazy — click the down arrow at the end of the field and Quicken displays a pop-up calendar (described in Chapter 4) from which you can select the appropriate month and day.

2. Record the name of the business you paid with a credit card.

Move the cursor to the Payee field and enter the name of the person or business you paid. If the restaurant is "Mommasita's Cantina," for example, type **Mommasita's Cantina** into the Payee field.

3. Enter the charge amount.

Move the cursor to the Charge field and enter the total charge amount — 30.47 in this example. Don't type a dollar sign, but do type the period to indicate the decimal place and cents.

4. (Optional) Enter a memo description.

Move the cursor to the Memo field and type the specific reason you're charging the item, such as a special date with your spouse or an important business meeting.

5. Enter the category.

Move the cursor to the Category field, activate the drop-down list box, and select the appropriate category. A restaurant charge might be categorized as "Entertain," for example.

6. Record the charge.

Select Record, or press Enter with the cursor in the Category field Either way, tell Quicken you want to record the charge. Quicken beeps and then calculates both the new credit card balance and the remaining credit limit. Quicken then moves the cursor to the next slot in the register.

Figure 10-5 shows the charge at Mommasita's Cantina. Good food and reasonable prices — you can't ask for much more than that.

By the way, I'm not making fun of Mexican restaurants nor of Mexican food. I love both. The nicest restaurant that I've ever eaten in was a Mexican restaurant in the Zono Rojo in Ciudad de Mexico. I actually wonder why they let me in, given the way I was dressed: a T-shirt, Bermuda shorts, thongs, and a stupid grin.

Changing charges you've already entered

Use the arrow keys or click the mouse to highlight the charge you want to change. Use the Tab and Shift+Tab keys or the mouse to move the cursor to the field that contains the misinformation you want to fix, fix the entry, and then record the transaction. That's easy enough, isn't it?

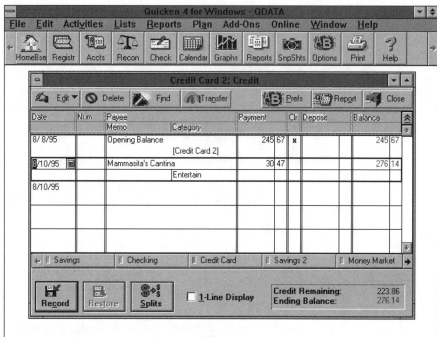

Figure 10-5:
The charge at Mommasita's Cantina.

Paying credit card bills

If you're tracking the credit card account balance with a credit card account like I'm describing here, Quicken provides two ways for you to pay a credit card bill.

If you're not using a credit card account, you record the check you sent to pay a credit card bill in the same way you record any other check.

A most bodacious way to pay a credit card bill

This is pretty simple, so don't blink your eyes because you may miss the action.

Look at your credit card statement. Decide how much you want to pay. Select the bank account on which you'll write the check. Then write the check and record it in the bank account register — but as a transfer to the credit card account.

You're done. If you have questions, take a peek at the highlighted check transaction shown in Figure 10-6. It pays $100 of the credit card balance. The only trick — if you want to call it that — is that the credit card account is specified as the account to which the money is transferred. (You can see the other account by selecting the transfer transaction and pressing Ctrl+X.)

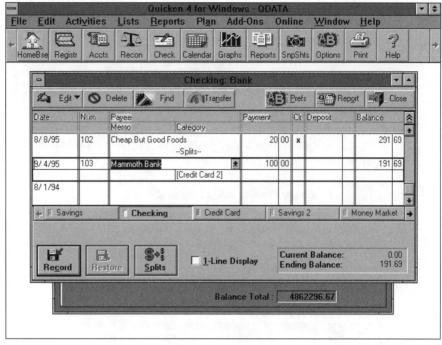

Figure 10-6:
A check that
pays a
portion of a
credit card
balance.

If you look at the credit card account register now, you see that this check
reduces the credit card balance by $100.

A less bodacious way to pay a credit card bill

You can also tell Quicken that you want to pay some portion of the credit card
bill as part of reconciling the credit card's account balance.

I think this method is slightly more difficult, but if you want to reconcile your
credit card account, think about using this second method. If you are reconciling a credit card statement and paying some portion of the credit balance at the
same time, you may find this method more convenient. Who knows?

I describe how to reconcile a credit card account in the very next section.

That Crazy Reconciliation Trick

You know that trick where you compare your checking account records with
your bank's records of your checking account? The one where you calculate the
difference between what you think is your account balance and what the bank

thinks is your balance? And this difference is supposed to equal the total of the transactions floating around out there in the system? You can do this same trick on your credit card account.

The actual reconciliation — neat and straight-up

To reconcile a credit card account, first get your credit card statement. Next, display the credit card account in a register window.

What the nasty credit card company says

To tell Quicken what that nasty credit card company says, follow these steps, and put on some music if you can't seem to get the rhythm thing right.

1. **Choose the Recon icon from the iconbar.**

   Quicken displays the Credit Card Statement Information dialog box, as shown in Figure 10-7.

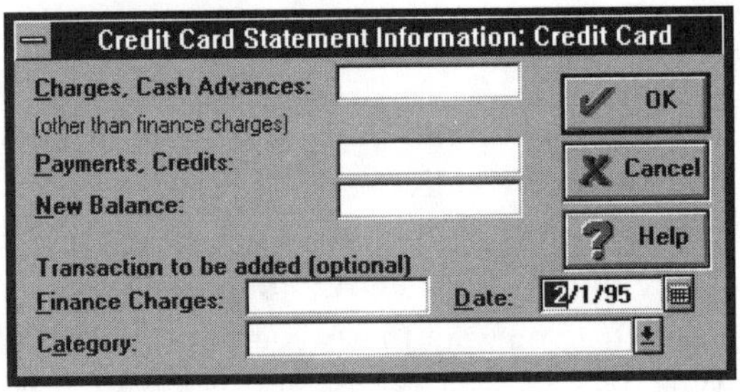

Figure 10-7:
The Credit
Card State-
ment Infor-
mation
dialog box.

2. **Enter the charges and cash advances that your statement shows.**

   Move the cursor to the Charges, Cash Advances text box and then type the number.

3. **Enter the payment and credits that your statement shows.**

   You know the drill: move the cursor and type the number, tap your foot and swing your partner, do-si-do.

4. **Enter the new balance shown on the credit card statement.**

   Now I bet this is a surprise. Go ahead and enter the figure — even if you just can't believe you charged that much.

5. **Enter the monthly interest charged by using the Finance Charges text box.**

   Pause for a moment of silence here if this is a sad, sad topic for you.

6. Assign the monthly interest to the appropriate spending category, such as "Int Exp."

Move the cursor to the Category text box and type the category name. (This is getting boring, isn't it? Move and type. . . . Move and type. . . . That's all I ever seem to say.) Remember that you can click the little down arrow at the end of the text box to see a list of categories to choose from.

7. Choose OK.

Quicken displays the Pay Credit Card Bill window (see Figure 10-8). You use it to tell Quicken which credit card charges and payments appear on your statement. (This step is akin to looking at a bank statement and noting which checks and deposits have cleared the bank.)

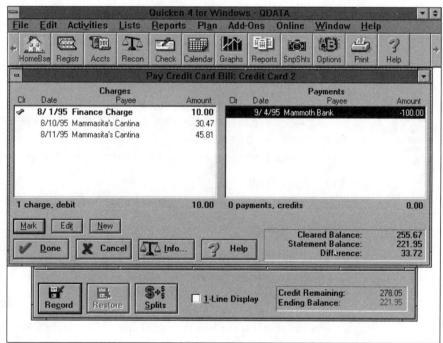

Figure 10-8:
The Pay
Credit Card
Bill window.

Ouch! Did I really spend that much?

After you give Quicken an overview of your credit card situation, you can note which charges have cleared and which charges haven't cleared.

If you're comfortable whipping through a bank reconciliation, you can probably do this with your eyes closed. If you need some help, leave your eyes open so you can read these steps:

1. **Find the first charge listed on the credit card statement.**

2. **Mark the charge as cleared.**

   Charges are listed in the left list box. Hmmm. It's not really any of my business, but maybe someone's eating at Mommasita's a bit too often?

   Scroll through the transactions listed in the Pay Credit Card Bill window until you find the charge and then click on the charge. Or highlight the charge using the arrow keys and then press the spacebar or select the Mark button. Quicken adds the checkmark symbol (✔) in front of the list entry in the Clr column to mark this charge as cleared and then updates the cleared statement balance.

3. **Enter any missing charges.**

   If you can't find a charge, you probably did not enter it in the Quicken register yet. Activate the credit card account register and then enter the charge into the register in the usual way — except enter an asterisk into the Clr column. You can do this by choosing the Edit command button. This identifies the charge as one that's already cleared. When you finish, return to the Pay Credit Card Bill window.

   To quickly go to the Credit Card register, you can also click on it with the mouse — if you can see it. Or, if you can't see the Credit Card register, you can also use the Window menu.

4. **Repeat steps 1, 2, and 3 for charges listed on the credit card statement.**

   Or until you're blue in the face.

5. **Find the first payment or credit listed on the credit card statement.**

   The payments and credits appear in the right list box. There's only one of these in Figure 10-8. It's the $100 payment to the credit card company, Mammoth Bank.

6. **Mark the payment or credit as cleared.**

   Scroll through the transactions listed on the Pay Credit Card Bill window until you find the first payment or credit and then click it. Or highlight the credit and then press the spacebar or select the Mark command button. Quicken adds the checkmark symbol in front of the list entry to mark the payment or credit as cleared and then updates the cleared statement balance.

7. **Enter any missing payments or credits.**

   If you can't find the payment or credit — and you probably know this — it means you haven't entered them into the Quicken register yet. Activate the credit card account register and then enter the payment or credit into the register in the usual way, except put an asterisk in the Clr column. Return to the Pay Credit Card Bill window when you finish.

8. Repeat steps 5, 6, and 7 for payments or credits listed on the credit card statement.

If you record a transaction wrong, do this

As you're looking through the credit card statement, you may discover that you incorrectly recorded a transaction. If this happens, select the incorrect transaction with the mouse or arrow keys. Then select the Edit command button. Quicken not only displays the Credit Card register so that you can make the needed fixes, it also highlights the transaction you need to fix.

Oh, that explains things

After you mark all the cleared charges and payments, the difference between the cleared balance for the credit card and the statement's ending balance should equal zero.

Figure 10-9 shows how this looks. By the way, it's darned easy to reconcile with fictitious data.

Finishing the reconciliation

If the difference does equal zero, you're cool. You're golden. You're done. (This sort of makes you sound like chicken, doesn't it?)

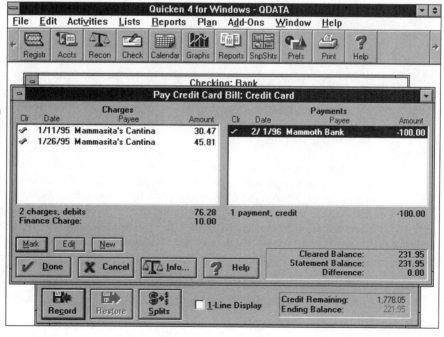

Figure 10-9: When the difference between the cleared balance and the statement balance equals zero, the reconciliation is complete.

All you need to do is select Done to tell Quicken you're finished. Quicken displays a congratulations message telling you how proud it is of you and then asks if you want to print a reconciliation report.

If you want to save a tree, skip the report. If you like paperwork, own stock in a paper company, or have a friend in the timber industry, print the report.

As part of finishing up, Quicken changes all the asterisks to Xs. There isn't any great magic in this. Quicken just does this to identify the transactions that have already been through the reconciliation process.

If the difference doesn't equal zero, you've got a problem. If you select Done in spite of the problem, Quicken will provide some cursory explanation as to why your account doesn't balance via a message. This message also tells you that you can force the two amounts to agree by pressing Enter.

You know what, though? Forcing the two amounts to agree isn't a very good idea. To do this, Quicken adds a cleared transaction equal to the difference. (Quicken will ask for a category if you choose the adjustment route.)

Despite the ease of making adjustments, a much better way is to fix the reason for the difference.

Chapter 7 provides some ideas for trying to figure out why a bank account that should balance won't. You can apply the same list of 10 tips to credit card reconciliations if you're in a bad way.

Postponing the inevitable

You can postpone reconciling the account by selecting the Cancel command button. Quicken then gives you the option to save your work-in-progress or to just abandon all hope and try again sometime in the future. (If you choose the Don't Save option, Quicken erases all the information you entered and puts you back to square one.)

If you indicate you want to save your work, Quicken basically leaves your reconciliation work half done. Transactions that you marked as cleared still show the asterisk in the Clr text box. You'll still have an inexplicable difference between the credit card statement and your register. Even so, postponing a reconciliation is usually better than forcing the cleared balance to equal the credit card statement balance. By postponing a reconciliation, you can hopefully find the problem or problems. You can fix them. Then you can restart the reconciliation and finish your work. (You restart a reconciliation the same way you originally start one.)

Paying the bill as part of the reconciliation

When you finish the reconciliation, Quicken politely asks if you want to pay the bill. Figure 10-10 shows the Make Credit Card Payment dialog box, which is the tool Quicken uses to collect the necessary data.

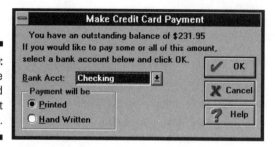

Figure 10-10:
The Make
Credit Card
Payment
dialog box.

You can probably figure out how to use this baby yourself, but hey, I'm on a roll, so here are the steps:

1. **Enter the bank account on which you'll write the check.**

   Activate the Bank Acct drop-down list box and select the account. Notice that the screen tells you what your register shows as the credit card balance, not what your credit card statement shows. I thought this was a nice touch.

2. **Indicate whether you'll print a check with Quicken or write one by hand.**

   Mark the Payment will be Printed option button if you want to print a check with Quicken. Mark the Payment will be Hand Written if you'll write a check by hand.

3. **Choose OK.**

   If you told Quicken that you want to print a check, Quicken displays the Write Checks window so that you can tell Quicken to print a check. (See Chapter 5 for information on how to do this.) If you told Quicken that you want to write a check, Quicken displays the register window in which you can add the missing information to complete the transaction. (See Chapter 4 for information on this.) Quicken assumes that you want to pay the entire credit card balance.

4. **Enter the check into the Write Checks window or the register window.**

   Describe the check as one that you will either print with Quicken or write by hand.

As I said earlier in this chapter, this usually isn't the easiest way to pay a credit card bill. But, hey, you're an adult. You make your own choices.

So What about Debit Cards?

Debit cards, when you get right down to it, aren't really credit cards at all. They're more like bank accounts. Rather than withdrawing money by writing a check, however, you withdraw money by using a debit charge.

While a debit card looks (at least to your friends and the merchants you shop with) like a credit card, you should treat it like a bank account.

In a nutshell, here's what you need to do:

- ✔ Set up a bank account with the starting balance equal to the deposit you make with the debit card company.

- ✔ When you charge something using your debit card, record the transaction just as you would record a regular check.

- ✔ When you replenish the debit balance by sending more money to the debit card company, record the transaction just as you would record a regular deposit.

If all this sounds pretty simple, it is. In fact, I'd go so far as to say that if you've been plugging along, doing just fine with a bank account, you'll find keeping track of a debit card as easy as eating an entire bag of potato chips.

The IntelliCharge Hoopla

IntelliCharge refers to a special credit card account — specifically provided for people who have the Quicken Visa credit card.

The big hoopla concerning this account is that you don't have to enter the credit card transactions into a register. Rather, you retrieve them from a floppy disk (which the Quicken credit card people send you) or by using a modem.

Is IntelliCharge something you should look into? Does it really save you time? Is it a good deal? Inquiring minds want to know, so I'll tell you what I think. (I should point out that what I'm about to say next is just my humble opinion.)

Although there isn't an annual fee for the credit card and the interest rate is competitive, IntelliCharge, at least as I'm writing this, still isn't all that cheap. The monthly delivery fee for the floppy disk is $4.50. Then the monthly modem charge is $3, so you're looking at $40 to $50 bucks a year.

For this, of course, you save some data-entry time, so maybe it is worth it. (If you're a heavy hitter running $20,000 or $30,000 a month in charges through your account, your time savings will be substantial.)

One thing that bothers me about the whole deal, however, is that you're really just receiving an electronic version of your statement. Reconciling your bank statement against, well, your bank statement isn't going to make a whole heck of a lot of sense. (Golly gee, Batman, the charge to Mulva's Pet School appears on both statements, too!)

Another thing is that you do have some extra fiddling to do. Now there's nothing particularly complicated about grabbing credit card charges off a floppy disk. Nor are there any special magic tricks you need to know to use a modem. (There is a secret handshake your computer and the Quicken credit card computer do every time they want to talk, but you'll get the scoop on this once you join the club.) Nevertheless, the fiddling takes some time.

IntelliCharge is kind of a cool idea, but it has some drawbacks. It won't eliminate the record keeping you have to do. And hey, it's not free.

Chapter 11
Other People's Money

In This Chapter

▶ When to track loans, mortgages, and other debts

▶ Setting up liability accounts

▶ Calculating the payment principal and interest portions of a payment

▶ Recording loan payments

▶ Handling mortgage escrow accounts

▶ Adjusting principal-interest breakdowns

▶ Scheduling automatic loan payments

A popular financial self-help writer thinks that one of the secrets to financial success is using other people's money: the bank's, the mortgage company's, the credit people's, your brother-in-law's. . . . You get the idea.

Me? I'm not so sure that other people's money is the key to financial success. I do know that borrowing other people's money can turn into a nightmare.

Quicken can help you out here. No, the folks at Intuit won't make your loan payments for you. But in a way, they do something even better. They provide you with a tool to monitor the money you owe other people and the costs of your debts.

Should You Bother to Track Your Debts?

I think it's a good idea to track your debts — car loans, mortgages, student loans, and so on — when lenders fail to tell you the amount you're paying in annual interest or the amount you owe after each and every payment.

If your lenders are doing a good job at keeping you informed, I don't think there's much sense in using Quicken for this purpose. Heck, it's their money. They can do the work, right?

Let me make one more observation. If lenders have half a clue, they send you a 1098 tax form at the end of every year. The number shown on that form equals your tax deduction if the interest stems from a mortgage, business, or investment loan. Note that personal interest expenses aren't deductible anymore, so there's little reason to track them unless you really want to be mean to yourself.

How Do I Get Started?

To track other peoples' money with Quicken, you must set up a *liability account*. Liability is big word — which is why accountants love it. (Say liability really slowly and you realize what a silly-sounding word it is. *Lie-a-bill-it-tee.*)

But it's easy to set up one of these babies. Just remember that you must set up a liability account for every loan or debt: your mortgage, your car loan, your student loan, and so on, "ad nauseam."

Setting up a liability account for an amortizing loan

An *amortized loan* is one on which you make regular, equal-sized payments. Over time, the principal portion of each payment pays off, or amortizes, the loan principal. If you borrowed money to purchase a house, a car, a Winnebago, or anything else that's really expensive and lasts for several years, chances are that your loan is of the amortizing variety.

Here's the recipe for setting up a liability account:

1. **Click the Accts icon on the iconbar.**

   Quicken, now well accustomed to your sure-footed direction, displays the Account List window.

2. **Select the New button in the Account List window.**

   Quicken, with little or no complaint, displays the Create New Account dialog box.

3. **Unmark the Guide Me check box if it's marked.**

   If you've worked with Quicken's accounts a bit, you don't need the Quicken guide to help.

4. **Click the Liability option button.**

   Quicken displays the Create Liability Account dialog box, as shown in Figure 11-1.

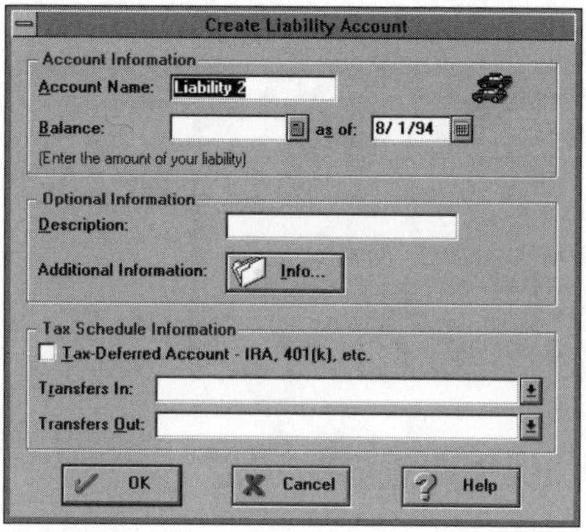

Figure 11-1:
The Create
Liability
Account
dialog box.

5. Name the liability.

Enter something clever (and hopefully useful) in the Account Name text box.

6. Enter the balance of your loan after your last payment.

(If you don't have this figure — and who does? — call your lender.) Move the cursor to the Balance text box and type the amount that you owe.

7. Enter the date of your last payment in the As of Date text box.

This date is the date as of which you owe the balance you entered in step 6. Enter the date in MM/DD/YY fashion. (For example, type **05/31/95** for May 31, 1995.)

8. (Optional) Enter a description of the account.

If the account name isn't descriptive enough, you might enter the account number or the name of the lender, for example. You can click Info to collect additonal information. Just fill out the dialog box Quicken displays.

9. Click OK.

Quicken diplays a message box that asks if you'd like to set up an amortized loan for the new liability account.

10. If you want to set up an amortized loan, choose Yes.

Quicken displays the Set Up Loan dialog box (see Figure 11-2). If you don't want to indicate that the loan is amortized, select Cancel when Quicken displays the message box that asks if you'd like to set up an amortized loan. You're done.

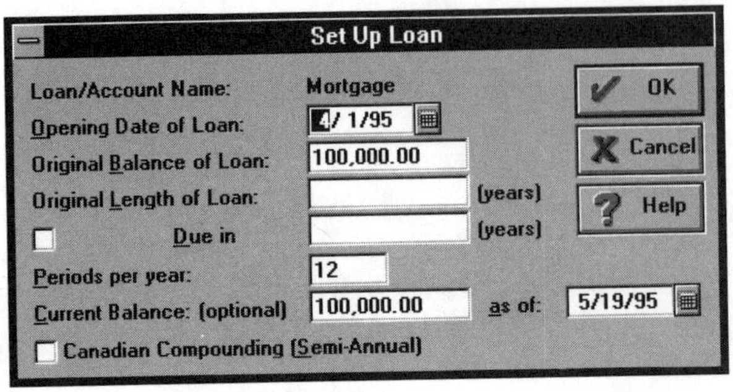

Figure 11-2:
The Set Up
Loan dialog
box.

11. **Enter the date you borrowed the money in the Opening Date of Loan text box.**

Quicken needs to know this date so that it can calculate the interest the loan started to accrue when you borrowed the money. The program suggests the As of Date you supplied when you set up the liability account.

12. **Enter the original loan balance.**

Quicken plugs the number you set as the liability account starting balance into the Original Balance of Loan text box. If this amount isn't current, no problem. Move the cursor to the Original Balance of Loan text box and then enter the amount you originally borrowed.

13. **Enter the loan term in years in the Original Length of Loan text box.**

If you set up a 30-year mortgage, for example, enter **30**. There's one tiny trick to entering this figure: if you set up a loan that includes a balloon payment, enter the number of years over which the loan will be fully amortized. For example, loan payments might be calculated based on a 30-year term, but the loan might require a balloon payment at the end of seven years. In this case, enter **30** in the Original Length of Loan text box.

14. **(Optional) Record any balloon payment provisions.**

If a loan includes a balloon payment provision, mark the check box that appears to the left of the Due In text box. Then enter the number of years in which the balloon payment is due in the Due In text box. If a balloon payment is due in seven years, for example, enter **7** (even though the loan is amortized over 30 years).

15. **Enter the number of loan payments you're required to make in a year in the Periods per year text box.**

If you make monthly payments, for example, enter **12**.

16. **Verify the current balance.**

The Current Balance text box also displays what you entered as the liability account's starting balance. If the balance isn't correct, fix it. You know the drill by now. Just move the cursor to the text box and pound a few number keys.

17. **(Optional) Mark the Canadian Compounding check box if your loan uses semiannual compounding.**

18. **Choose OK.**

    Quicken displays the Set Up Loan Payment dialog box. See Figure 11-3.

19. **Enter the interest rate in the Current Interest Rate text box.**

    Be sure to enter the rate as a decimal value. If a loan charges 8⅞ percent interest, for example, enter **8.875**. Quicken then calculates the loan payment and enters this figure in the Principal and Interest text box.

20. **Verify the principal and interest payment calculated by the program.**

    If it's wrong, you can keep going, but let me point out a minor but annoying problem. You probably entered incorrectly one of the loan calculation inputs, such as the loan balance, the loan term, or the interest rate. It's also possible that you incorrectly marked that Canadian Compounding check box. Fortunately, these errors are only a minor bummer. Later in the chapter (in the "Fixing Loan Stuff" section), I describe how to restart.

21. **(Optional) Indicate any amounts you pay besides principal and interest.**

    Click the Split button. Quicken displays the Splits window, which you can use to describe any additional amounts the lender requires you to pay. In the case of a mortgage, for example, you might be required to pay property taxes or private mortgage insurance. After you enter information and click the OK button, Quicken calculates the full payment and redisplays the Set Up Loan Payment dialog box.

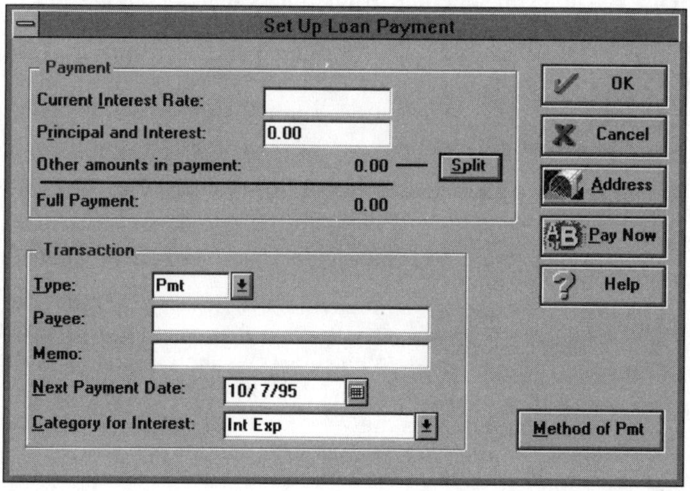

Figure 11-3:
The Set Up Loan Payment dialog box.

22. Indicate how you make payments.

Select one of the payment transaction types listed in the Type drop-down list box. Pmt means that you hand-write checks, Chk means that you print checks by using Quicken, and Epmt means that you use CheckFree to make electronic payments.

If you print checks by using Quicken and want to put the payee's address on the check, click the Address button in the Set Up Loan Payment window. Quicken displays a dialog box you can use to input the payee's address.

23. Type the lender's name in the Payee text box.

This is just the name of the person or business who loaned you the money.

24. (Optional) Enter a memo description.

Does the lender always get mixed up when you send the check? Stick the loan account number in the check's Memo text box. Personally, I refrain from using this text box to comment on the fairness of the bank's interest rate, to mock the intelligence of the loan payment processors, or to perform other emotionally gratifying but generally unproductive acts.

25. Enter the date of your next loan payment in the Next Payment Date text box.

26. Enter the Interest Category.

Activate the Category for Interest drop-down list box and select the appropriate category.

Quicken lets you schedule or memorize loan payments and CheckFree electronic payments so that it can remind you of the payment or even make the payment automatically. I'm going to assume that you don't want to be doing this kind of stuff — at least not yet. If I'm assuming incorrectly, click the Method of Pmt button. Then fill out the dialog box that appears. It's not all that difficult.

If you're still confused, I talk about how you can use the Financial Calendar to schedule loan payments later in the chapter.

27. (Optional) Indicate that you want to make the loan payment immediately.

If you want to make the loan payment right this exact minute, select Pay Now. Quicken displays a message box that asks from which account the payment should be made. You select the account by using the message box's drop-down list box. Then click OK. Quicken enters the payment in the register and displays the View Loans dialog box. If you choose to make the payment immediately, this step is the last one you perform.

28. With the Set Up Loan Payment dialog box displayed, select OK.

Quicken removes the Set Up Loan Payment dialog box so that you can see the View Loans dialog box (which has been hidden the whole time). Figure 11-4 shows this dialog box, which summarizes the loan you've set up, lists payments, and displays an amortization schedule for the loan. You can noodle around with the View Loans dialog box for a while. When you're done noodling, close the dialog box. You do so by double-clicking the dialog box's control menu icon.

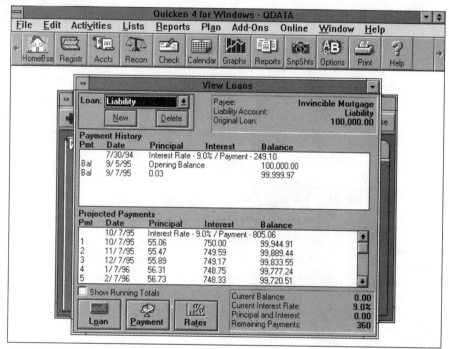

Figure 11-4:
The View Loans dialog box.

Mark the Show Running Totals check box to direct Quicken to calculate the interest and principal you've paid on a loan.

Fixing loan stuff

Nobody's perfect, right? It's possible that you made a tiny little mistake in setting up either the loan or the loan payment. It doesn't need to be a major financial or personal crisis, however. Just use the View Loans dialog box to identify the incorrectly described loan and then make your corrections. (See Figure 11-4.) If the View Loans dialog box isn't displayed, choose the Loans command from the Activities menu.

Once you see the View Loans dialog box, activate the Loan drop-down list box and select the loan you want to change. Quicken gives you all the dirt on the selected loan in the View Loans dialog box.

Changing loan or loan payment information

If you want to change something about the loan, click the Loan button. Quicken displays the Set Up Loan dialog box (see Figure 11-2). Make your changes and select OK. To change something about the payment, click the Payment button. Quicken displays the Set Up Loan Payment dialog box. (See Figure 11-3.) Make your changes and select OK. I describe how the Set Up Loan and Set Up Loan Payment dialog boxes work in the previous section.

Working with adjustable rate loans

Before I wrap up this discussion, let me mention a couple other things. If you're working with a variable rate loan, you can click the Rates button to display the Loan Rate Changes dialog box (see Figure 11-5). This dialog box has a very simple purpose in life: it lists the interest rates you entered for a loan and the dates these interest rates were used in loan calculations.

Figure 11-5:
The Loan
Rate
Changes
dialog box.

If you want to record new interest rates — because you have a variable rate loan and the interest rate changes, for example — click the New button in the Loan Rate Changes dialog box. Quicken displays the Insert an Interest Rate Change dialog box, as shown in Figure 11-6.

Figure 11-6:
The Insert
an Interest
Rate Change
dialog box.

Enter the new interest rate in the Interest Rate text box. Quicken then recalculates the loan payment and sticks the new loan payment figure into the Regular Payment text box.

Use the Effective Date box to indicate when the new interest rate becomes effective. You can either type in a date or activate the drop-down list box and select a date from the calendar.

Adding and removing loans

You can add and delete loans by using the View Loans dialog box.

Delete a loan that you no longer need or shouldn't have added in the first place by selecting the loan from the Loan drop-down list box. Then select Delete.

You can add loans from the View Loans dialog box, too. (See Figure 11-4.) To do so, click the View Loans dialog box's New button. Quicken displays the Set Up Loan Account dialog box. Using option buttons, it asks whether you are borrowing money or lending money. The button you mark tells Quicken to set up an asset account or a liability account. (Note, then, that by using this approach you can set up loan accounts for which you are the lender in addition to loan accounts for which you are the borrower.) Using the appropriate text box, give a name to the loan account and then click OK. Quicken walks you through that sequence of steps to set up the loan that I described earlier. For example, you fill out both the Set Up Loan dialog box (Figure 11-2) and the Set Up Loan Payment dialog box (Figure 11-3).

Delivering a Pound of Flesh (a.k.a. Making a Payment)

After you set up a liability account, you're ready to give the lender his pound of flesh — that is, make a payment. Before you say that this phrase is just some sort of populist bull-dweeble, I want to remind you that this metaphor comes from Shakespeare — Shylock uses it in *The Merchant of Venice*.

Recording the payment

After you set up the loan and the loan payment, you're ready to record the payment in (drum roll, please)... the register.

I'm trying to make the old Quicken register more exciting for you because you're probably becoming pretty darn familiar with it. And familiarity, as they say, breeds contempt.

Anyway, complete the following steps to record a payment:

1. Display the register window or theWrite Checks window.

If the bank account on which you write checks to make loan payments isn't selected, you must select it first. (You can do so by clicking the Accts icon on the iconbar.)

2. Enter the check date.

3. If you're using the register window, enter the check number. (If you're using the Write Checks window, of course, you don't enter the check number because Quicken will do this for you later.)

4. Get the memorized loan transaction.

Quicken automatically memorizes loan payment transactions (which means that it stores the transactions in a list so that you can use them again). Move the cursor to the Payee text box and begin typing the name of the lender. Quicken QuickFills the Payee text box with the complete lender name. Press Enter or Tab. Quicken QuickFills the register field with the memorized transaction information and then it displays the Confirm Principal and Interest dialog box, as shown in Figure 11-7.

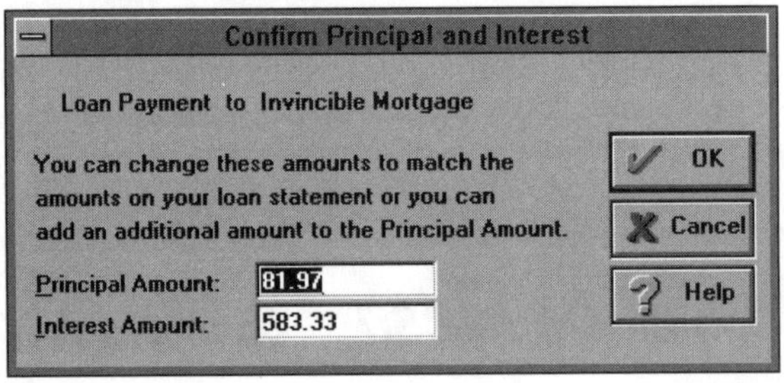

Figure 11-7:
The Confirm Principal and Interest dialog box.

Confirm Principal and Interest

Loan Payment to Invincible Mortgage

You can change these amounts to match the amounts on your loan statement or you can add an additional amount to the Principal Amount.

Principal Amount: 81.97
Interest Amount: 583.33

✓ OK
✗ Cancel
? Help

---

5. Correct the interest or principal amount if either is wrong.

Quicken fills in the text boxes in the Confirm Principal and Interest dialog box with its calculations of the principal and interest portions of the loan payment. If the figures are incorrect, enter the correct amounts in the Principal Amount and Interest Amount text boxes.

6. Click OK.

Quicken enters the loan payment in the Bank Account register.

7. Record the transaction in one of the usual ways.

Select the Record button. Press Ctrl+Enter. Clap your hands three times in a row. Wait, that last one doesn't work, does it? Just kidding...

Figure 11-8 shows the Splits window. The loan payment is split between principal and interest.

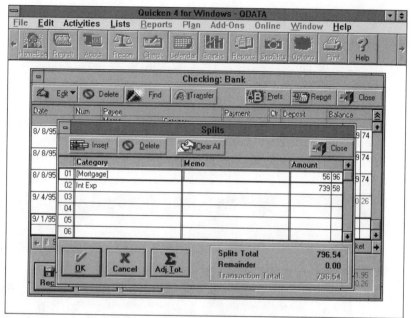

This transaction is tricky because you're both assigning to an expense category and transferring to a liability account. Splitting loan payments is as close as you'll get to rocket science in your financial record keeping.

Handling mortgage escrow accounts

We should talk about one minor mortgage record-keeping annoyance — mortgage escrow accounts.

If you have a mortgage, you know the basic procedure. Although your mortgage payment may be $800 a month, your friendly mortgage company (while insisting that they trust you completely) makes you pay an extra $150 a month for property taxes and other such things. In other words, even though you're paying only $800 a month in principal and interest, your monthly payment to the mortgage company is, according to this example, $950 ($800 + $150).

The mortgage company, as you probably know, saves this money for you in an *escrow account* or a set of escrow accounts. A couple of times a year they pay your property taxes, and a time or two a year they pay your homeowner's insurance. If you have private mortgage insurance, they may pay this fee every month as well. And so it goes.

The question, then, is how to treat this stuff. As with most things, there's an easy way, which is rough, dirty, and unshaven, and there's a hard way, which is precise, sophisticated, and cumbersome.

You can choose whichever method you want. It's your life.

The rough, dirty, and unshaven method

Suppose you do pay an extra $150 a month. You can treat this extra $150 as another expense category, such as Other Housing or Property Expenses. (I'm just making up these categories. If you can think of better ones, use your own.)

Nice. Easy. No fuss. These words and phrases pop into my head when I think about the rough, dirty, and unshaven method of mortgage escrow record keeping. Figure 11-9 shows a sample Splits window filled out this way.

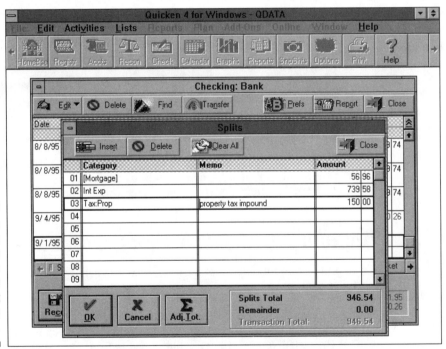

Figure 11-9:
A mortgage payment with an escrow account treated as an expense.

I use the rough, dirty, and unshaven method. Let me make a confession, though. This approach doesn't tell you how much moola you have stashed away in your escrow accounts. It also doesn't tell you how much you really spend in the way of homeowner's insurance, what you're entitled to claim as a property tax deduction, or how much they're bleeding you for private mortgage insurance.

To get these figures, you have to peruse the monthly and annual mortgage account statements — that is, if you get them. Or you have to call the mortgage lender and rattle a cage or two.

The precise, sophisticated, and cumbersome approach

You say you can't live with the uncertainty, the stress, the not knowing? There's another approach just for you.

You can set up an *asset account* for each of the escrow accounts for which the mortgage company collects money.

You set up asset accounts as you set up other liability accounts. Because I already explained this process, I'll just refresh your memory quickly. You need to set up an asset account with its starting balance equal to the current escrow account balance. To do so, display the Account List window and click the New button to indicate that you want to create a new account. Identify the account as an asset account and give it a name. Then tell Quicken how much money is in the account as of a specific date.

If you've set up an account or two in your time, this process should take you about 40 seconds.

After you set up your asset account and record its current balance, you're ready to cruise. Record payments in the escrow as account transfers whenever you record the actual loan payment. Figure 11-10 shows an example of how the Splits window looks when you do so, assuming that there's only one escrow account.

You need to do one other thing. When you set up an escrow account, you must record the payments that the bank makes from your escrow account to the county assessor (for property taxes) and to the insurance company (for things like homeowner's and private mortgage insurance). You don't know when these payments are really made, so watch your monthly mortgage account statements.

When the mortgage company disburses money from the escrow account to pay, for example, your first property tax assessment, you need to record a decrease equal to the payment for property taxes and then categorize the transaction as a property tax expense. This process isn't tricky in terms of mechanics, as shown in Figure 11-11, the Asset Account register. The account increases every loan payment (see the second transaction). The account decreases when there's a disbursement (see the third transaction).

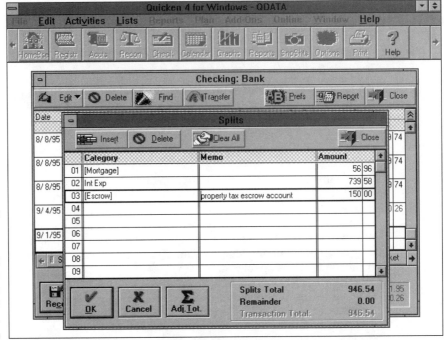

Figure 11-10:
A Splits window that transfers money to an escrow account.

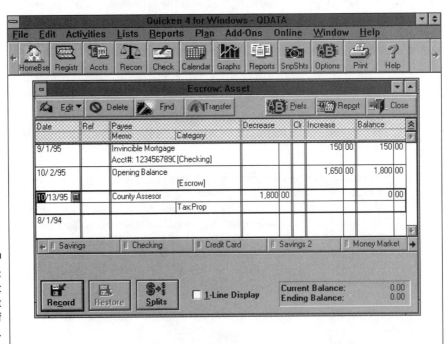

Figure 11-11:
The asset account version of the register.

Basically, the Asset Account register mirrors the Bank Account register. The only difference is that the Payment and Deposit fields in the latter are labeled Decrease and Increase in the former.

This second approach doesn't seem like all that much work, does it? And if you use this approach, you can track escrow balances and escrow spending precisely. You can, for example, pull your property tax deduction right from Quicken. Jeepers, maybe I should try the sophisticated approach next year.

Your Principal-Interest Breakdown Won't Be Right

I don't want to bum you out, but your principal interest breakdown will often be wrong. You might calculate interest expense as $712.48, for example, when your bank calculates it as $712.47. A few pennies here, a few pennies there, and pretty soon your account balance and interest expense tallies are, well, a few pennies off.

So you can't change the world

You can try calling the bank, telling them what bozos they are, and then demanding that they correct your balance. (If this approach works for you, let me know.)

Or (and this method is really more practical) you can adjust your records to agree with the bank's. Here's how:

1. **Display the register for the liability.**

2. **Choose the Update Balances command from the Activities menu. Then choose the update Cash Balance command from the menu that appear next to Update Balances.**

   (Go ahead. Tap your keys very hard if you're angry that the bank won't adjust their records.) Quicken displays the Update Account Balance dialog box, as shown in Figure 11-12.

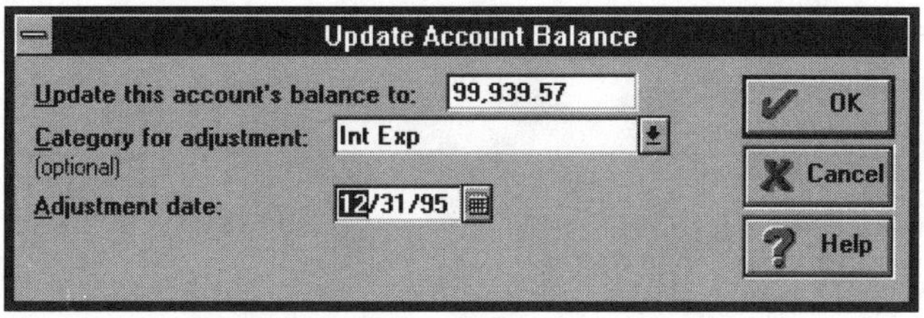

Figure 11-12:
The Update
Account
Balance
dialog box.

Update Account Balance

Update this account's balance to: `99,939.57`

Category for adjustment: `Int Exp`
(optional)

Adjustment date: `12/31/95`

✔ OK

✘ Cancel

? Help

3. **Enter the correct (that is, the one the bank says is correct) account balance.**

   Type the correct figure in the Update This Account's Balance To text box. (The amount probably comes from the year-end or month-end loan statement.)

4. **Enter your interest expense category.**

   Type the correct category name in the Category for Adjustment text box. (To see a list of categories, activate the drop-down list box.)

5. **Enter the last day of the month or year for which you're making the adjustment.**

   Enter a transaction date in the Adjustment Date text box. (The trick here is to use a transaction date that sticks the transaction that fixes the principal-interest split into the right month or year.)

6. **Record the adjustment.**

   When the Adjust Account Balance window correctly describes the needed adjustment, select OK.

Do you think this adjustment business is kooky?

Does the whole adjustment transaction business make sense to you? At times it can seem kind of backwards, so let me throw out a quick observation.

Remember that as you record loan payments, you split the loan payment between the interest expense category and a principal account transfer that reduces the liability. Here's the tricky part: when the liability gets reduced either too much or not enough, you need to fix both the liability balance *and* the principal-interest split.

Let me give you an example. Suppose that over the course of a year you record $.17 too little interest expense and therefore record $.17 too much principal reduction, despite your best efforts to be accurate. You need to increase the liability account balance by $.17 in this case, but you also need to increase the interest expense figure by $.17. By entering the interest expense category in the Category For Adjustment field, Quicken does these adjustments for you. Pretty cool, huh?

Automatic Loan Payments

Quicken has a couple of nifty features called Scheduled Transactions and the Financial Calendar that can help you with automatic loan payments.

The Financial Calendar and Scheduled Transactions features may be useful in other instances as well. For example, a business might use the Scheduled Transactions and the Financial Calendar to schedule and plan employee payroll checks, tax returns, and deposits.

Scheduling a loan payment

If a loan payment occurs regularly, you can set it up as a scheduled payment. When you do so, Quicken automatically records the payment for you based on a schedule.

Consider this example. Suppose that on the fifth day of every month your mortgage company taps your checking account for the full amount of your mortgage payment. (You, of course, have already authorized them to do so. They can't take your money willy-nilly.) In this case, you can tell Quicken to record the mortgage payment on the fifth of each month. Kind of handy, right?

Follow these steps to set up such a scheduled transaction:

1. **Choose the Financial Calendar command from the Activities menu or click the Calendar icon.**

   Quicken displays the Financial Calendar window, as shown in Figure 11-13. It shows a calendar for the current month and a list of transactions.

2. **Display the first month for which you want to schedule the transaction.**

   Using the Pre_v_ and Nex_t_ buttons, select the starting month for the scheduled transaction.

3. **Identify the scheduled transaction and date.**

   Select the transaction for which you want to create a schedule. In Figure 11-13, for example, you might want to schedule the Mammoth Bank loan payment transaction to fall on the 5ht. To do so, select the transaction by clicking it. Then drag the transaction to the 5th. When you release the mouse button, Quicken displays a dialog box that asks you to confirm the principal and interest breakdown (see Figure 11-14). You won't know whether the breakdown is correct until you see the bank statement, so click OK. Quicken displays the Drag and Drop Transaction dialog box (see Figure 11-15).

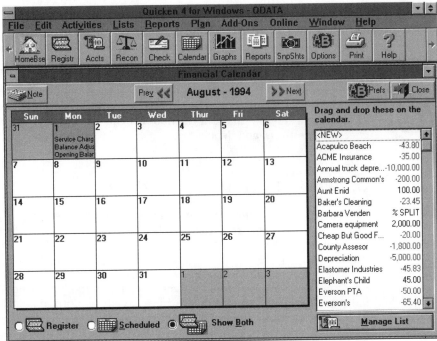

Figure 11-13:
The
Financial
Calendar.

4. Verify the date.

The date is probably correct, but because you're new to this scheduled transactions stuff, Quicken gives you a second chance. The date shown should be the next date you want the transaction recorded.

5. Identify the account from which the payment should be made.

Activate the Account drop-down list box and then select the appropriate account.

6. Verify that the transaction type is payment.

Activate the Type drop-down list box and select Payment. (Of course, if you were setting up some other type of payment, you might choose something else.)

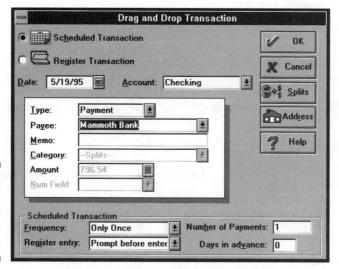

Figure 11-14:
The Drag
and Drop
Transaction
dialog box.

7. **Verify that the payee and memo fields are correct.**

They probably are. But I have kind of a compulsive personality. Since I've been telling you to check all this other stuff, I thought I'd also suggest you check these two fields.

8. **Indicate how often the scheduled transaction should occur.**

Activate the Frequency drop-down list box. Then select the frequency. (Initially, the drop-down list box shows Only Once.) For a monthly mortgage payment, for example, you would select Monthly.

9. **Tell Quicken whether you want to double-check the scheduled transaction before it actually gets entered in the register.**

This is easy. Just activate the Register entry drop-down list box to select the Prompt Before Entry choice.

10. **Indicate the number of payments Quicken should schedule.**

Move the cursor to the Number Of Payments text box. Then, enter a number. If you're setting up a 30-year mortgage with monthly payments and you think you'll be using Quicken for 30 years, enter 360. (You can do the math, too, I know, but 12 months times 30 years equals 360 payments.)

11. **Indicate the number of days in advance you want to be reminded of the scheduled payment.**

Move the cursor to the Days In Advance text box and enter a number. This input actually determines how many days in advance Quicken starts reminding you about a scheduled transaction using the Reminders window. (The Reminders window appears when you first start Quicken, as mentioned in Chapter 1. It also appears whenever you choose the Reminders command from the Activities menu.)

12. **Click OK.**

Quicken adds the transaction to its scheduled transaction list.

Quicken takes the Paul Masson approach to finance — it will enter no transaction before its time. So when the time is right — meaning next month on the fifth for this example — Quicken enters the transaction automatically. Furthermore, Quicken enters the transaction automatically each month until you tell it to stop.

More stuff about scheduled transactions

You already know the most important thing about scheduled transactions: how to set one up. Here are some other nuggets of knowledge that you might find useful.

Quicken identifies a calendar day for scheduled transactions by marking the day with the color green. You can see which transactions are scheduled for a day by clicking that day.

Another thing: you don't have to use the Financial Calendar to set up scheduled transactions. You can use the Scheduled Transactions command on the Lists menu instead. This command displays a window that lists all scheduled transactions and provides buttons that you can use to add, edit, or delete scheduled transactions. The functions of this window are pretty straightforward. To delete a scheduled transaction, for example, just select it from the list and choose Delete.

More stuff about the Financial Calendar

The iconbar at the top of the Financial Calendar provides some other tools you may want to use. I'm not going to spend a lot of time on them; you'll have more fun trying them out yourself than you would reading about them. Nevertheless, let me give you a bird's-eye view:

- The Prefs button displays a dialog box you can use to modify the appearance of the Financial Calendar. If you choose this command, for example, you can mark an option button that adds a graph to the bottom of the Financial Calendar window. The graph shows your account balances.

- The Note button lets you post a note on a calendar day. You use this feature to create reminder notes. For example, you might want to post a note saying, "Remember Wedding Anniversary," on the big day. When you click this button, Quicken displays a dialog box in which you type the message. Then you select Save. Quicken's Billminder utility displays your calendar notes. The program also marks the calendar day with a little yellow square — a miniature Post-It Note. Click the square to read the message.

✔ The Close button removes the Financial Calendar from the Quicken desktop. But, shoot, you probably figured that out already, didn't you?

The option buttons at the bottom of the Financial Calendar let you specify what transactions should appear on the Financial Calendar. You could have probably guessed this on your own, but if you mark Register, all the transactions from the register appear. (This looks a little cluttered as you might guess.) If you mark Scheduled, only scheduled transactions appear. If you mark Show Both, well, then both the register transactions and the scheduled transactions appear.

✔ The Manage List button in the lower right corner of the Financial Calendar window displays the Memorized Transactions List. You can use it to edit, delete, and add memorized transactions. The transactions shown in that list box along the right edge of the Financial Calendar window, by the way, are memorized transactions.

The 5th Wave

By Rich Tennant

"OH SURE, $1.8 MILLION DOLLARS SEEMS LIKE ALOT RIGHT NOW, BUT WHAT ABOUT RANDY? WHAT ABOUT HIS FUTURE? THINK WHAT A COMPUTER LIKE THIS WILL DO FOR HIS S.A.T. SCORE SOMEDAY."

Chapter 12
Mutual Funds

∙ ∙

In This Chapter

▶ Knowing when to use Quicken's investment recordkeeping

▶ Setting up a mutual fund investment account

▶ Recording your initial mutual fund investment

▶ Buying mutual fund shares

▶ Recording mutual fund profits

▶ Selling mutual fund shares

▶ Adjusting your mutual fund shares

▶ Adjusting mutual fund price information

∙ ∙

*I*don't mean to scare you, but I think investment recordkeeping is Quicken's most complicated feature. So it's time to get down to business. Time to stop pussyfooting around. Time to earn my pay.

To Bother or Not to Bother?

Quicken's investment recordkeeping feature lets you do three important things:

✔ Track your interest and dividend income

✔ Track real and potential capital gains and losses

✔ Measure an investment's performance by calculating an internal rate of return

If you're a serious investor, these things probably sound worthwhile. But before you invest any time learning how Quicken's investment recordkeeping works, be sure that you need all this power.

Are your investments tax-deferred?

If your investments are tax-deferred (if, for example, you're using individual retirement accounts (IRAs), 401Ks, or Keoghs), you don't really need to track investment income and capital gains and losses. Tax-deferred investments have no effect on your personal income taxes. You get a tax deduction for the money you stick into IRAs, for example, and anything you take out is taxable.

With tax-deferred investments, you record all that you should need to know via your checking account. Checks earmarked for investment are categorized as "IRA Deductions," for example, while investment account withdrawals deposited into your checking account are categorized as "Income."

Are you a mutual fund fanatic?

If you're a fan of mutual funds, you won't need Quicken to measure the fund's annual returns. The fund manager provides these figures for you in quarterly and annual reports.

Some investors don't need Quicken

Let me give you an example of someone who doesn't need to use Quicken's investments feature — me. Once upon a time I bought and sold common stocks, fooled around with half a dozen mutual funds, and learned firsthand why junk bonds are called junk bonds. Over the last few years, though, I've simplified my financial affairs considerably.

I don't invest directly in stocks, bonds, or mutual funds these days; instead, I stick money into an IRA. My investments don't produce taxable dividends or interest income, nor do they produce taxable or tax-saving capital gains or losses. Money I put into the IRA is tax-deductible. And money I ultimately take out of the IRA will be taxable.

I'm also sticking with a handful of mutual funds, but I don't need to calculate the annual return — that's what mutual fund managers do. So I don't need to separately figure, for example, what my shares of Vanguard Index Trust delivered as an annual return when I include both the 3 percent dividend and the 10 percent price drop.

Because I don't need to track investment income, or track capital gains and losses, or calculate the progress of my investment portfolio, I don't need Quicken's investment recordkeeping for my personal use.

Many investors do need Quicken

Of course, many people do benefit from Quicken's investment recordkeeping. If you routinely buy stocks and bonds, you probably want to calculate your annual returns. What's more, if you try to monitor your capital gains and losses intelligently — and you should — you want to know which securities have gone up and which have gone down.

The size of your investment portfolio isn't an issue. For example, I have two daughters who are saving money for college. (Actually, in a cruel twist of fate, *I* am saving; they're simply accumulating.) Although Beth and Britt haven't saved much money, and although they use mutual funds to keep things simple, they do three things that cause nightmarishly complex recordkeeping for their poor, overworked, and grossly underpaid accountant — dad: they reinvest their quarterly dividend income, pay annual maintenance fees, and coerce their parents into adding more money to their investment portfolios.

What's the big deal? All three things adjust the *basis* in the fund. And when Beth and Britt sell their mutual fund shares, their gain (or loss) will be determined by subtracting the basis from the sales proceeds.

The bottom line: Even though Beth and Britt don't have much money, I need to use Quicken to track their investments.

Tracking a Mutual Fund

If you still think that you need to track a mutual fund investment, you need to know how to set up a mutual fund account and then record your investment activities.

Even if you don't invest in mutual funds, you shouldn't skip this section.

Setting up a mutual fund investment account

Setting up an investment account works the same way as setting up any other account:

1. **Choose the Accts icon from the iconbar.**

   Quicken, ever the faithful companion, displays the Account List window.

2. **Select the New button on the Account List window.**

   Quicken dutifully displays the Create New Account window. If you've seen one Create New Account window, you've seen them all — so I won't show them all as figures.

3. **Make sure that the Guide Me check box is unmarked before you click.**

4. **Select the Investments button.**

   Quicken displays the Create Investment Account dialog box (see Figure 12-1).

5. **Name the investment.**

   Move the cursor to the Account Name text box and enter a name for the mutual fund. If you're investing in the Vanguard Index 500 Trust mutual fund, for example, you might type **Vanguard Index**.

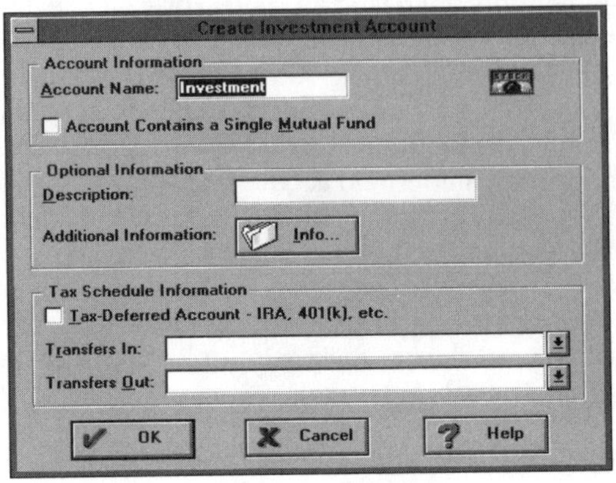

Figure 12-1:
The Create
Investment
Account
dialog box.

6. **Mark the Account Contains A Single Mutual Fund Check Box.**

   This tells Quicken, "Yeah, this is a mutual fund investment account."

7. **Mark the Tax-Deferred Account - IRA, 401(k), Etc. check box if the investment is tax-deferred.**

   This tells Quicken that this information doesn't affect your taxes. As I mentioned earlier, I can't think of a good reason for tracking a tax-deferred mutual fund. But, hey, I just work here.

8. **(Optional) Enter a description for the account.**

   Move the cursor to the Description text box and type a description.

9. **Click OK.**

   Quicken displays a message asking whether it should add a Portfolio View icon to your iconbar. Go ahead and click Yes.

   Quicken displays the Set Up Mutual Fund Security dialog box, shown in Figure 12-2. The Name text box will show the name you entered in step 5.

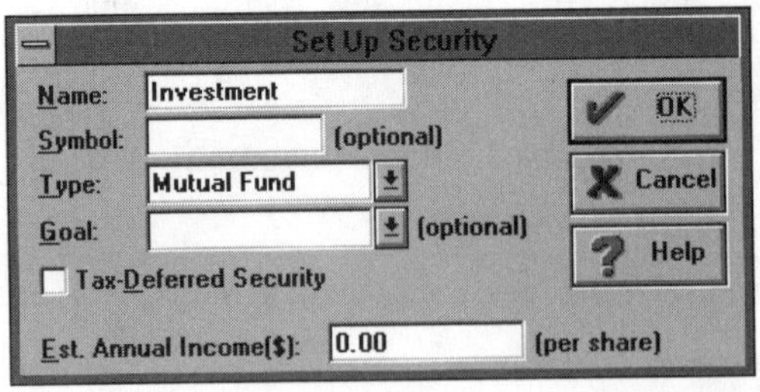

Figure 12-2:
The Set Up
Mutual Fund
Security
dialog box.

10. **(Optional) Enter the mutual fund symbol.**

    If you're going to download share price information via a modem, move the cursor to the Symbol text box and enter the mutual fund's stock symbol.

11. (Optional) Indicate the type of investment you're setting up.

Choose an investment type (bond, cd, mutual fund, or stock) from the Type drop-down list box.

12. (Optional) Indicate why you're investing.

Choose your goal (college fund, growth, high risk, income, or low risk) from the Goal drop-down list box. This investment stereotyping seems sort of goofy, though. Are there really people who want high-risk investments? Reminds me of an old joke: How do you accumulate a million dollars in the stock market? Start with two million in the stock market.

13. (Optional) Enter the annual estimated income.

If you want, enter an estimate of the annual investment profits produced in the Est. Annual Income($) text box. (There's an on-screen Portfolio View window that summarizes this information. I'll talk about the Portfolio View window at the end of this chapter.)

14. Click OK.

Quicken redisplays the Account List window — except now it lists the new investment account.

Recording your initial investment

After you set up a mutual fund investment account, you can record an initial purchase of fund shares.

Of course, you need to know the original price of those first shares. So dig through that kitchen drawer where you stuff bank statements, financial records, and those kooky birthday cards from Aunt Enid.

When you find the proper paperwork that shows the number of shares you purchased and the price per share, here's what you do:

1. Select the investment account.

Display the Account List window; then highlight the investment account (with the arrow keys or by clicking the mouse). Select the Open button. Quicken displays the Create Opening Share Balance dialog box (shown in Figure 12-3), which asks for your starting account balance.

2. Enter zeros into the Number Of Shares and Price Per Share text boxes. Then click OK.

In other words, don't enter anything into the Create Opening Share Balance dialog box. You don't — I repeat, don't — want to record your initial purchase with this dialog box.

Quicken displays the Investment Account register window (see Figure 12-4). You're in the big leagues now.

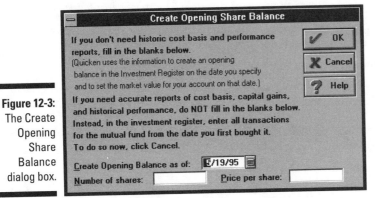

Figure 12-3:
The Create
Opening
Share
Balance
dialog box.

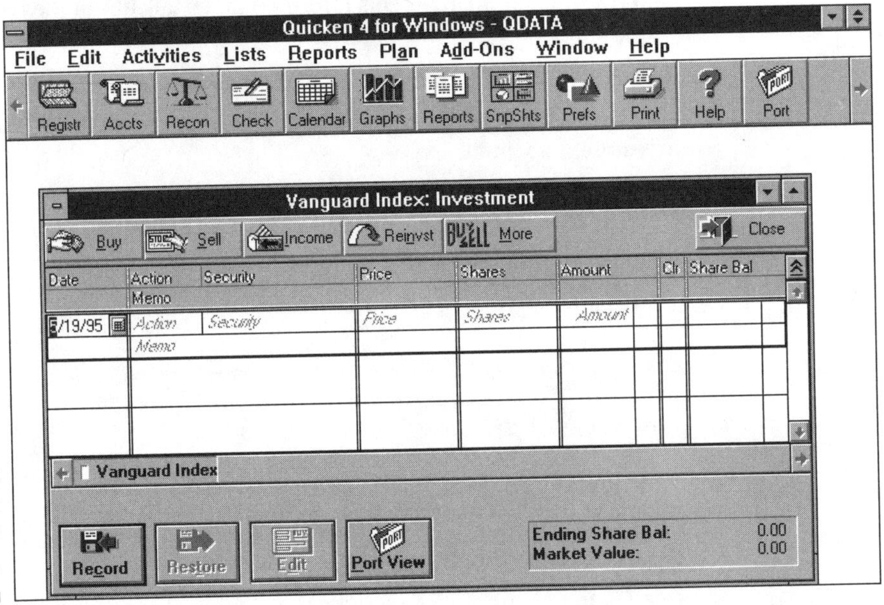

Figure 12-4:
The
Investment
Account
register
window.

3. **Enter the date you first purchased fund shares into the first row's Date field.**

   Move the cursor to the Date field and type the date using the MM/DD/YY format. Enter May 23, 1987, for example, as **5/23/87**. You also may select the date from the pop-up calendar.

4. Indicate that you're recording the prior purchase of shares.

When you move the cursor to the Action field, Quicken displays a down-arrow box, indicating a drop-down list box. From the drop-down list box, select ShrsIn. This tells Quicken, "Yeah, I've purchased some shares of this mutual fund, but I don't want you to adjust my checking account because I bought them a long, long time ago and I recorded the transaction then."

TIP

In some Quicken windows, drop-down list boxes don't appear until you move the cursor onto the field.

5. Accept the suggested security name.

The security name is the mutual fund account's name. Move the cursor past the Security field to the Price field.

6. Indicate what you paid per share.

With the cursor on the Price field, enter the share price. You can enter a fractional price — such as 10 ¼ — but your mutual fund shares probably cost something in dollars and cents — such as 10.25.

7. Indicate the size of your purchase.

Tell Quicken the size of your initial investment — either total number of shares or total price.

To enter the total number of shares, move the cursor to the Shares field (fractional shares are OK).

To enter the total price, move the cursor to the Amount field.

Quicken calculates the piece of data you didn't enter. Let's say, for example, you spent $500 to purchase 48.7805 shares of a mutual fund that cost $10.25 per share. If you enter the share price as $10.25 and the number of shares as 48.7805, Quicken calculates the total price. If you enter the share price as $10.25 and the total purchase as $500, Quicken calculates the number of shares purchased.

Life doesn't get much better than this, huh?

8. (Optional) Enter a memo description.

If you want to tie the purchase to a confirmation order number, for example, enter the data into the Memo field. I suppose you could use this field to record anything: Kilroy was here. Save the Whales. Don't tread on me.

9. Record the initial purchase of mutual fund shares.

Select the Record button.

Quicken beeps in agony and then records the transaction into the register. Figure 12-5, for example, shows a register that records a $500 purchase of shares in the Vanguard Index mutual fund.

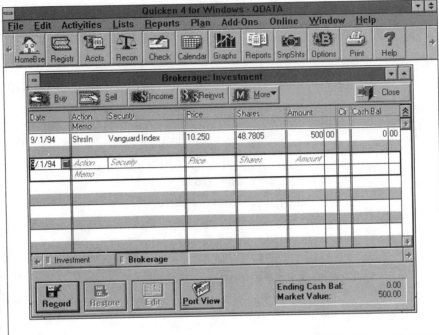

Figure 12-5:
The record
of an initial
purchase of
mutual fund
shares.

Buying near

As you purchase shares — by sending a check to the mutual fund management
company or by reinvesting dividends and capital gain distributions — you
should record these transactions in the Investment register.

By writing a check

If you buy shares by writing a check, there are two ways to enter a description
of the shares you've purchased.

I think the easier way is to enter the transaction directly into the Investment
register, much as you enter checks and deposits into a bank account register.
To record the purchase this way:

1. **Enter the purchase date into the first empty row's Date field.**

2. **Indicate that you're purchasing new shares by check.**

   Move the cursor to the Action field. From the Action drop-down list box,
   select the BuyX action. (You also can type the Action abbreviations
   directly into the field.)

3. **Accept the suggested security name.**

4. **Indicate what you paid per share.**

5. **Indicate the size of your purchase.**

   Tell Quicken the size of your investment — either total number of shares or total price.

6. **(Optional) Enter a memo description.**

7. **Enter the commission or fee that you paid.**

   Move the cursor to the Comm Fee field and enter the commission or fee you paid to purchase the shares. (This figure will be included in the amount shown in the Amount field.)

8. **Enter the bank account on which you'll write the check that pays for the shares.**

   From the Xfer Acct drop-down list box, select the account name.

9. **Enter the account transfer amount.**

   Move the cursor to the XFer Amt field and press Enter. Quicken beeps with enthusiasm and then records the purchase of new shares. You are now, by definition, a capitalist. Congratulations!

   Figure 12-6 shows a new shares purchase transaction recorded in the Investment register.

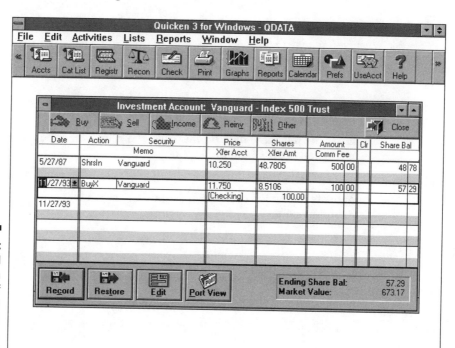

Figure 12-6:
The record of a purchase of additional mutual fund shares.

Quicken offers another way to record a shares purchase: the Buy Shares dialog box (see Figure 12-7) prompts you to enter the same information that you record when entering a mutual shares purchase transaction directly into the Investment register. Quicken then records the transaction into the register.

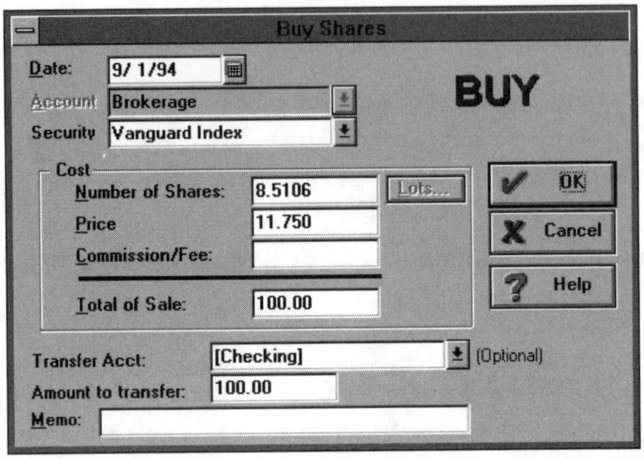

Figure 12-7:
The Buy
Shares
dialog box.

To display the Buy Shares dialog box, select the Buy button, which appears at the top of the Investment register window.

By reinvesting dividends, interest, or capital gains

When you reinvest your dividends, interest, or capital gains, you also have two methods available for recording the transaction: using the register or using the Reinv button. Here again, I like the register approach, so I'll describe it first.

You can record your reinvestment transactions, which buy new shares, by first displaying the Investment register and then by following these steps:

1. **Enter the purchase date (in this case, the reinvestment date) into the next empty row's Date field.**

2. **Tell Quicken that you're purchasing new shares by reinvesting.**

   Activate the Action drop-down list box and select one of the following Reinvest actions:

   - ReinvDiv (reinvest dividends)
   - ReinvInt (reinvest interest)
   - ReinvLg (reinvest long-term capital gains)
   - ReinvSh (reinvest short-term capital gains)

Use the arrow keys or the mouse to select the appropriate reinvestment action and press Enter. Quicken enters the reinvestment abbreviation in the Action field. You also can type these abbreviations directly in the field after you've memorized them.

You don't need to determine whether the amounts you reinvest are dividends, interest, long-term capital gains, or short-term capital gains because the mutual fund statement tells you this. If you reinvest more than one type of gain, however, you need to record more than one transaction. For example, if the $50 you reinvest is part long-term capital gain and part dividend income, you need to record two transactions: one for the long-term capital gain reinvestment and one for the dividend income reinvestment.

3. **Accept the suggested security name.**

4. **Indicate the price per share that you paid.**

5. **Indicate the size of your purchase.**

   You can give Quicken either the number of shares you're purchasing or the total dollar amount of the transaction.

6. **(Optional) Type a brief explanation of the transaction into the Memo field.**

7. **Enter the commission or fee that you paid in the Comm Fee field.**

   The commission fee is included in the figure shown in the Amount field.

8. **Record the reinvestment transaction.**

   Select the Record button.

Figure 12-8 shows $56.88 of dividends being reinvested in the mutual fund by buying shares that cost $13.65 a piece. Other reinvestments work basically the same way — except you use a different reinvestment action.

As mentioned earlier, the second way to record amounts you reinvest is to use the Reinvst button. After you choose this command, Quicken displays the Reinvest Income dialog box (see Figure 12-9).

To describe an amount you're reinvesting, just fill in the text boxes, which are similar to the fields you fill in when you record the reinvestment directly into the register. When you select OK, Quicken takes the information you entered into the text boxes and records the reinvestment into the investment register.

Although you can record reinvestment transactions either directly into the register or by using the Reinv button, using the Reinv button does possess a noteworthy advantage. When you use the register approach, you need to record one transaction for each type of income reinvested. When you use the

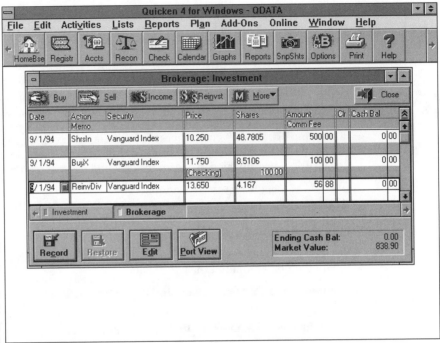

Figure 12-8:
How you record the reinvestment of dividends.

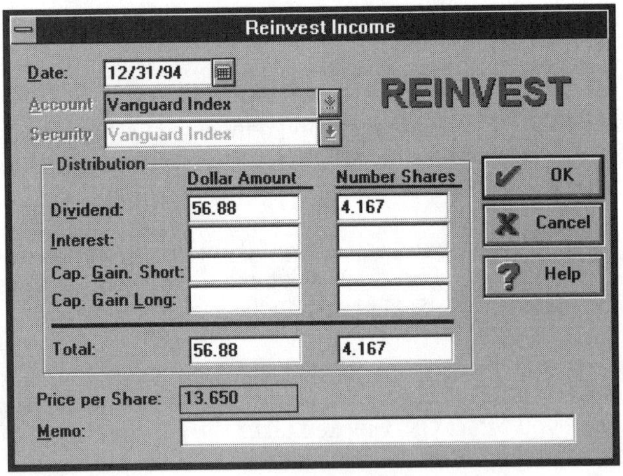

Figure 12-9:
The Reinvest Income dialog box.

Reinv command, however, you can record the reinvestment of each type of income at the same time: dividends, interest, short-term capital gains, and long-term capital gains. All you need to do is fill out more than one set of Dollar Amount and Number Shares text boxes. The Reinvst command then enters the separate transactions — one for each type of income — into the register.

Recording your profits

Every so often, you may receive distributions directly from the mutual fund company. Retirees, for example, often direct mutual fund managers to send dividend checks and capital gains directly to them rather than to have the amounts reinvested.

To record these kinds of distributions, you go through a process very similar to those described earlier. For example, if you want to record an income transaction directly into the Investment register, you follow these steps:

1. **Enter the distribution date into the next empty row's Date field.**

2. **Tell Quicken that you're receiving a distribution from the mutual fund.**

   Activate the Action drop-down list box and select the appropriate action to describe the distribution: DivX, to indicate that you're depositing dividends; CGLongX, to indicate that you're depositing long-term capital gains; or CGShortX, to indicate that you're depositing short-term capital gains. Again, when you've memorized these abbreviations — DivX, CGLongX, and CGShortX — you also can type them directly into the Action field.

   You don't need to determine for yourself whether a distribution is a dividend, a long-term capital gain, or a short-term capital gain because the mutual fund statement makes the distribution clear.

3. **Indicate the dividend or capital gains distribution amount.**

   Enter the amount in the Amount text box.

4. **(Optional) Type a brief description of the distribution in the Memo field.**

   Be creative — type your wedding anniversary, the name of your dog, or even a piece of data related to the dividend or distribution.

5. **Indicate into which bank account you'll deposit the dividend or distribution.**

   Activate the Xfer Account drop-down list box and select the account into which you'll deposit the money.

6. **Record the dividend or distribution transaction.**

   You can record the dividend in a bunch of ways, but why not just click the Record button? Quicken records the reinvestment — Bip. Bap. Boom. It's just that quick.

Figure 12-10 shows $50 of dividends being deposited into a checking account cleverly named Checking.

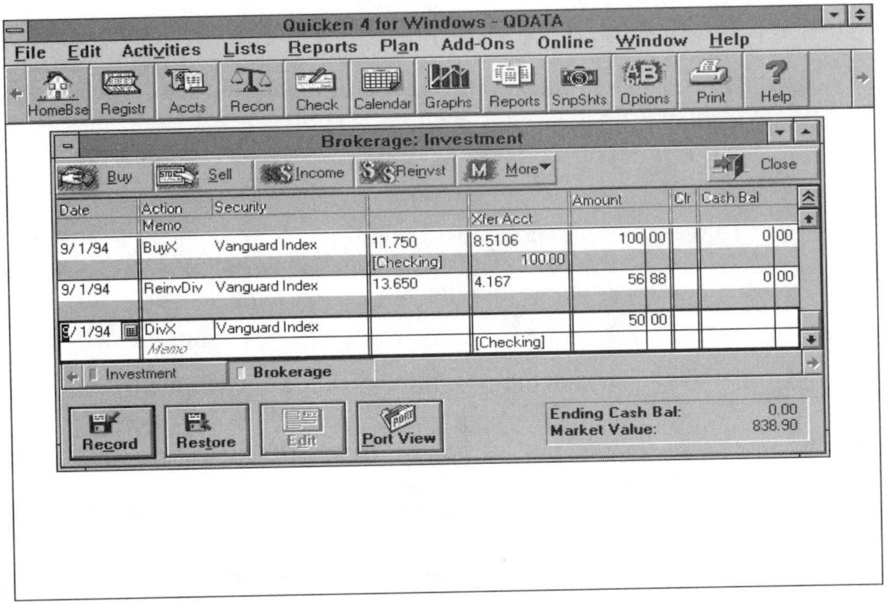

Figure 12-10:
How you record a dividend distribution.

If you don't want to enter the transaction directly into the Investment register, click the Income button. Quicken displays the Record Income dialog box (see Figure 12-11).

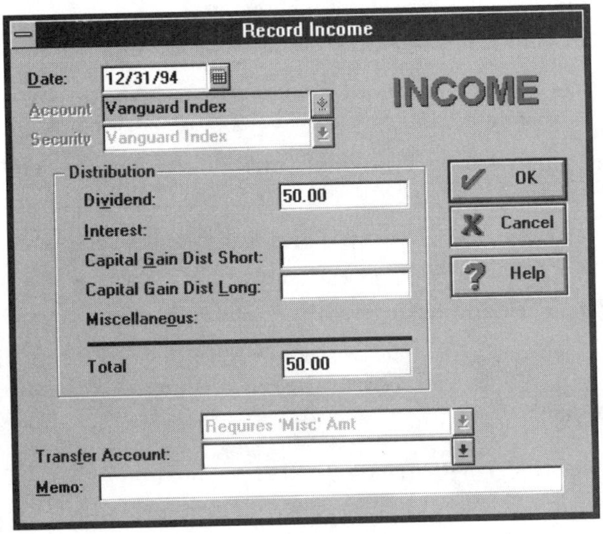

Figure 12-11:
The Record Income dialog box.

You record an income transaction in the Income dialog box in the same way that you record it directly in the register. You describe the income amount, category, and the account into which the dividend, interest, or capital gains check is deposited.

As with the Reinvst command, an advantage of the Income command is that you can record several types of income in one fell swoop. Quicken uses the information you type in the Income dialog box to enter up to four income transactions into the Investment register.

Selling dear

Selling mutual fund shares works basically the same way as buying them. You can record the sale of shares either directly into the register or by using the Sell command.

If you want to record the sale of shares directly into the register, do the following:

1. **Enter the sale's date into the next empty row's Date field.**

2. **Tell Quicken that you're selling shares.**

   Activate the Action drop-down list box and select the SellX action. (Note that you also can type **SellX** directly into the field.)

3. **Accept the suggested security name.**

4. **Indicate the price per share that you received.**

   With a little luck, your sale's price is more than you paid.

5. **Indicate the size of your sale by giving Quicken either the number of shares you sold or the total dollar amount of the sale.**

   Quicken calculates whatever you don't enter. For example, if you tell Quicken how many dollars you sell, it calculates the number of shares you sell by dividing the total sales amount by the price per share. If you tell Quicken how many shares you sell, it calculates the total sales amount by multiplying the number of shares by the price per share. I guess this is a handy feature.

6. **(Optional) Type a brief description of the sale in the Memo field.**

7. **Enter the bank account into which you'll deposit the sale's proceeds.**

   Activate the Account drop-down list box and select the appropriate account.

8. **Enter the account transfer amount.**

   Move the cursor to the XFer Amount field and enter the transfer amount. This amount is what you'll actually deposit into the transfer account. The transfer amount equals the total sales price less the commission you paid.

9. Enter the commission or fee you paid to sell the shares in the Comm Fee field.

No wonder Bernie, your broker, does so well, huh? He makes money whether you do or not.

10. Select the Record button.

Quicken displays a message box that asks whether you want to specifically identify the shares you're selling. You get to answer yes or no.

11. (Optional) Indicate whether you want to use Specific Identification.

Quicken displays the Yes or No message box that asks whether you want to identify specifically which lots you're selling.

Choose No if you're selling all the shares because specific identification makes no difference in your case.

Choose Yes if you aren't selling all your shares. Now you can pick and choose which shares to sell so that you can minimize the capital gains taxes you'll owe (good idea, huh?). Quicken displays the Specific Identification of Shares dialog box, shown in Figure 12-12.

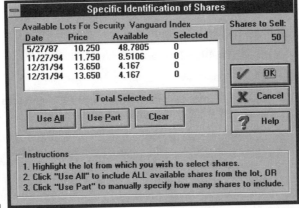

Figure 12-12:
The Specific
Identification
of Shares
dialog box.

12. (Optional) Identify which lots you're selling.

What you do now is pick and choose which lots to sell to minimize the capital gains taxes you owe. A *lot* is simply a batch, or set, of shares that you purchased at one time. If you sell the most expensive lots, you reduce your capital gains and the taxes on those gains.

To pick an entire lot, double-click it or select it with the mouse and choose the Use All button.

To pick a portion of a lot, select it and choose the Use Part button. Quicken displays the Specify Quantity dialog box that allows you to indicate how many shares of the lot you want to sell. To do this, just enter the number of shares into the Quantity text box. (I didn't provide a screen shot of this simple dialog box because all it has is one input field for Quantity.)

To clear your selections and start over, choose the Clear button.

After the Specific Identification of Shares dialog box correctly shows all the shares you want to sell, select OK. Quicken records the sell transaction in the register.

Figure 12-13 shows shares being sold to pay for Beth's first-quarter college tuition. Just a few pages ago, she was just a little girl. And now she's leaving home. She grew up so fast!

If you don't want to record a sell transaction directly into the register, you can use the Sell button. After you click the button, Quicken displays the Sell Shares dialog box, which collects the same information in its text boxes that you enter in the register's fields (see Figure 12-14). To identify shares specifically, choose the Lots button.

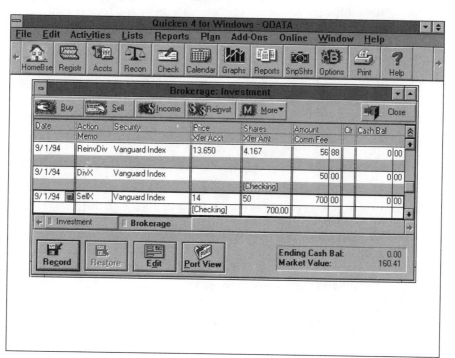

Figure 12-13:
How you record the sale of the mutual fund shares.

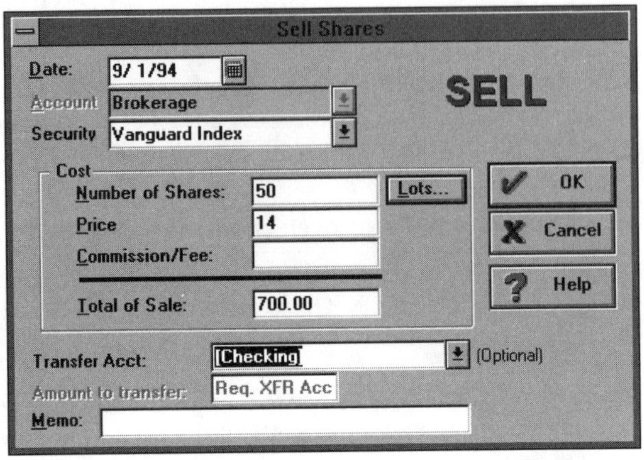

Figure 12-14:
The Sell
Shares
dialog box.

What if you make a mistake?

If you make a mistake, don't worry — it's not a problem. You can edit an investment transaction in the investment register the same way you edit check and deposit transactions in a bank account register. For example, you can click the fields with the incorrect entries, fix them, and then record the new, corrected transaction.

You also can select the transaction and choose the Edit button. Quicken then displays the investment dialog box that lets you change each of the pieces of the transaction. The dialog box that Quicken displays mirrors the investment dialog box you could have used originally to record the transaction. For example, the dialog box to edit a sell shares transaction looks like the Sell Shares dialog box shown in Figure 12-14.

Slightly tricky mutual fund transactions

I didn't describe every possible mutual fund transaction — although I have described every one I've encountered in the last 10 or 12 years. You should know, however, that Quicken does let you record three additional transactions by specifying several almost-magical actions: shares out, stock split, and reminder transactions.

Removing shares from an account

You can tell Quicken to remove shares from an account without moving the money represented by the shares to some other account. Why would you want to remove a *shares out* transaction? I can think of two situations: when you erroneously add shares to the account with the shares in (ShrsIn) action and now you need to remove them, or when you use an investment account to record old investment activity, such as activity from last year.

The first instance is self-explanatory because you are simply correcting an error that you made. In the second case, however, you don't want to transfer the proceeds of a mutual fund sale to a checking account because the money from the sale is already recorded as a deposit at some point in the past.

You can record a shares out transaction directly into the register by moving the cursor to the next empty row of the register and specifying the action as ShrsOut. Next, fill in the rest of the fields in the investment register the same way you would for a regular ol' sell transaction. The only difference is that you won't give an Xfer Account.

You also can record a shares out transaction with a dialog box. Click the More button, choose the ShrsOut command, and fill in the Date and Number Of Shares text boxes on the Move Shares Out dialog box.

The stock split and then doubled

Stock splits don't occur very often with mutual funds; however, when they do occur, the mutual fund manager, in effect, gives you a certain number of new shares (such as two) for each old share you own.

To record a stock split, you use the StkSplit action. Then you indicate the ratio of new shares to old shares. For a two-for-one split, for example, you indicate that you get two new split shares for each old unsplit share. The whole process is really pretty easy.

You can record a stock split by moving the cursor to the next empty row of the register and using the StkSplit action. You also can choose the More button, select the StkSplit command from the menu, and fill out the dialog box that asks about the split date, the new shares, the old shares, and, optionally, the share price after the split.

Quicken, will you remind me of something?

A reminder transaction is the electronic equivalent of a yellow sticky note. If you put a reminder transaction in the investment register, Quicken's Billminder utility tells you there's a reminder message on the reminder date. You can't goof up anything by trying out reminders, so if you're curious, enter a reminder transaction for tomorrow and see what happens.

You can post a reminder note by moving the cursor to the next empty row of the register and using the Reminder action. Or you can choose the More button, select the Reminder command from the menu, and fill out the dialog box that asks you to fill out information about the reminder.

Oops, my mutual fund shares are wrong

It's very possible that you may end up with share count errors in your mutual fund account. Sometimes the error occurs because calculations have been rounded differently in Quicken than by your mutual fund manager. If you sell shares for $13.65 and receive $838.89 for the transaction, for example, Quicken may calculate the number of shares sold in a different manner than does your mutual fund manager.

To fix these sorts of errors, just make a *shares adjustment*. A shares adjustment changes the number of shares Quicken shows for a mutual fund to whatever you set. To do a share adjustment, choose the Update Balances command from the Activities menu and then choose the Update Share Balance command from the Update Balances menu. Quicken displays the Update Share Balance dialog box, shown in Figure 12-15.

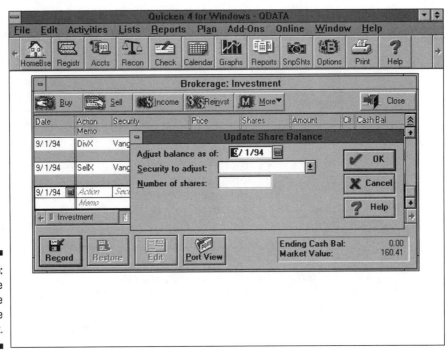

Figure 12-15:
The Update
Share
Balance
dialog box.

To use this dialog box, just specify the correct number of shares, enter the date that reflects the corrected figure, and select OK. By using either the ShrsIn or ShrsOut action, Quicken adds an adjustment transaction to the register to fix the shares balance for the mutual fund.

Reports

I just want to say one thing about Quicken reports as they relate to your investments: *remember that the reports are there.* (For more information, see Chapter 6.)

Menu commands and other stuff

For the most part, the commands and menus available for an investment account are the same as those available for all the other accounts Quicken supplies. I've written about the commands that I think are most helpful to new users in the preceding chapters of this book. If you have a question about how the Void Transaction command works, for example, refer to the Index, where you will be directed to a specific discussion of that command.

Updating Securities Prices

You can collect current market prices and store this information with your accounts. Just display the investment account that has the mutual fund shares. Then click the Port View button or choose the Portfolio View command from the Activities menu. Either way, Quicken displays the Portfolio View window (see Figure 12-16).

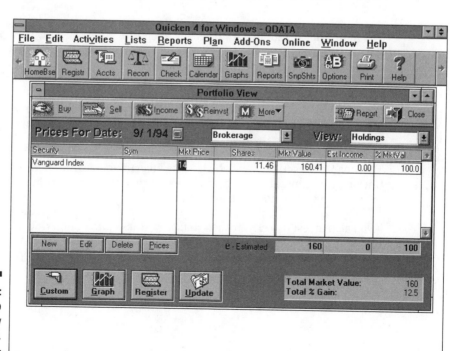

Figure 12-16: The Portfolio View window.

The Portfolio View window

You can do more with the Portfolio View window than just update share prices. For example, if you take a close look at Figure 12-16, notice that the row of buttons at the top of the window is the same one that appears at the top of the register: Buy, Sell, Income, Reinvst, and Move. You can use these buttons to enter investment transactions.

You can choose the Report button to display an on-screen report of the securities you hold.

The Prices Date Field lets you specify the date on which you want to see and set market prices and values. The Account drop-down list box lets you choose which account you want to see. And the View drop-down list box allows you to view the type of information you see in the window. (Quicken provides different views of the information.)

The Custom button lets you create customized views of the Portfolio View window. (These different views show or emphasize different types of information.) The Prices button lets you see and modify a historical list of share prices. The Graph button allows you to plot the information shown in the Portfolio View window in a chart.

I'm not going to go into more detail here about what all these extra whistles and bells do. If you're a serious investor, however, take the time to explore these commands. You may gain some interesting insights into your investments.

To record the current market price for a security, use the arrow keys or click the mouse to highlight the security. Then move the cursor to the Mkt Price field and enter the current price. You also can use the + and - keys to change incrementally the per share price by an eighth, or $.125.

Quicken updates the Total Market Value figure shown in the lower right corner of the register window. After you update the market price, you can return to the register by choosing the Register button.

This chapter describes how you use the investments feature in Quicken for tracking your mutual funds. If you invest exclusively in mutual funds, the information you've now picked up should be all you need.

If you also invest directly in such things as stocks and bonds, you may want to turn to the next chapter. It describes how you use a Quicken investment account to track a brokerage account.

The 5th Wave

By Rich Tennant

"WE OFFER A CREATIVE MIS ENVIRONMENT WORKING WITH STATE-OF-THE-ART PROCESSING AND COMMUNICATIONS EQUIPMENT; A COMPREHENSIVE BENEFITS PACKAGE, GENEROUS PROFIT SHARING, STOCK OPTIONS, AND, IF YOU'RE FEELING FUNKY AND NEED TO CHILL OUT AND RAP, WE CAN DO THAT TOO."

Chapter 13
Stocks and Bonds

● ●

In This Chapter

▶ Setting up a brokerage account

▶ Describing the securities in a brokerage account

▶ Transferring cash to and from a brokerage account

▶ Buying stocks and bonds from a brokerage account

▶ Recording dividends, capital gains, and other investment income from securities held in a brokerage account

▶ Recording margin interest, miscellaneous income and expenses, and return of capital

▶ Updating securities prices

▶ Adjusting your brokerage cash balance

▶ Adjusting your brokerage account shares

● ●

Tracking a Brokerage Account

When you understand how Quicken handles mutual fund investments, you'll find it a snap to work with a brokerage account. (Quicken calls this type of account a *cash investment account.*)

Setting up a brokerage account

Setting up a brokerage account is similar to setting up a regular mutual fund account except for a couple of minor but predictable differences. Because you're still fairly new to this process, I'll go through it step by step:

1. **Choose the Accounts icon from the iconbar.**

   Quicken, ever the faithful companion, displays the Account List window.

2. **Click the New button in the Account List window.**

   Quicken displays the familiar Create New Account dialog box.

3. Click the Investments button.

Make sure that the Guide Me check box isn't marked when you click. The Quicken guide is useful for people just starting out, but you probably don't need it if you're now working with Quicken investment accounts.

Quicken displays the Create Account Investment dialog box (see Figure 13-1).

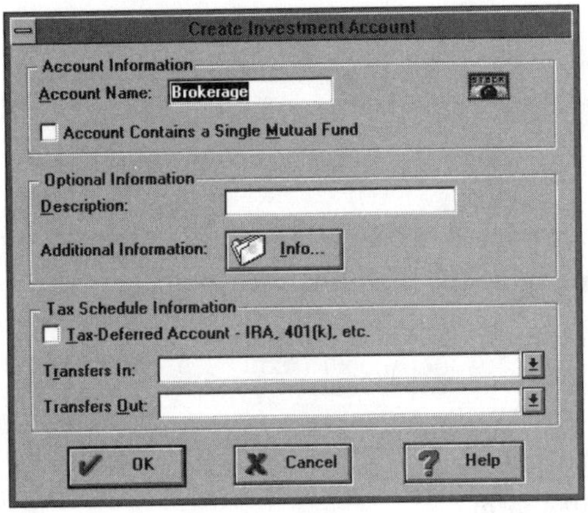

Figure 13-1:
The Create
Investment
Account
dialog box.

4. Name the investment.

Move the cursor to the Account Name text box and type the name of the broker. Or, if you don't have trouble remembering your broker's name, you can identify this account as the one you use to track your brokerage account with a name like Brokerage. (I entered this name in Figure 13-1.)

5. Leave the Account Contains A Single Mutual Fund check box unmarked.

Leaving this check box unmarked tells Quicken that the investment account is being used to track a brokerage account.

6. (Optional) Enter a description of the account.

You can use the Description text box to store extra information about the account.

7. Mark or unmark the Tax-deferred Account check box as appropriate.

Basically, this check box tells Quicken whether the dividends, interest, and capital gains for this account affect your taxable income.

8. Click OK.

Quicken redisplays the Account List window. If you want to begin entering investment transactions, select the account and then click the Open button. Quicken displays an investment register window, as shown in Figure 13-2.

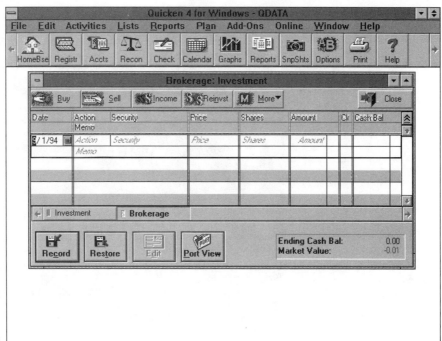

Figure 13-2:
A typical
investment
register
window.

Setting up security lists

Your account contains more than one type of *security.* You might have shares of Boeing, General Motors, or Chase Manhattan. You name it, and someone owns it.

You need to create a list of the securities — stocks, bonds, and so on — that your account holds.

To do so, complete the following steps after you set up the brokerage account:

1. Choose the Security command from the Lists menu.

Quicken displays the Security List window (see Figure 13-3). Note that any mutual funds you've already set up appear in the list as securities.

2. Click the New button in the Security List window.

Quicken displays the Set Up Security window, as shown in Figure 13-4.

3. Enter a name for the security by using the Name text box.

4. (Optional and probably crazy) Enter the stock symbol for the security in the Symbol text box.

This step allows you to download share price information from a modem.

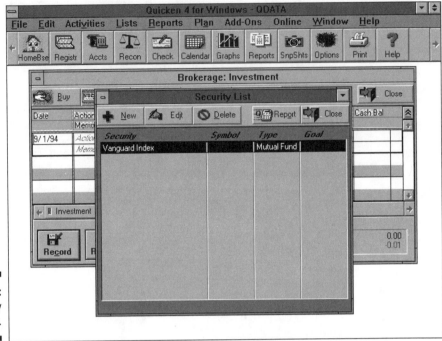

Figure 13-3:
The Security
List window.

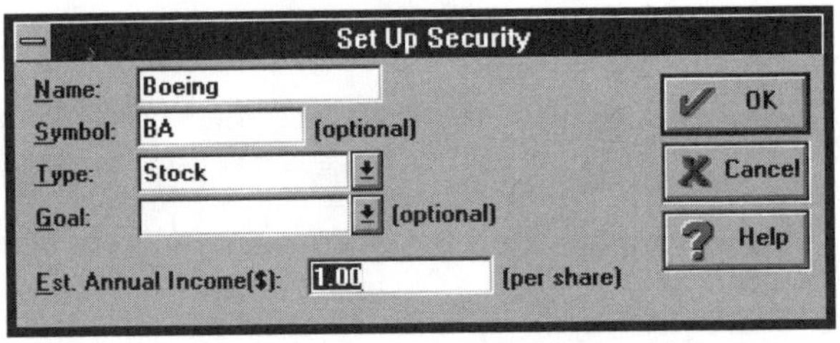

Figure 13-4:
The Set Up
Security
dialog box.

5. **(Optional) Indicate which type of security you're setting up.**

    Activate the Type drop-down list box and then select one of the types
    listed: bond, CD, mutual fund, or stock.

6. **(Optional) Indicate the purpose for which you're investing.**

    Activate the Goal drop-down list box and then select one of the goals
    listed: college fund, growth, high risk, income, or low risk.

    You can use the Lists menu's Security Type and Investment Goal com-
    mands to display lists of the security types and investment goals. You can
    also use these commands to create new security types and investment
    goals — Sure-fire, Easy money, or Unconscionable profits, for example.

I don't think this option is all that important. If you want to use it, choose the Security <u>T</u>ype or Investment <u>G</u>oal command and then click the New button in the dialog box that appears. Quicken displays another dialog box, in which you enter your new type or goal.

7. Select OK.

Quicken redisplays the Security List window. It now lists the new stock, bond, or any other item you added.

8. Practice, practice, practice.

As necessary, repeat steps 1 through 7 until you're sick to death of doing so or until you've described each of the securities in your brokerage account.

Treat mutual fund shares that you hold in a brokerage account the same way that you treat other stocks and bonds that you hold in the account. If you're confused, think of it this way: while many mutual funds are sold by brokers to their clients, some mutual funds are sold by the mutual fund manager directly to the public.

I don't want to get into the subject of load mutual funds versus no-load mutual funds, but if you're interested in how these two types of funds work, flip open the *Wall Street Journal* and look for advertisements from no-load fund managers such as Vanguard, Scudder, and T. Rowe Price. Give one of them a call, and they'll tell you why they think you should bypass the middleman — your broker. Next, talk to a broker, who will tell you why you *shouldn't* bypass the middleman. Then you make the call.

What? You want *my* opinion? With much trepidation, I'll give it to you: I always use no-load mutual funds, so I'm a big fan of the do-it-yourself approach. However, I also think that a good broker — good is the operative word here — is well worth the commission fee if the broker helps you avoid expensive mistakes. I'm probably in enough hot water at this point from both sides, so I'll stop here.

Working with cash

One of the differences between a brokerage account and a mutual fund account is that a cash management, or *money market,* account is attached to the brokerage account.

When you initially set up a brokerage account, your money goes into this account. (The broker buys you a doughnut and coffee in this meeting so that you'll put lots and lots of money into your new account, remember?)

You purchase your first shares with the cash from this account. And when you sell shares, all cash proceeds go into this account.

Transferring cash to and from an account

Because you work with cash in a brokerage account, you need to know how to record the cash that flows in and out of the account.

To record the cash you transfer into a brokerage account, specify the action as XIn. To record the amount of a cash transfer, enter the dollar amount in the Amount field.

Figure 13-5 shows cash being transferred into a brokerage account. Notice that the lower right corner of the register window displays the cash balance.

To record the cash you transfer out of a brokerage account, specify the action as XOut. To record the amount of a cash transfer, again enter the dollar amount in the Amount field.

To record cash in and cash out actions, activate the Action drop-down list box and choose either the XOut (Cash Out) action or the XIn (Cash In) action.

Sure, it's not all that complicated. But you'll impress your friends.

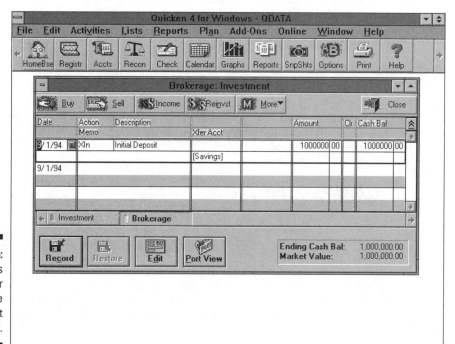

Figure 13-5:
Cash goes into your brokerage account first.

Adding shares to a brokerage account

Add shares to your account when you need to store the shares in the account but don't want them to affect your brokerage account cash or other checking account. As with mutual fund ShrsIn transactions, you would probably add shares only when you first set up a brokerage account.

I describe this process in detail in the preceding chapter, so I won't repeat that discussion here. But note that you can enter a ShrsIn transaction either directly in the register or by using a dialog box that prompts you for needed bits of information. To access the Shares In dialog box, click the Buy/Sell Other button and then choose the ShrsIn command from the menu Quicken displays.

Figure 13-6 shows a ShrsIn transaction listing the amount and cost of shares previously purchased. I want to assure you that I'm not suffering delusions of grandeur. Nor have I won the lottery. These transactions are fake.

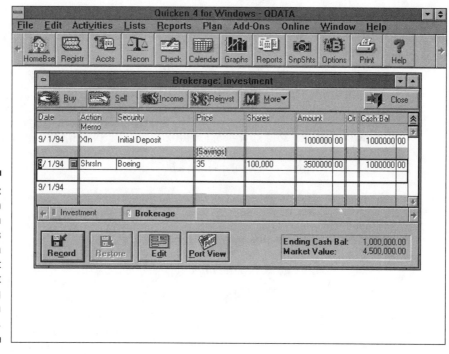

Figure 13-6:
A ShrsIn transaction adds shares to an account without adjusting the cash balance.

Removing shares from a brokerage account

The ShrsOut, or Remove Shares, transaction works roughly the same way. When you have already recorded the cash proceeds of a sale, you can take shares out of an account without adjusting the cash balance of the brokerage account or other checking account.

As with ShrsIn transactions, you can enter a ShrsOut transaction directly in the register. Or you can choose the More button, choose the ShrsOut command, and then fill in the necessary information in the dialog box.

Buying near and selling dear

Buying and selling securities in a brokerage account is very similar to buying and selling shares of a mutual fund. For example, you can enter buy and sell transactions in the register directly or use the Buy and Sell buttons. You fill out almost the exact same set of fields, but there are a couple of minor differences.

One key difference between a brokerage account and a mutual fund account is that when you buy or sell a brokerage account share, Quicken wants to know where you got or stashed the cash.

When the cash comes from or goes into the brokerage account, you use actions to indicate it. Remember that for mutual funds you use the BuyX action to indicate that you bought shares of a mutual fund using cash from another account — usually a checking account. Similarly, you use the SellX action to indicate that you sold shares of a mutual fund and then put the cash proceeds into another account — again, probably a checking account. (The old under-the-mattress approach is, of course, a little passé.)

In a brokerage account, you can use the same actions if you buy with cash from another account or you deposit the cash from a sale into another account. When the cash stays in the brokerage account, you use two new actions. The Buy action indicates that the cash used to buy a security comes from the brokerage account's cash. The Sell action indicates that the cash earned from selling a security goes into the brokerage account cash.

If you use the Buy Shares dialog box or the Sell Shares dialog box to describe the investment transaction, Quicken provides an optional Transfer Acc text box. If you fill in this text box, Quicken knows that you're recording a BuyX or SellX transaction because you're moving the cash someplace else. If you don't fill in this text box, Quicken assumes that you're recording a regular Buy or Sell transaction (which means that you're leaving the cash in your brokerage account).

The other difference between a brokerage account and a mutual fund account stems from the fact that a brokerage account can have more than one security. Therefore, you must tell Quicken which security you're buying or selling.

Figure 13-7 lists four brokerage account transactions in the register. The first transaction shows shares of Boeing purchased with cash from the brokerage account. The second shows shares of Boeing purchased with cash from a checking account. The third shows proceeds from the sale of shares of Boeing going back into the brokerage account as cash. The fourth shows the proceeds of the sale of shares of Boeing going into a checking account. You're now a churning hunk of burning funk. Your broker will love you.

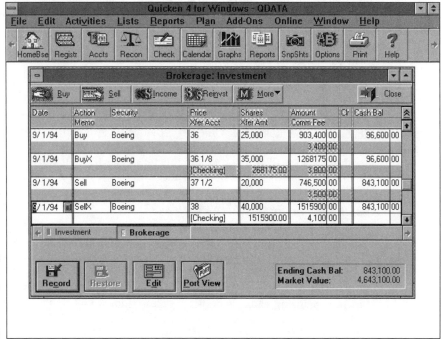

Figure 13-7:
Sample Buy
and Sell
transactions.

Dividends, capital gains, and other goodies

You could probably guess as much, but the whole brokerage account cash business also comes into play with dividends and capital gains.

When an investment action involves cash, Quicken must know whether the cash goes into or out of the brokerage account or into or out of some other account (such as your checking account). If the action indicates cash going into or out of another account, it ends in the letter X. Quicken supplies equivalent actions for cash going into or out of the brokerage account.

When you record dividends received on stock held in a brokerage account, you must specify where the dividend money goes — into the brokerage account or into some other account. For example, you use either the Div or DivX action to record a dividend directly in the register. To indicate that your dividend money goes back into the brokerage account as cash, use the Div action. To indicate that your dividend money goes into another account, use the DivX action and then designate the account. (The DivX action works for brokerage accounts in the same way that it works for mutual fund accounts. Remember, though, to specify the security on which you received the dividend check.)

Record capital gain distributions directly in the register in the same way that you record dividends directly in the register. Again, you must specify where the money ends up. To indicate that your capital gains distribution money goes back into the brokerage account as cash, use either the CGLong (for long-term capital gains) or the CGShort (for short-term capital gains) action. To deposit your capital gains distribution someplace else, use either the CGLongX or the CGShortX action. When you specify either of these actions, you also need to tell Quicken into which account you put the money.

When you describe a dividend, interest income amount, or capital gain in the Record Income dialog box, Quicken provides an optional Transfer Account text box. If you fill in this text box, Quicken knows that you're moving the cash to another location. If you don't fill in this text box, Quicken knows that you're leaving the cash in your brokerage account.

I still don't get it — where's the cash?

I hope the logic of this "Where's the cash?" business makes sense. Again, the whole thing boils down to one burning question: where does the cash go or come from when you're talking about a brokerage account?

This advice is sort of funny, but let me suggest something. If this all seems terribly confusing, put this book down and think about this for a few minutes over the next day or so. I bet things will click for you, and suddenly the answer to the "Where's the cash?" question will become crystal clear.

Other not-so-tricky transactions

Quicken lets you record all sorts of transactions in a brokerage account. Not only can you do reminder and stock split actions (described for mutual fund accounts in Chapter 12), but you can also do a bunch of other things.

I'll briefly describe these other transactions and demonstrate them by using the register transactions shown in Figure 13-8.

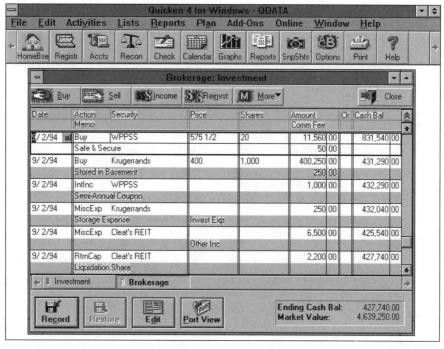

Figure 13-8:
Example
transactions
I'll use to
explain
other
record-
keeping
tricks.

Bonds, James' bonds

The first transaction shown in Figure 13-8 records the purchase of some bonds. Note that the bond price is given in dollars and cents.

Why do I bring this up? If you invest in bonds, you know that a bond's price is actually quoted as a percentage of its face value. A bond that sells for $950 with a face value of $1,000, for example, is quoted as 95 because the $950 price is 95 percent of the $1,000 face value. Quicken, however, doesn't let you describe a bond's price as a percent. So you enter the bond price as its price in dollars and cents.

Going for the gold

The second transaction in Figure 13-8 shows the purchase of some Krugerrands (one-ounce gold coins minted by South Africa). For this transaction, the price is the price per Krugerrand, and the shares figure is actually the number of ounces (equal to the number of Krugerrands). Because Quicken doesn't supply price-per-ounce and number-of-ounces fields, you insert the information into the Price and Shares fields. That makes sense, right?

Recording interest income

To record interest income directly in the register, use the IntInc action (the third transaction shown in Figure 13-8). Note that you should identify the security paying the interest. (In the figure, the WPPSS bonds pay the interest.)

If you want to use the dialog box approach to record interest income, choose the Income button and complete the Income dialog box.

By the way, you also use the IntInc action or the Income button for recording interest income of certificates of deposit and other debt securities you purchase.

Are you on the margin?

The MargInt, or margin interest, action records margin interest expense directly in the register. The MargInt command appears in the menu that Quicken supplies after you click the Buy/Sell Other button.

I'll assume that if you're on the margin roller coaster, you're a smart cookie and can figure out how to fill in the blanks Quicken supplies when you specify the action as MargInt or choose the MargInt command.

I talk about the two ways of recording investment transactions with the More button in the preceding chapter. Even so, let me provide a quick review.

When you select the More button, Quicken displays a menu of kooky investment actions like MargInt. You then choose the investment action that corresponds to the transaction you want to record. Quicken displays a dialog box that provides text boxes in which you describe the transaction. When you press Enter, Quicken takes the stuff you entered and records the transaction in the register.

Paying miscellaneous expense

Sometimes you need to pay an expense. I've never seen one occur for a stock or bond — but my investing has been pretty conventional. Expenses sometimes do arise with mutual fund shares (which can be stored in a brokerage account), real estate partnership interests (which can be treated like common stock shares), or precious metal investments (which can also be treated like common stock shares).

If you need to pay a fee for account handling or for storing those South African Krugerrands you've been hoarding, for example, you can record such an expense directly in the register by using the MiscExp action. Categorize the expense by selecting an expense category from your regular category list. Or you can choose the More button and then choose the MiscExp command.

The fourth transaction listed in Figure 13-8 shows a miscellaneous expense associated with the Krugerrand investment. Note the category, Invest Exp.

Listing miscellaneous income

No big surprise here. Because you have a MiscExp action, Quicken also provides a MiscInc, or Miscellaneous Income, action.

This investment transaction is very similar to the miscellaneous expense transaction. You use the miscellaneous income transaction to record investment income that can't be recorded by using one of the other investment income actions — dividends, interest income, or capital gains distributions.

I've seen this used mostly in relation to investments in things other than stocks and bonds. For example, in a real estate limited partnership the quarterly distributions that the general partner makes aren't interest or dividends; rather, they are rental income. In this case, you can use the MiscInc action on the Income command. Quicken lets you specify an income category for the transaction, so you can use the income category you set up to track rental income.

The fifth transaction in Figure 13-8 is a miscellaneous income transaction showing money you received for your share of a real estate investment trust's (Cleat's REIT) quarterly net rental income.

Recording a return of capital

One final thing: the old return of capital trick. Sometimes, the money you receive because you own a security isn't really income. Rather, it's a refund of part of the purchase price.

Consider this example. You buy a mortgage-backed security — such as a Ginnie Mae bond — for which the *mortgagee* (the person who borrowed the mortgage money) pays not only periodic interest but also a portion of the mortgage principal.

Obviously, you shouldn't record the principal portion of the payment you receive as income. You must record this payment as a mortgage principal reduction or — in the parlance of investment recordkeeping — as a return of capital.

As another example, suppose you invest in a limited partnership or real estate investment trust that begins liquidating. Some of the money the investors receive in this case is really a return of their original investment, or a return of capital.

To record a return of capital action, specify the investment action as RtrnCap or click the <u>M</u>ore button and choose RtrnCap. The sixth transaction listed in Figure 13-8 shows a return of capital transaction associated with the Cleat's REIT security.

More Quick Stuff about Brokerage Accounts

Let me tell you a couple other quick things. You'll almost certainly find these tidbits helpful.

Monitoring and Updating Securities Values

Regardless of whether you're working with a mutual fund account or with securities in a brokerage account, you can collect current market prices and store them with Quicken's account information.

To do so, display the investment account with the mutual fund shares or the securities you want to update. Then choose the Portfolio View command from the Activities menu or choose the Port View button at the bottom of the register window. Quicken displays the Portfolio View window. (See Figure 13-9. I show this window in Chapter 12, but, heck, let's see it again.)

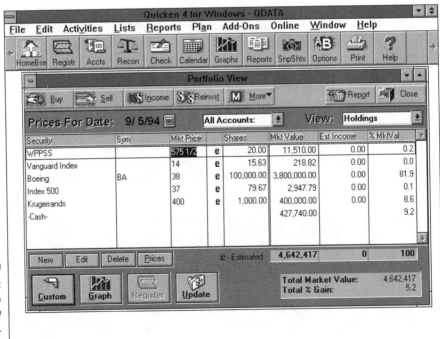

Figure 13-9:
The Portfolio
View
window.

Although I'm not a big fan of using the Portfolio View window for looking at mutual funds, it makes a lot of sense for viewing a brokerage account. Why? Because it shows you the value of each of the securities in your portfolio. (You don't really need this information in a mutual fund account because you've got only one security. The account balance shows you the mutual fund investment's value.)

To record the current market price for a security, use the up-arrow and down-arrow keys to highlight the security. Next, move the cursor to the Markt Price field and enter the current price. You can also adjust a price by eighths by using the − and + keys. The − key subtracts an eighth, or $.125, from the price shown. The + key adds an eighth, or $.125, to the price shown.

After you update the market price for each security, select the Prices. Quicken updates the market value figure shown in the lower right corner of the window.

I provide a quick overview of what the other Portfolio View buttons do in the preceding chapter. So if you have a question about what the Graph button does, for example, you can look there.

Adjusting errors

You can adjust the cash balance in a brokerage account and the shares balance in brokerage accounts if for some reason the figures are incorrect.

Oops, my brokerage cash balance is wrong

To adjust the cash balance in a brokerage account, choose the Update Balances command from the Activities menu. Quicken displays another menu. Select Update Cash Balance.

Quicken next displays a dialog box that lets you specify the correct cash balance and the date as of which the figure you enter is correct. Fill in the text boxes and select OK. Quicken adds an adjustment transaction to the register to fix the cash balance. (If you add cash, Quicken uses the MiscInc action. If you subtract cash, Quicken uses the MiscExp action.)

Oops, my brokerage account shares balance is wrong

To adjust the shares balance for a security in a brokerage account, choose Update Balances from the Activities menu. Quicken displays a menu asking whether you want to update the cash balance or the shares balance. Select Update Share Balance.

Quicken next displays a dialog box that lets you specify the security, the correct shares balance, and the date as of which the figure you enter is correct. Fill in the text boxes and select OK. Quicken adds an adjustment transaction to the register to fix the shares balance for the security you specified. (Quicken uses the ShrsIn and ShrsOut actions to make these adjustments.)

Chapter 14
Petty Cash and Mad Money

. . . .

In This Chapter

▶ Setting up a cash account

▶ Entering cash transactions

▶ Handling checks you cash

▶ Updating your petty cash or mad money balance

. . . .

*Y*ou can track petty cash in your business as well as the petty cash in your wallet (and we all have extra petty cash in our wallets, don't we?) by using a special Quicken cash account. To track the cash, you must set up a cash account and then enter the increases and decreases into the cash account's register. Sure — this isn't exactly rocket science — but shoot, I thought I'd just quickly go over this stuff to show you how easy it really is. OK?

Adding a Cash Account

To set up a cash account, you follow roughly the same steps as you do for a bank account. Because you've probably already set up a bank account, you can move quickly through the following steps for setting up a cash account:

1. **Choose the Accts icon from the iconbar.**

   Quicken displays the Account List window. You remember this puppy, the one you've seen a thousand times already.

2. **Select the New command button on the Account List window to set up a new account.**

   Quicken, of course, is no dummy, so it displays the Create New Account window shown in Figure 14-1.

3. **Select cash account.**

   You know how to do this, don't you? You just click the Cash button. (Be sure to unmark the Guide Me check box before you click.)

Figure 14-1:
The Create
New
Account
window.

4. Click OK.

Quicken, ever mindful of your purpose, displays the Create Cash Account dialog box, as shown in Figure 14-2.

5. Name the account.

Move the cursor to the Account Name text box and type a name.

6. Enter the cash balance you're holding.

Move the cursor to the Balance text box and enter the balance value by using the number keys.

7. Enter the account balance date.

Move the cursor to the As Of (or date) text box and type the two-digit month number, the two-digit date number, and the two-digit year number (probably the current date).

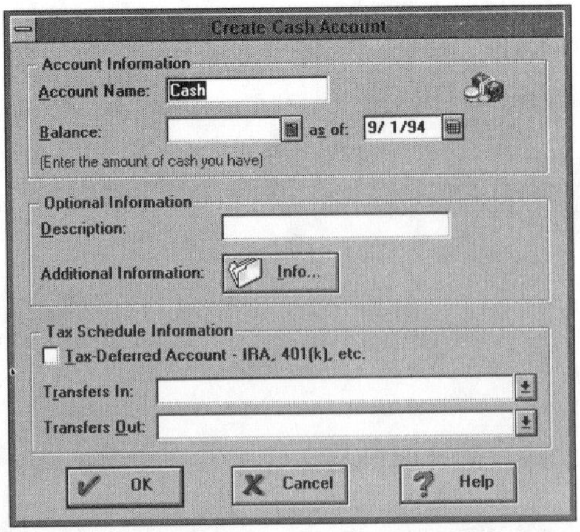

Figure 14-2:
The Create
Cash
Account
dialog box.

8. **(Optional) Indicate whether the account is tax-deferred.**

Click the Tax-Deferred check box to mark the box if the cash account is a tax-deferred account, like an IRA. (Almost certainly the account isn't tax-deferred.)

9. **(Optional) Enter a description for the account.**

You can enter whatever you want as a description — petty cash, mad money, slush fund, and so on — to help you more easily identify this particular account when you've got a bunch of different accounts set up.

10. **Click OK.**

Quicken redisplays the Account List dialog box. Well, golly, it shows the new cash account.

Tracking Cash Inflows and Outflows

After you set up a cash account, you can use it to track the cash you receive and spend in the same way you track the deposits and checks for a bank account.

To record your cash inflows and outflows, use the register window. To display the register window for the cash account you just set up, for example, open the Account List window by choosing the Accts icon from the iconbar and then select the cash account from the window list in the window. Then click th Open button. Figure 14-3 shows the cash account version of the register window.

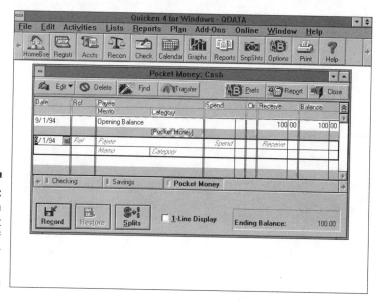

Figure 14-3:
The cash account version of the register window.

To record the amount of money you spend, fill in the Date, Payee, and Spend fields. To record the amount of money you receive, fill in the Date, Payee, and Receive fields. To track the reasons you're receiving and spending the cash, use the Memo and Category fields.

About Checks You Cash Instead of Deposit

By the way, you don't necessarily need to set up a cash account if you like to spend cash (rather than, say, write checks or charge on a credit card). If you just cash a check and you do have a bank account set up, there's another way that may be simpler: just use the Splits window to show both the income category (Salary, for example, for an individual) and the way you're going to use the money.

For example, if you cash a $1,000 check and you plan to use the $1,000 for spending money, you may show a positive $1,000 in the Salary category and a minus $1,000 in the Entertainment spending category. Figure 14-4 shows this trick.

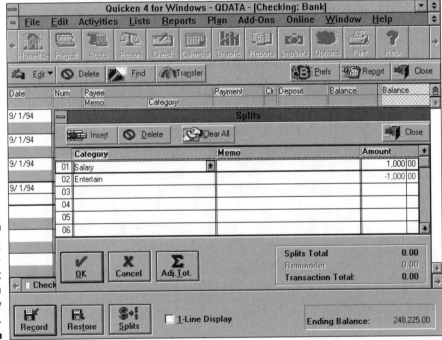

Figure 14-4:
A zero-amount transaction is one handy trick.

Note that the transaction shown in Figure 14-4 produces a transaction that equals zero. This is correct. Cashing the check that you never deposited doesn't affect your checking account balance. But by filling out the Splits window as shown in Figure 14-4, you do end up recording both the $1,000 of income and the $1,000 of expense.

Don't worry. I won't ask why you're carrying around $1,000 in cash.

Updating Cash Balances

You can update a register's cash balance to reflect what you actually have in petty cash, your wallet, under the mattress, in the cookie jar, or wherever else you keep your cash by doing the following steps:

1. **Display the account cash register.**

2. **Choose the Update Balances command from the Activities menu.**

3. **Choose the Update Cash Balance command from the Update Balances menu.**

   Quicken displays the Update Account Balance dialog box, as shown in Figure 14-5.

Figure 14-5:
The Update
Account
Balance
dialog box.

Update Account Balance		
Update this account's balance to: `75`		✓ OK
Category for adjustment: `Entertain` ▼ (optional)		✗ Cancel
Adjustment date: `2/ 1/95`		? Help

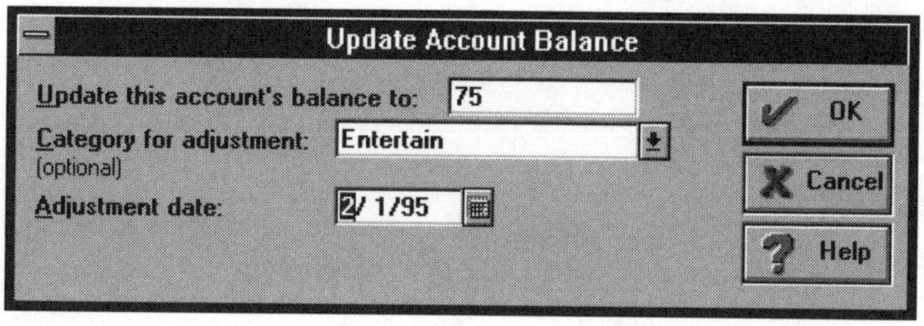

4. **Enter the actual cash balance into the Update This Account's Balance To text box.**

5. **Choose the category that you want to update in the Category For Adjustment drop-down list box.**

   After you click the arrow to the right of the drop-down list box, you get a list of all the categories that you have set up. Oh, one other thing: ignore the fact that Quicken says the Category is optional. You should *always* categorize.

6. **Enter a date in the Adjustment Date text box.**

7. **When you're finished, click OK.**

   Quicken updates the cash account's balance.

Part IV
Serious Business

The 5th Wave   By Rich Tennant

I WILL REMEMBER MY PASSWORD TO THE PAYCHECK FILE.
I WILL REMEMBER MY PASSWORD TO THE PAYCHECK FILE.
I WILL REMEMBER MY PASSWORD TO THE PAYCHECK FILE.

In this part...

1f you use Quicken in a business, you'll find it helpful to get some information about how to use it for payroll, customer receivables, and vendor payables. Sure, you could learn these things by sitting down with your certified public accountant, having a cup of coffee, and paying about $100 an hour.

Or you can read on, pretend we're chitchatting over coffee, and save the $100.

Chapter 15
Payroll

In This Chapter

▶ Creating categories and accounts you need to prepare payroll

▶ Getting an employer ID number

▶ Where to get Social Security, Medicare, and federal income taxes withholding information

▶ Calculating an employee's gross wages, payroll deductions, and net wages

▶ Recording a payroll check in Quicken

▶ Making federal tax deposits

▶ Filing quarterly and annual payroll tax returns

▶ Producing annual wage statements such as W-2s

▶ Handling state payroll taxes

*M*any people use Quicken in a business. Many businesses have employees. Many employees want to be paid on a regular basis. Methinks, therefore, that many people will find help on preparing the payroll helpful.

Getting Ready for Payroll

To prepare payroll checks and summarize the payroll information that you need to prepare quarterly and annual returns, you need to set up some special accounts and categories. You also need to do some paperwork stuff. I'll describe how to do both things in this section.

Getting Quicken ready

To do payroll in Quicken, you'll need to set up several liability accounts, a payroll expense category, and several payroll expense subcategories. Fortunately, none of this is particularly difficult.

I'm going to describe how you do this for purposes of United States federal income and payroll taxes. If you employ people in one of the states that has a state income tax — California, say — you may also have state payroll taxes to deal with. But you can track and process these the same way you process the federal taxes.

I should say that the same thing is probable if you employ people outside the United States. But, hey, there are like a couple hundred countries in the world. So check with someone from the country of employment for specific advice.

Setting up liability accounts

You need to set up three liability accounts to deal with federal payroll and income taxes: one named *Payroll-SS* to track Social Security, one named *Payroll-MCARE* to track Medicare, and one named *Payroll-FWH* to track federal income taxes owed. (I should confess that these aren't my names. They're the names Quicken expects you to use.)

To set up a liability account for any of these payroll tax liabilities, follow these steps:

1. **Choose the Accts icon from the iconbar.**

   Quicken displays the Account List window. You've probably seen this dialog box about a hundred times before. If you want to see the dialog box right now, though, choose the Accts icon and look at your screen.

2. **Choose the <u>N</u>ew command button in the Account List window.**

   Quicken displays the Create New Account window. If you've been reading this book cover-to-cover, you've seen this baby a bunch of times before. If you want or need to see it now, though, you can just follow along on-screen.

3. **Click the <u>L</u>iability button.**

   This tells Quicken you're going to set up a Liability account. (Be sure that you've marked the Guide Me check box before you click. It'll make things go much faster.)

   Quicken displays the Create Liability Account dialog box, as shown in Figure 15-1.

4. **Enter the appropriate account name: Payroll-SS, Payroll-MCARE, or Payroll-FWH.**

   Move the cursor to the <u>A</u>ccount Name text box and type in the right name.

   If your state has an income tax, you'll also want to set up a Payroll-SWH liability account.

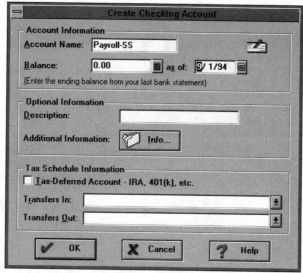

Figure 15-1:
The Create
Liability
Account
dialog box.

The only trick to naming other payroll tax liability accounts is that you
need to start each liability account name with the word *Payroll.* No, this
isn't some rule I made up arbitrarily. There really is a reason for this. The
Quicken Payroll report prints information on all the accounts and categories that start with the word *Payroll.*

5. **Enter the current amount you owe for the payroll tax liability.**

   Move the cursor to the Balance text box and enter whatever you already
   owe. Or if you're just starting and you owe nothing, enter **0.** (If you do owe
   something but you don't have a clue in the world as to how much, the
   easiest thing to do is to figure out what you owe now, before going any
   further. Sorry.)

6. **Enter the A̲s Of date.**

   Move the cursor to the a̲s of (or date) text box. Enter the date on which you
   owe the balance you entered in step 3. This is probably the current date.

7. **Optionally, enter a description, if you want, in the D̲escription (optional)
   text box.**

   I think the standard payroll tax liability names are pretty obvious, so I just
   go with them alone.

8. **Select OK.**

   Quicken adds the new liability account and displays a message box that
   asks whether you want to set up an amortized loan for this liability (see
   Figure 15-2).

Figure 15-2:
The
message
box Quicken
displays to
ask whether
you want to
set up an
amortized
loan.

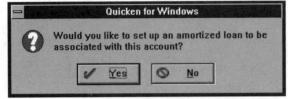

9. **Select No.**

This tells Quicken that you don't want to set up an amortized loan for the liability account. Quicken, only slightly bent out of shape, redisplays the Account List window.

10. **Repeat steps 2 through 10 for each of the other payroll tax liability accounts you want to add.**

Remember that you need at least three payroll tax liability accounts — Payroll-SS, Payroll-MCARE, and Payroll-FWH — for the people you employ in the United States. And if you live in a state with income taxes, you either need to move, or you need to set up a fourth account: Payroll-SWH.

Setting up a payroll expense category

You'll also need to set up a payroll expense category, which isn't tough. Here's all you have to do:

1. **Choose the Category & Transfer command from the Lists menu.**

Quicken, with no hesitation, displays the Category & Transfer List window. Figure 15-3 shows this puppy.

2. **Choose the New command button.**

Quicken displays the Set Up Category dialog box (see Figure 15-4).

3. **Enter Payroll as the category name.**

Move the cursor to the Name text box and type **Payroll**, as shown in Figure 15-4.

4. **Optionally, enter a description of the category.**

If you want, you can type a description in the Description text box. Figure 15-4 shows the description I chose: Payroll expenses. But I'm not particularly creative. You may be able to think of something far better.

5. **In the Type section, mark the Expense option button.**

This tells Quicken you're setting up an expense category. But you probably know this, right?

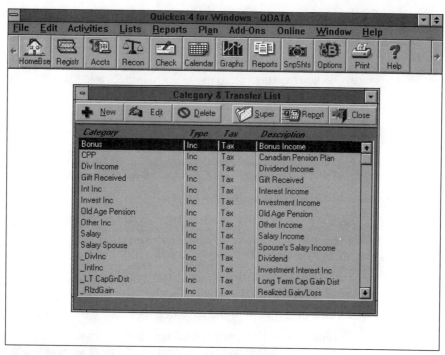

Figure 15-3:
The
Category &
Transfer List
window.

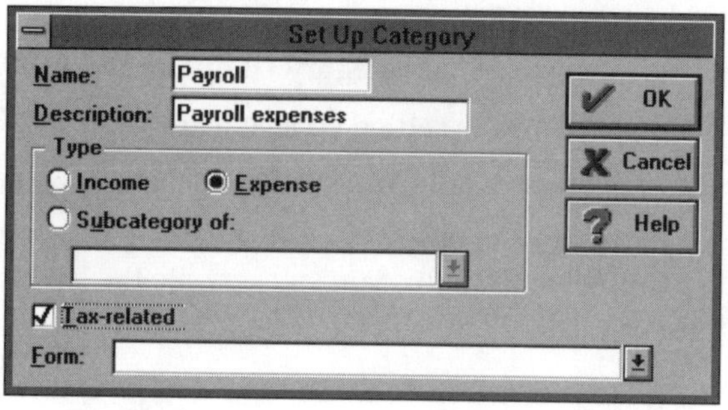

Figure 15-4:
The Set Up
Category
dialog box.

6. Indicate whether the payroll tax is tax deductible.

If you're going to be preparing payroll for a business, mark the Tax-related check box. If you're going to be preparing payroll for a household employee — like a nanny, say — don't mark the Tax-related check box. All this little check box really does is tell Quicken that this category should be included on the Tax Summary report. Household employee payroll expenses aren't tax deductible — as you probably know.

7. Select OK.

Quicken adds the category to the category list and redisplays the Category & Transfer List window. You've almost completed this part of the mission, Commander Bond.

Setting up the payroll subcategories

There's one other thing you need to do to get Quicken ready for payroll. You need to set up subcategory expenses for employee gross wages, the company's share of the Social Security taxes, and the company's share of the Medicare taxes. Quicken expects you to use *Gross, Comp SS,* and *Comp MCARE* as subcategory names. So that's what you'll do, okay?

1. **Display the Category & Transfer List window if it isn't already displayed.**

   Choose the Category and Transfer list command from the lists menu. If you can't remember what this window looks like, refer to Figure 15-3.

2. **Choose the New command button.**

   Quicken displays the Set Up Category dialog box (refer to Figure 15-4).

3. **Enter the appropriate payroll expense subcategory name: Gross, Comp SS, or Comp MCARE.**

   For example, move the cursor to the Name field and type **Gross** or **Comp SS** or **Comp MCARE**.

4. **Enter a description of the subcategory in the Description text box.**

   Because the subcategory names are a little more cryptic, you may want to use the Description text box to document things such as the fact that Comp SS means *Company Social Security.*

5. **In the Type section, select the Subcategory Of option button.**

   This option tells Quicken you're setting up a subcategory.

6. **Indicate that the subcategory falls into the Payroll expense category.**

   Move the cursor to the Subcategory Of text box and type **Payroll**. Or because this is a drop-down list box, you can activate the list box and select the payroll expense category from it.

7. **Select OK.**

   Quicken adds the subcategory to the category list and redisplays the Category & Transfer List window.

8. **Repeat steps 2 through 7 for each of the remaining payroll expense subcategories you need.**

Remember that for employees working in the United States, you need at least three subcategories: Gross (for tracking gross wages), Comp SS (for tracking Company Social Security taxes), and Comp MCARE (for tracking employer Medicare taxes).

Congratulations, James! You saved the world again. You created the liability accounts and categories that you need to track the amounts you pay employees and the payroll taxes you withhold and owe.

TIP

Quick Pay

I'm assuming that you aren't using QuickPay here. But you should know that QuickPay is a software program provided by Intuit. QuickPay works with Quicken to calculate things like gross wages, federal and state income taxes, and Social Security and Medicare taxes. In my humble opinion, QuickPay isn't necessary or all that handy if you only have one or two employees or employees that are always paid the same amount. For example, if your only employee is a nanny or a secretary and the person is paid a straight salary, I don't think you save time by using QuickPay.

If you have a few employees, though, and they're paid an hourly rate and work different numbers of hours every week, get smart. Simplify your financial life and your payroll bookkeeping by buying QuickPay. In your situation, you'll find QuickPay invaluable and well-worth the $50 or so Intuit charges. And, no, I don't earn a sales commission by getting you to buy more software from Intuit.

Getting the taxes stuff right

There are also a couple of other things you need if you want to do payroll the right way.

Requesting (or demanding) an employer ID number

First, you need to file an SS-4, or Request for Employer Identification Number form, with the Internal Revenue Service (IRS) so you can get an employer identification number. You can get this form by calling the IRS and asking for one. Or if you have a friend who's an accountant, he or she may have one of these forms. (See, there is a reason to invite people like me to your dinner parties.)

In one of its cooler moves, the IRS changed its ways and now lets you apply for and receive an employer identification number over the telephone. You still need to fill out the SS-4 form, however, so you can answer questions the IRS asks during the short telephone-application process. (You also need to mail or fax the form to the Service after you have your little telephone conversation.)

So what about Social Security, Medicare, and withholding taxes?

You need to do two things before you can know how to handle all those taxes. First, you need your employees to fill out a W-4 form to let you know what filing status they will use and how many personal exemptions they will claim. Guess where you get blank W-4 forms? That's right . . . from your friendly IRS agent.

The second thing you need to do is get a Circular E Employer's Tax Guide publication. The Circular E publication is the pamphlet that tells you how much you should withhold in federal income taxes, Social Security, and Medicare from a person's salary. You can get this form and the additional federal and state forms that you must fill out to satisfy the government requirements for hiring employees, too, just by calling those friendly people at the Internal Revenue Service.

Paying someone for a job well done

After you tell Quicken to get ready to do payroll and you collect the needed tax information, you're ready to pay someone.

Figuring out the gross wages figure

This should be pretty easy. Does Raoul make $14 an hour? Did he work 40 hours? Then you owe him $560 because $14 times 40 equals $560. Is Betty's salary $400 a week? Then you owe her $400 for the week.

All that deductions stuff

Your next step — after you know how much you're supposed to pay Raoul or Betty — is to figure out what big brother says you must withhold.

To figure this out, you need both Raoul's and Betty's W-4s to find out their filing status and personal exemptions. Then just flip to the page in the Circular E that describes withholding for a person claiming that filing status and paid by the week.

If Raoul is single and claims just one personal exemption, for example, you would flip to the page like the one shown in Figure 15-5. Remember that Raoul is paid weekly. I circled the number in the table in Figure 15-5 that shows what Raoul is supposed to pay in federal income taxes, Social Security, and Medicare.

And about Betty? Remember that Betty's pay is $400 a week. If Betty's filing status is married filing joint and with three personal exemptions, you would flip to the page that resembles Figure 15-6. Again, I circled the number in the table in Figure 15-6 that shows what Betty is supposed to pay.

SINGLE Persons–WEEKLY Payroll Period
(For Wages Paid After December 1990)

At least	But less than	0	1	2	3	4	5	6	7	8	9	10
		And the number of withholding allowances claimed is— / The amount of income tax to be withheld shall be—										
$540	$550	$95	$83	$72	$60	$53	$47	$41	$35	$29	$22	$16
550	560	98	86	75	63	55	49	42	36	30	24	18
560	570	101	89	77	66	56	50	44	38	32	25	19
570	580	103	92	80	69	58	52	45	39	33	27	21
580	590	106	95	83	71	60	53	47	41	35	28	22
590	600	109	97	86	74	63	55	48	42	36	30	24
600	610	112	100	89	77	65	56	50	44	38	31	25
610	620	115	103	91	80	68	58	51	45	39	33	27
620	630	117	106	94	83	71	60	53	47	41	34	28
630	640	120	109	97	85	74	62	54	48	42	36	30
640	650	123	111	100	88	77	65	56	50	44	37	31
650	660	126	114	103	91	79	68	57	51	45	39	33
660	670	129	117	105	94	82	71	59	53	47	40	34
670	680	131	120	108	97	85	74	62	54	48	42	36
680	690	134	123	111	99	88	76	65	56	50	43	37
690	700	137	125	114	102	91	79	68	57	51	45	39
700	710	140	128	117	105	93	82	70	59	53	46	40
710	720	143	131	119	108	96	85	73	62	54	48	42
720	730	145	134	122	111	99	88	76	64	56	49	43
730	740	148	137	125	113	102	90	79	67	57	51	45
740	750	151	139	128	116	105	93	82	70	59	52	46
750	760	154	142	131	119	107	96	84	73	61	54	48
760	770	157	145	133	122	110	99	87	76	64	55	49
770	780	159	148	136	125	113	102	90	78	67	57	51
780	790	162	151	139	127	116	104	93	81	70	58	52
790	800	165	153	142	130	119	107	96	84	72	61	54
800	810	168	156	145	133	121	110	98	87	75	64	55
810	820	171	159	147	136	124	113	101	90	78	66	57
820	830	173	162	150	139	127	116	104	92	81	69	58
830	840	176	165	153	141	130	118	107	95	84	72	60
840	850	179	167	156	144	133	121	110	98	86	75	63
850	860	182	170	159	147	135	124	112	101	89	78	66
860	870	185	173	161	150	138	127	115	104	92	80	69
870	880	187	176	164	153	141	130	118	106	95	83	72
880	890	190	179	167	155	144	132	121	109	98	86	74
890	900	193	181	170	158	147	135	124	112	100	89	77
900	910	196	184	173	161	149	138	126	115	103	92	80
910	920	199	187	175	164	152	141	129	118	106	94	83
920	930	201	190	178	167	155	144	132	120	109	97	86
930	940	204	193	181	169	158	146	135	123	112	100	88
940	950	207	195	184	172	161	149	138	126	114	103	91
950	960	210	198	187	175	163	152	140	129	117	106	94
960	970	213	201	189	178	166	155	143	132	120	108	97
970	980	215	204	192	181	169	158	146	134	123	111	100
980	990	219	207	195	183	172	160	149	137	126	114	102
990	1,000	222	209	198	186	175	163	152	140	128	117	105
1,000	1,010	225	212	201	189	177	166	154	143	131	120	108
1,010	1,020	228	215	203	192	180	169	157	146	134	122	111
1,020	1,030	231	218	206	195	181	172	160	148	137	125	114
1,030	1,040	234	221	209	197	186	174	163	151	140	128	116
1,040	1,050	237	224	212	200	189	177	166	154	143	131	119
1,050	1,060	240	227	215	203	191	180	168	157	145	134	122
1,060	1,070	243	231	218	206	194	183	171	160	148	136	125
1,070	1,080	246	234	221	209	197	186	174	162	151	138	128
1,080	1,090	250	237	224	211	200	188	177	165	154	142	130
1,090	1,100	253	240	227	214	203	191	180	168	156	145	133
1,100	1,110	256	243	230	217	206	194	182	171	159	148	136
1,110	1,120	259	246	233	220	208	197	185	174	162	150	139
1,120	1,130	262	249	236	224	211	200	188	176	165	153	142
1,130	1,140	265	252	239	227	214	202	191	179	168	156	144
1,140	1,150	268	255	243	230	217	205	194	182	171	159	147
1,150	1,160	271	258	246	233	220	208	196	185	173	162	150
1,160	1,170	274	262	249	236	223	211	199	188	176	164	153
1,170	1,180	277	265	252	239	226	214	202	190	179	167	156
1,180	1,190	281	268	255	242	229	216	205	193	182	170	158
$1,190 and over		Use Table 1(a) for a **SINGLE person** on page 22. Also see the instructions on page 20.										

Page 25

Figure 15-5: Raoul's tax deductions stuff.

WARNING!

Always use up-to-date information. The numbers you use for federal income tax withholding change annually. Therefore, don't use the tables shown in Figures 15-5 and 15-6. They will be out-of-date by the time you read this.

Social Security and Medicare amounts are figured by multiplying the gross wage figure by a set percentage. Social Security is 6.2 percent of the gross wages up to a specified limit — roughly $60,000 in 1994. The Medicare tax is 1.45 percent of the gross wages. (Be sure to check your faithful Circular E if you think limits come into play for a particular employee. Note, too, that as I'm writing this, Congress is fiddle-faddling with the tax laws again.)

MARRIED Persons—WEEKLY Payroll Period
(For Wages Paid After December 1990)

And the wages are—		And the number of withholding allowances claimed is—										
At least	But less than	0	1	2	3	4	5	6	7	8	9	10
		The amount of income tax to be withheld shall be—										
$0	$70	$0	$0	$0	$0	$0	$0	$0	$0	$0	$0	$0
70	75	1	0	0	0	0	0	0	0	0	0	0
75	80	1	0	0	0	0	0	0	0	0	0	0
80	85	2	0	0	0	0	0	0	0	0	0	0
85	90	3	0	0	0	0	0	0	0	0	0	0
90	95	4	0	0	0	0	0	0	0	0	0	0
95	100	4	0	0	0	0	0	0	0	0	0	0
100	105	5	0	0	0	0	0	0	0	0	0	0
105	110	6	0	0	0	0	0	0	0	0	0	0
110	115	7	0	0	0	0	0	0	0	0	0	0
115	120	7	1	0	0	0	0	0	0	0	0	0
120	125	8	2	0	0	0	0	0	0	0	0	0
125	130	9	3	0	0	0	0	0	0	0	0	0
130	135	10	3	0	0	0	0	0	0	0	0	0
135	140	10	4	0	0	0	0	0	0	0	0	0
140	145	11	5	0	0	0	0	0	0	0	0	0
145	150	12	6	0	0	0	0	0	0	0	0	0
150	155	13	6	0	0	0	0	0	0	0	0	0
155	160	13	7	1	0	0	0	0	0	0	0	0
160	165	14	8	2	0	0	0	0	0	0	0	0
165	170	15	9	2	0	0	0	0	0	0	0	0
170	175	16	9	3	0	0	0	0	0	0	0	0
175	180	16	10	4	0	0	0	0	0	0	0	0
180	185	17	11	5	0	0	0	0	0	0	0	0
185	190	18	12	5	0	0	0	0	0	0	0	0
190	195	19	12	6	0	0	0	0	0	0	0	0
195	200	19	13	7	1	0	0	0	0	0	0	0
200	210	21	14	8	2	0	0	0	0	0	0	0
210	220	22	16	10	3	0	0	0	0	0	0	0
220	230	24	17	11	5	0	0	0	0	0	0	0
230	240	25	19	13	6	0	0	0	0	0	0	0
240	250	27	20	14	8	2	0	0	0	0	0	0
250	260	28	22	16	9	3	0	0	0	0	0	0
260	270	30	23	17	11	5	0	0	0	0	0	0
270	280	31	25	19	12	6	0	0	0	0	0	0
280	290	33	26	20	14	8	2	0	0	0	0	0
290	300	34	28	22	15	9	3	0	0	0	0	0
300	310	36	29	23	17	11	5	0	0	0	0	0
310	320	37	31	25	18	12	6	0	0	0	0	0
320	330	39	32	26	20	14	8	1	0	0	0	0
330	340	40	34	28	21	15	9	3	0	0	0	0
340	350	42	35	29	23	17	11	4	0	0	0	0
350	360	43	37	31	24	18	12	6	0	0	0	0
360	370	45	38	32	26	20	14	7	1	0	0	0
370	380	46	40	34	27	21	15	9	3	0	0	0
380	390	48	41	35	29	23	17	10	4	0	0	0
390	400	49	43	37	30	24	18	12	6	0	0	0
400	410	51	44	38	32	26	20	13	7	1	0	0
410	420	52	46	40	33	27	21	15	9	2	0	0
420	430	54	47	41	35	29	23	16	10	4	0	0
430	440	55	49	43	36	30	24	18	12	5	0	0
440	450	57	50	44	38	32	26	19	13	7	1	0
450	460	58	52	46	39	33	27	21	15	8	2	0
460	470	60	53	47	41	35	29	22	16	10	4	0
470	480	61	55	49	42	36	30	24	18	11	5	0
480	490	63	56	50	44	38	32	25	19	13	7	0
490	500	64	58	52	45	39	33	27	21	14	8	2
500	510	66	59	53	47	41	35	28	22	16	11	3
510	520	67	61	55	48	42	36	30	24	17	11	5
520	530	69	62	56	50	44	38	31	25	19	13	6
530	540	70	64	58	51	45	39	33	27	20	14	8
540	550	72	65	59	53	47	41	34	28	22	16	9
550	560	73	67	61	54	48	42	36	30	23	17	11
560	570	75	68	62	56	50	44	37	31	25	19	12
570	580	76	70	64	57	51	45	39	33	26	20	14
580	590	78	71	65	59	53	47	40	34	28	22	15
590	600	79	73	67	60	54	48	42	36	29	23	17
600	610	81	74	68	62	56	50	43	37	31	25	18
610	620	82	76	70	63	57	51	45	39	32	26	20
620	630	84	77	71	65	59	53	46	40	34	28	21

Page 26 — (Continued on next page)

Figure 15-6:
Betty's tax deductions stuff.

Figuring out someone's net wages

Table 15-1 summarizes the payroll calculations shown in Figures 15-5 and 15-6.

Does Table 15-1 make sense? If it doesn't, take another look at the marked information in Figures 15-5 and 15-6 and read my earlier discussion of how to figure out deductions stuff. All I've really done in the table is reorganize some information, calculate the Social Security and Medicare taxes, and show how Raoul's and Betty's gross pay gets nickeled and dimed by the various taxes they owe.

Table 15-1		Payroll for Raoul and Betty	
Item	*Raoul*	*Betty*	*Explanation*
Gross wages	$560.00	$400.00	Hey, it's their pay
Withholding	$089.00	$032.00	From Circular E
Social Security	$034.72	$024.80	6.2 percent of gross wages
Medicare	$008.12	$005.80	1.45 percent of gross wages
Net Wages	$428.16	$337.40	What's left over

What about other taxes and deductions?

If you have other taxes and deductions and you understand how the federal income taxes, Social Security taxes, and Medicare taxes work, you won't have any problem working with the other taxes — no matter what they are.

State income tax withholding, for example, works like the federal income tax withholding. (Of course, you need to get the state's equivalent to the Circular E guide.)

In general, other taxes and amounts paid by the employee get treated similarly.

In fact, the only thing that you need to be careful about is what affects employees' gross pay for income taxes but not their Social Security taxes — things like 401K deductions and certain fringe benefits. If you have these kinds of things to deal with and you need help, just ask your accountant. (It's just too difficult — and actually kind of dangerous, too — for me to provide general answers that will work for everyone who reads this paragraph. Sorry.)

Recording a payroll check

After you make the tax deduction and net wages calculation, you're ready to record the check. This is a little bit complicated, but stick with me, partner. We'll get through it in no time.

If Raoul and Betty are milling around your computer, whining and saying things like, "Gee, Boss, how much longer? I want to get to the bank before it closes," tell them to cool their heels for about three minutes.

Suppose that you're going to record the check using the register window for your checking account (see Figure 15-7). (As you know, recording the check into the Write Checks window works the same basic way. The difference is that by using the Write Checks window, you can print the payroll check.)

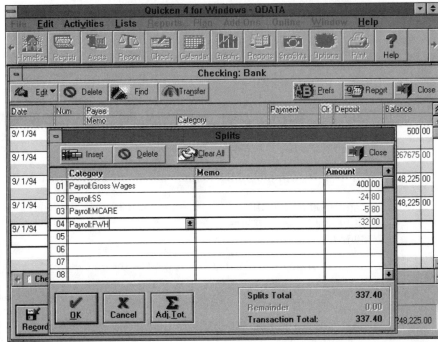

Figure 15-7:
The Quicken register window and Splits window recording Betty's $400 of wages and her $337.40 payroll check.

After you display the checking account register window and highlight the first empty row of the register, follow these steps.

1. **Enter the date of the payroll check in the Date field.**

2. **Enter the payroll check number in the Num field.**

3. **Enter the employee name in the Payee field.**

4. **Enter the net wages amount in the Payment field.**

5. **Open the Splits window (refer to Figure 15-7).**

   You can do this by choosing the Splits command button.

6. **In the first row of the Splits window, enter the category and gross wages amount in the correct fields.**

   Enter the category **Payroll:Gross**. The amount, of course, should be the gross wages figure (400.00 in the example).

7. **Enter the employee's Social Security tax withheld and account in the second row of the Splits window.**

   Instead of a category in the Category field, enter the liability account **[Payroll-SS]**. The amount of the Social Security tax withheld should be 6.2 percent of the employee's gross wages (24.80 in this example). Enter this in the Amount field.

8. **Enter the employee's Medicare tax withheld and account in the third row of the Splits window.**

   In the Category field, enter the liability account **[Payroll-MCARE]**. The amount of the Medicare tax withheld should be 1.45 percent of the employee's gross wages (5.80 in this example).

   Figure 15-7 shows the Quicken register window and Splits window filled out to record Betty's $400 of wages, the taxes poor Betty has to pay on these earnings, and the net wages figure of $337.40. If you have questions about any of these figures, take a peek again at Table 15-1, shown earlier.

9. **Optionally, if you plan to print this paycheck on a payroll check that has a remittance advice or payroll stub, press the PgDn key not twice but thrice.**

   (An *advice* is accounting jargon for the little slip of paper that's attached to the actual check form.)

   Only the first 16 lines of the Splits window print on a payroll stub. So by using lines 17 and higher for the employer portions of the payroll tax, you won't confuse the employee about employee versus employer payroll taxes.

10. **On the next two empty lines of the Splits window, enter the employer's matching share of the Social Security you have to pay.**

    If the employee pays $24.80 of Social Security tax, for example, use the first empty line to enter $24.80 of expense categorized to the Payroll:Comp FICA expense category. Enter **-24.80** in the Amount field and **Payroll:Comp SS** in the Category field.

    Then use the second empty line to record $24.80 of payroll SS tax liability using the [Payroll-SS] account. Enter **24.80** in the Amount field and **[Payroll-SS]** in the Category field.

11. **On the next two empty lines of the Splits window, enter the employer's matching share of the Medicare tax you have to pay.**

    If the employer pays $5.80 of Medicare, for example, use the first empty line to enter $5.80 of expense categorized to the Payroll:Comp MCARE expense category. Enter **-5.80** in the Amount field and **Payroll:Comp MCARE** in the Category field.

Then use the second empty line to record $5.80 of payroll FICA tax liability using the **[Payroll-MCARE]** account. Enter **5.80** in the Amount section and **[Payroll-MCARE]** in the Category section.

Figure 15-8 shows the Social Security and Medicare payroll tax information.

The accounts you use to show the payroll taxes withheld and owed are liability accounts. By looking at the account balances of these accounts, you can easily see how much you owe the government.

12. **If you have other employer-paid payroll taxes, record these following the employer's matching share of Social Security and Medicare.**

    You can use this same basic approach to record federal and state unemployment taxes.

13. **When you finish entering the employer-paid payroll taxes, select OK to close the Splits window.**

14. **To record the payroll check and related employer-paid payroll tax information, select Record.**

You did it! You recorded a payroll check and the related payroll taxes. Maybe it wasn't all that much fun. But at least it wasn't very difficult.

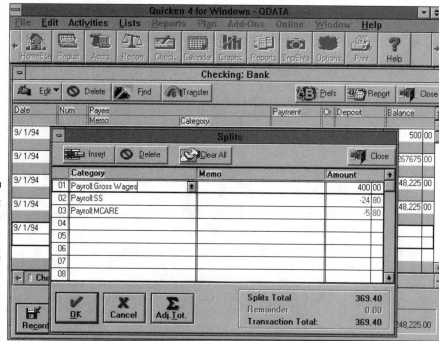

Figure 15-8:
The employer's matching share of Social Security and Medicare taxes.

Making Tax Deposits

Make no mistake. Big Brother wants the money you withhold from an employee's payroll check for federal income taxes, for Social Security, and for Medicare. Big brother also wants the payroll taxes you owe — the matching Social Security and Medicare taxes, federal unemployment taxes, and so on.

Then, every so often, you need to pay Big Brother the amounts you owe.

Making this payment is actually simple. Just write a check payable for the account balances shown in the payroll tax liability accounts. If you have only written the one check to Betty (as shown in Figures 15-7 and 15-8), for example, your payroll liability accounts would show balances as follows:

Liability Account	Amount
Payroll-SS	$49.60
Payroll-MCARE	$11.60
Payroll-FWH	$32.00
	———
Total	$93.20

Notice that the Payroll-FICA account balance and the Payroll-MCARE account balance include both the employee's Social Security and Medicare taxes and the employer's Social Security and Medicare taxes.

Then you write a check for the $93.20 you owe (see Figure 15-9). The only tricky thing about this transaction is that you're transferring the check amount to the payroll liability accounts rather than assigning the check amount to a payroll tax category. In effect, you're transferring money from your checking account to the government to pay off the payroll taxes you owe.

The first time you see this sort of transfer, it can be a little confusing. So take a minute to think about this. If you write the check to the government, your checking account doesn't have the money in it any more, and you don't owe them the money any more. Therefore, the checking account balance and the liability account balance both need to be decreased. In Quicken, the way you do this is with an account transfer.

When do you make payroll tax deposits? The general rule about United States federal tax deposits is this: If your accumulated payroll taxes are less than $500 for the quarter, you can just pay the taxes the following month with your quarterly return. (This is called the De Minimis rule — named after the Congresswoman Dee Minimis? Naw!) If you owe $500 or more, other special rules

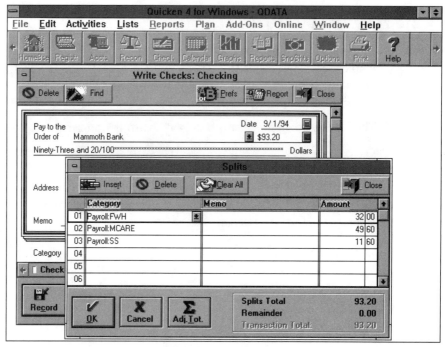

Figure 15-9:
The check
and split
transaction
information
when you
pay the IRS.

come into play that determine whether you pay deposits monthly or semi-monthly. Whether you're supposed to do the monthly or semi-monthly thing basically depends on how much payroll deposit money you paid last year.

If you owe a lot of money, you're required to deposit it almost immediately. For example, if you owe $100,000 or more, you need to make the payroll tax deposit by the next banking day. There are some nuances to these, so unless you don't owe very much and therefore can fall back on the De Minimis rule, you may want to consult a real, live tax advisor (or call the Internal Revenue Service).

To make a payroll tax deposit, just mail your check with a federal tax deposit coupon to a financial institution qualified as a depository for federal taxes or to the Federal Reserve bank serving your geographical area. The IRS should have already sent you a book of coupons as a result of your asking for an employer ID number. And one other thing: make your check payable to the depository or to the Federal Reserve.

Filing Quarterly Payroll Tax Returns

At the end of every quarter, you need to file a quarterly payroll tax return. (By *quarters* here, I'm referring to calendar quarters. You don't do this four times on a Sunday afternoon as you or your couch-potato spouse watch football.)

If you're a business, for example, you must file a Form 941 — which is just a form you fill out to say how much you paid in gross wages, how much you withheld in federal taxes, and how much you owe for employer payroll taxes.

If you're not a business but you have got household employees — such as a nanny — you must file a Form 942. Again, this is just a form you fill out to say how much you paid in gross wages, withheld in federal taxes, and owe in payroll taxes.

To get the gross wages totals and the balances in each of the payroll tax liability accounts, print the Business Payroll report. To do this, activate the Reports menu and choose the Business command on the Business Reports Menu; and then choose the Payroll command. Quicken displays the Create Report dialog box, as shown in Figure 15-10.

Specify the range of dates as the start and end of the quarter for which you're preparing a quarterly report. Then select OK. Quicken produces a payroll report, which you can easily use to fill out the quarterly payroll tax return. Figure 15-11 shows the Payroll report. (As I mentioned earlier, what this report really does is summarize all the transactions that were categorized as falling into the Payroll expense category or transferred to an account named *Payroll (something)*.)

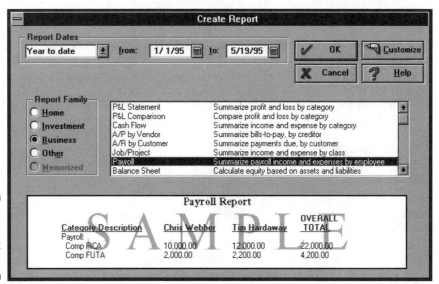

Figure 15-10:
The Create
Report
dialog box.

```
                        Payroll Report by Payee
                          1/1/95 Through 4/1/95
 5/19/95                                                              Page 1
 All Accounts
                                                       OVERALL
                    Category Description   Betty Ready   Mammoth Bank   TOTAL

 INCOME/EXPENSE
   EXPENSES
     Payroll:
       Comp MCARE          -5.80           0.00          -5.80
       Comp SS            -24.80           0.00         -24.80
       Gross              400.00           0.00         400.00

     Total Payroll        369.40           0.00         369.40

   TOTAL EXPENSES         369.40           0.00         369.40


   TOTAL INCOME/EXPENSE  -369.40           0.00        -369.40

   TRANSFERS
     TO Payroll-FWH         0.00         -32.00         -32.00
     TO Payroll-MCARE      -5.80         -49.60         -55.40
     TO Payroll-SS        -24.80         -11.60         -36.40
     FROM Payroll-FWH      32.00           0.00          32.00
     FROM Payroll-MCARE     5.80           0.00           5.80
     FROM Payroll-SS       24.80           0.00          24.80

   TOTAL TRANSFERS         32.00         -93.20         -61.20


   OVERALL TOTAL         -337.40         -93.20        -430.60
```

Figure 15-11:
The Payroll
report.

The compensation to employee total — $400 in the example — is the gross wages upon which your employer payroll taxes are calculated.

The company social security contribution and Medicare contributions are the amounts you recorded to date for the employer Social Security and Medicare taxes — so you need to double these figures to get the actual Social Security and Medicare taxes owed.

The TOTAL TRANSFERS line in the Payroll report represents the federal tax deposits you paid. (This appears on the next page of the report, so you can't see it on the screen.)

By the way, if your accountant is the person who will fill out the 941 or 942, you don't even need to read this stuff. Your accountant won't have any problem completing the quarterly payroll tax return using the Quicken Payroll report and in fact — I kid you not — will probably even enjoy it.

Those Pesky Annual Returns and Wage Statements

At the end of the year, there are some annual returns — like the 940 federal unemployment tax return — and the W-2 and W-3 wages statements you'll need to file.

As a practical matter, the only thing that's different about filling out these reports is that you need to use a payroll report that covers the entire year — not just a single quarter. So you need to enter the range of dates in the Payroll Report dialog box as January 1 and December 31.

The 940 annual return is darn easy if you've been wrestling with the 941 or 942 quarterly returns. The 940 annual return works the same basic way as those more difficult quarterly tax returns. You print the old payroll report, enter a few numbers, and then write a check for the amount you owe.

Note that you need to prepare any state unemployment annual summary first before preparing the 940 because the 940 requires information from the state returns.

For the W-2 statements and the summary W-3 (which summarizes your W-2s), you just print the old payroll report and then, carefully following directions, enter the gross wages, the Social Security and Medicare taxes withheld, and the federal income taxes withheld into the appropriate blanks.

If you have a little trouble, call the IRS. If you have a lot of trouble, splurge and have someone else do it for you. It doesn't take a rocket scientist to fill out these forms, by the way. Any experienced bookkeeper can do it for you.

Please don't construe my "rocket scientist" comment as personal criticism if this payroll taxes business seems terribly complicated. My experience is that some people — and you may very well be one of them — just don't have an interest in things like payroll accounting. If, on the other hand, you're a "numbers-are-my-friend" kind of person, you'll have no trouble at all once you learn the ropes.

Doing the State Payroll Taxes Thing

Yeah. I haven't talked about state payroll taxes — at least not in any great detail. I wish I could provide this sort of detailed, state-specific help to you. Unfortunately, doing so would make this chapter about 150 pages long. It would also cause me to go stark, raving mad.

My sanity and laziness aside, however, you still need to deal with the state payroll taxes. Let me say, however, that you apply to state payroll taxes the same basic mechanics you apply to the federal payroll taxes. For example, a state income tax works the same way as the federal income tax, employer-paid state unemployment taxes work like the employer-paid federal taxes, and employee-paid state taxes work like the employee-paid Social Security and Medicare taxes.

If you've tuned in to how federal payroll taxes work in Quicken, you really shouldn't have a problem with the state payroll taxes — at least, not in terms of mechanics.

Chapter 16
Receivables and Payables

. . . .

In This Chapter

▶ Setting up an account to track customer receivables

▶ Recording customer invoices

▶ Recording customer payments

▶ Tracking amounts your customers owe

▶ Handling customer receivables: a problem

▶ Describing vendor payables

▶ Handling vendor payables

▶ Tracking vendor payables

▶ Using the Billminder™ utility

. . . .

*Q*uicken, as a checkbook program, isn't really built for tracking the amounts that clients and customers owe you or that you owe your vendors, but you can do both if you don't have a long list of receivables or payables. This short chapter describes how you can handle both situations.

Preparing to Track Customer Receivables

To track customer receivables, you must set up an asset account just for tracking customer receivables. If you know how to set up an asset account, just do it. If you don't, follow the steps outlined below:

1. Display the Account List window.

Choose the Accts icon from the iconbar to display the window.

2. Select the New button on the Account List window.

Quicken displays the Create New Account dialog box. (Unmark the Guide Me check box if it's marked.)

3. Click the Asset button.

This tells Quicken that you're setting up a catch-all asset account to track something besides a bank account, cash, or your investments.

Quicken displays the Create Asset Account dialog box. Figure 16-1 shows this dialog box.

4. Name the account.

Move the cursor to the Account Name text box and type a name, such as *Acct Rec,* to identify the account as the one that holds your accounts receivable. But one of the fun things about being in your own business is that *you* get to make the decisions about what you name your accounts — so go for it, dude, and be creative.

5. Enter the starting balance as zero.

6. Accept the default date.

You don't need to enter a date because you aren't entering a starting balance.

7. (Optional) Enter a description for the account.

I don't know — how about something creative, like *Accounts Receivable?* Of course, if the name you choose is descriptive enough you don't need to use this optional description.

8. Leave the Tax-Deferred Account check box unmarked.

You don't need to use this check box for an accounts receivable account.

9. Select OK.

Quicken redisplays the Account List window. But, magically, the window now lists an additional account — the accounts receivable account you just created. (Actually, this isn't really magic — but you know that.)

To tell Quicken which account you want to work with, use the Account List window. Display the Account List window, highlight the account you want by using the arrow keys or the mouse, and then press Enter. Quicken selects the account and displays the register window.

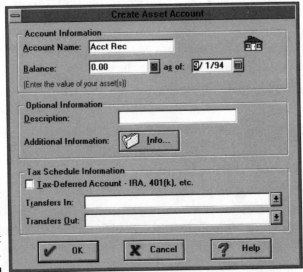

Figure 16-1:
The Create
Asset
Account
dialog box
for setting
up an asset
account.

Recording Customer Invoices and Payments

Because Quicken isn't designed to keep track of lots of receivables and doesn't generate its own invoices (see Chapter 2 for a refresher on what Quicken does and doesn't do), I think that the easiest approach to setting up an account is just to use Quicken to keep a list of your unpaid customer invoices. You could use a Quicken Other account to bill customers and track their invoices, but this approach requires Rube Goldberg*esque* complexity. What's more, if you do want to do all this complex stuff, you're really better off with a real small-business accounting system, such as Intuit's own QuickBooks.

Now, back to the chase...

Recording customer invoices

After you bill a customer, you just enter a transaction for the invoice amount in your Accounts Receivable account register. You can follow these steps for recording a customer invoice in the next empty slot in the Accounts Receivable register:

1. **Open the register window for the Accounts Receivable account.**

   To display the register window, choose the Accts icon from the iconbar and double-click the Accounts Receivable account.

2. **Enter the invoice date — the date you bill your customer or client — in the Date field.**

3. **Enter the invoice number in the Ref field.**

   The invoice number you enter is the number of the invoice you create yourself.

4. **Enter the customer or client name in the Payee field.**

   After the transaction has been recorded, the name now appears in the Payee drop-down list box, and you can select it from the list box anytime you activate the list.

Make sure that you use the same spelling of the customer's name every time you enter it because Quicken summarizes accounts receivable information by payee name; Quicken interprets *John Doe* and *Jonh Doe* as two different customers. In addition, you must take care with names because Quicken's QuickFill works quickly in assuming that you mean a particular account name. If you first enter a customer name as *Mowgli's Lawn Mower Repair,* for example, and then later you type **Mowg** as an account name, Quicken assumes that you're entering another transaction for *Mowgli's Lawn Mower Repair* and fills the Payee field with the complete name. You can avoid trouble in both these instances by activating the Payee drop-down list and selecting the payee name from the list.

5. **Enter the invoice amount in the Increase field.**

6. **Select Record to record the transaction.**

   If Quicken reminds you to enter a category, select the Yes (That's Right ... I Don't Want To Use A Category) option. You don't want to use a category in this step because you later categorize the invoice by using an income category when you record the customer deposit.

   Figure 16-2 shows a register entry for a $750 invoice to Mowgli's Lawn Mower Repair. The ending balance, shown in the lower right corner, is actually the sum of all the transactions shown in the register.

Recording customer payments

When you work with customer payments in Quicken, you actually need to do two things. First, you record the customer check as a deposit in your bank account and categorize it as falling into one of your income categories. Because you probably can record this information with your eyes closed and one hand tied behind your back, I won't describe the process again here.

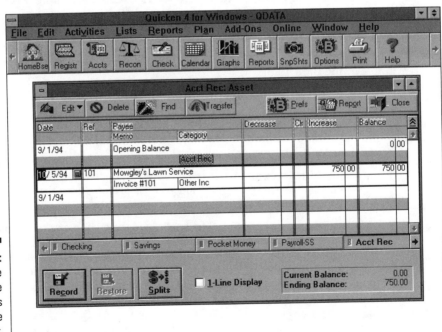

Figure 16-2:
An invoice
entry in the
Accounts
Receivable
register.

Second, you must update your accounts receivable list for the customer's payment. To update the list, display the Accounts Receivable account in the register window and mark the existing invoice the customer has paid by putting an asterisk in the Clr (or cleared) field. Figure 16-3 shows that the first $750 invoice to Mowgli's Lawn Mower Repair has been paid.

Note that I've gotten pretty crazy and entered some other invoices, too. (Hey, it's my job.)

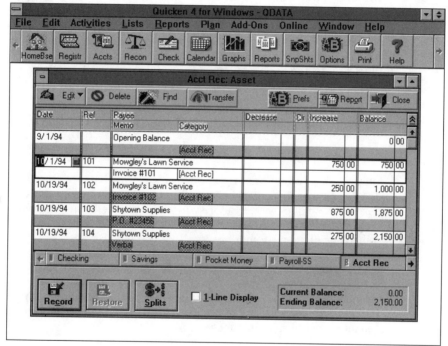

Figure 16-3:
The Accounts Receivable register with invoice #101 marked as paid.

Tracking Your Receivables

When you look at the Accounts Receivable register at this point, you can't tell the total of what your customers owe you. In Figure 16-3, for example, even though I've marked invoice 101 as paid, the account balance still shows $2,150 (the balance of all four invoices shown).

Discovering a dirty little secret about Quicken's A/R reporting

You have just discovered an unfortunate quirk in the way Quicken handles accounts receivable: the account balance for an asset account includes all the transactions entered in the register — even those you mark as being cleared. This quirk causes some problems. For example, you can't print an accurate balance sheet report because Quicken uses the account balance from an asset account on the balance sheet report, and this balance is not accurate.

Oh m' gosh — does this mean you can't track receivables this way? — naw. It does mean, however, that you can't use the accounts receivable account balance for anything because the balance is really a meaningless number. What's more, the accounts receivable, total assets, and net worth figures on the balance sheet reports are also meaningless numbers because the report uses the goofy accounts receivable account balances, too.

Producing an accurate balance sheet

Suppose that you do want to produce an accurate balance sheet. What do you do? You simply strip out the cleared transactions in a receivables register by deleting them one by one. Before you begin your deletions, however, print a copy of the Customer Receivables register. You may want to have a record someplace of the customer invoices that you billed.

What's that? You don't like the idea of stripping out the transactions? OK. If you're willing to go to slightly more work, you can fix the accounts receivable balance in another way. Using the Splits window (see Chapter 14), go through and add split transaction detail showing a reduction in the invoice total that results when the customer makes a payment.

For a $400 invoice on which the customer pays the $400, for example, the Splits window includes one line that records a positive number for the initial $400 invoice and another line that records a negative number for the $400 customer payment. So what you're left with is a transaction that equals zero because the split transaction amounts add up to zero.

You can overcome the problem of producing an accurate balance sheet with Quicken simply by printing an A/R by Customer business report to summarize who owes you and how much they owe.

The A/R by Customer report summarizes all uncleared transactions. To Quicken, however, the first transaction in this register, Opening Balance, looks like a customer — even though it is not a real account. So that this phantom customer doesn't appear on your report, either delete it or mark it as cleared.

To print the A/R by Customer business report, follow these simple steps:

1. **Open the Reports menu.**

2. **Choose the Business command to display the Business Reports menu.**

3. **Choose the A/R by Customer command from the Business Reports menu.**

   Quicken displays the standard Create Report dialog box. (Refer to Chapter 6 if you have questions about this dialog box.)

4. **Select Customize if you've already created other asset accounts.**

   Quicken displays the Customize A/R by Customer dialog box. Mark the Accounts option button. Your dialog box should look like the one you see in Figure 16-4.

5. **Select which accounts with uncleared transactions you want on the accounts receivable report.**

   Initially, Quicken selects all the asset accounts. To unselect an asset account, highlight it. Then to mark the account, click the mouse, or press the spacebar. (By the way, if you have only one asset account — the Accounts Receivable account — Quicken's initial selection is correct.)

6. **Choose OK.**

   Quicken produces a report that summarizes the uncleared transactions by payee names. Figure 16-5 shows the A/R by Customer report based on the three uncleared invoices shown in Figure 16-3.

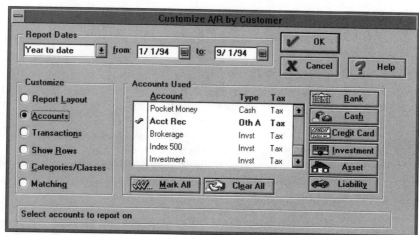

Figure 16-4:
The Customize A/R by Customer dialog box.

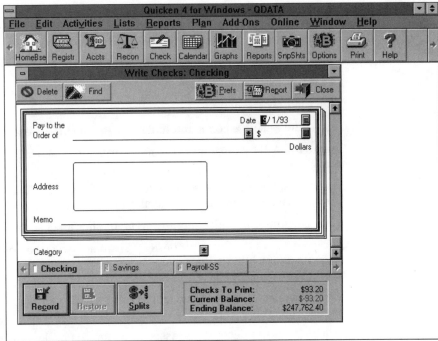

Figure 16-5:
The actual
A/R by
Customer
report.

Preparing to Track Vendor Payables

You really don't have to do anything special to begin tracking the amounts you know that you'll pay; however, you do need to have a bank account already set up. (I'm assuming you already have a bank account set up. If you don't — and it's almost impossible to believe that you don't — refer to Chapters 1 and 2.)

Describing your vendor payables

You describe your vendor payables by filling in the checks you use to pay a vendor's bills in the Write Checks window, as shown in Figure 16-6. Don't print the checks, though. Quicken tracks these unprinted checks because they represent your unpaid vendor invoices. That's it.

I'm super tempted to describe how you fill out the blanks of the Write Checks window — the result of the first tenet in the boring old computer writer's code of honor, "When in doubt, describe in detail." But really — and you probably know this — filling out the Write Checks window is darn easy.

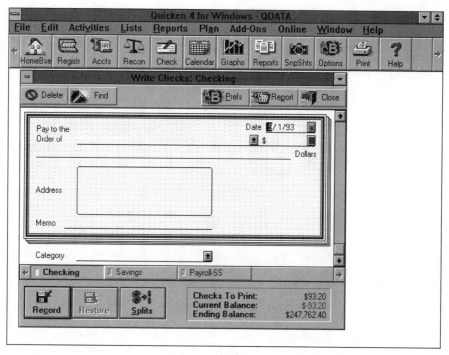

Figure 16-6:
The Write
Checks
window.

If you're not sure about how to fill out the Write Checks window, don't feel that you're stupid or that the process requires an advanced degree. After all, you're still getting your feet wet. So if you feel unsure of yourself, peruse Chapter 5 and then go ahead and wail away at your keyboard.

Tracking your vendor payables

Whenever you want to know how much money you owe someone, just print a report that summarizes the unprinted checks by payee name. Pretty easy, huh? All you have to do is print the A/P by Vendor business report. If you know how to print the report, go ahead. If you need a little help, here's a blow-by-blow account of the steps you need to follow:

1. **Open the Reports menu.**

2. **Choose the Business command to display the Business Reports menu.**

3. **Choose the A/P by Vendor command.**

   Quicken displays the Create Report dialog box, already filled out so that Quicken can print an A/P (Unprinted Chks) by Vendor report. Because I have explained this dialog box in Chapter 6, I didn't include it as a figure in this chapter.

How Quicken identifies an unprinted check

Here's a little tidbit of information you may (or may not) find useful. When you describe a check you want to print by using the Write Checks window, Quicken records the check in the register but uses the word *Print* in place of the check number. The word *Print* identifies the check as the one that you want to print and signals Quicken to look at the check and say to itself, "Aha! — an unprinted check!" *Print* is, to say the least, an important word.

If you're someone who's decided to get truly wild and crazy and use Quicken's electronic bill-paying feature, untransmitted payments show up in the register, too. This time, Quicken uses the word *XMIT* to look at and say, "Aha! — an untransmitted electronic payment!" Untransmitted payments, however, don't appear on the A/P (Unprinted Chks) by Vendor report. Go figure.

Electronic payments can be wild and crazy? What a concept! Yes, the entire Quicken program can be just that, if it means being fun and adventurous. You know, wild and crazy — as in ordering Thai food and saying, "Make that four stars, please." Or wild and crazy — as in not wearing any underwear. You understand.

4. Select OK.

Quicken summarizes the unprinted checks in your bank, cash, and credit card accounts. Figure 16-7 shows an example of this cute little report.

Explaining how Quicken handles payables

Before I conclude this wonderfully interesting, terribly exciting discussion about how you track unpaid bills in Quicken, let me make one final, quick point: an unprinted check gets counted as an expense only after you print it. Does this news sound like much ado about nothing? It probably is.

But let's take a minute to explain the accounting system that Quicken uses. For example, if you record a $1,000 check to your landlord on December 31 but you don't print the check until January, Quicken doesn't count the $1,000 as an expense in December. It instead counts the $1,000 as an expense in January of the next year.

By the way, the Quicken register will show two balances: the current balance, which shows, well, the current balance (the balance that's in your account even as you read this sentence) and the ending balance, which shows the unprinted checks.

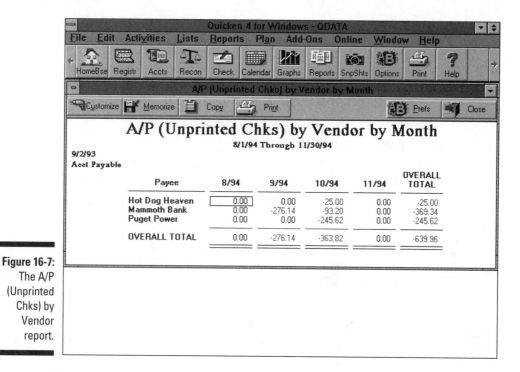

Figure 16-7:
The A/P
(Unprinted
Chks) by
Vendor
report.

If you know a little about cash-basis accounting versus accrual-basis accounting, you've probably already said to yourself, "Hey, man, Quicken uses cash-basis accounting." And you're right, of course.

This little subtlety between the two accounting systems can cause confusion, especially if you've already been working with a regular, full-featured accounting system that uses an accounts payable module with accrual-basis accounting. In one of these systems, the $1,000 check to your landlord probably gets counted as an expense as soon as you enter it in the system.

Meeting a New Friend Named Billminder

Bill, my affectionate nickname for Billminder, is a separate program in Quicken that will soon become a good friend of yours, too. You can tell Quicken to fix your computer so that the Billminder program runs every time you turn on your computer — a nice feature.

What Bill does is simple: he looks through your unprinted checks for any checks with dates falling on or before the current date. If Bill finds a check with such a date, he displays a message that says, "Hey, dude, you have checks that you need to print." Or, in the case where you have overdue checks, Bill displays a message that says, "Dude, the situation is getting gnarly — you've got some seriously overdue checks." (The messages don't use these exact words, by the way.)

To tell Bill you want him reminding you of the checks you need to print, follow these steps:

1. **Choose the Re_m_inders command from the Acti_v_ities menu.**

   In a surprising move, Quicken displays the Quicken Reminders window.

2. **Choose the _P_refs button.**

   Quicken displays the Billminder Preferences dialog box, where all the action happens — at least from Bill's perspective. Figure 16-8 shows the Billminder Preferences dialog box.

3. **Turn on the Billminder reminder feature.**

   To turn on Bill, just mark the _T_urn on Billminder check box.

   Billminder also keeps its eyes open for scheduled transactions, investment reminder messages, and notes you've posted on the Financial Calendar.

4. **Enter a value in the only text box on the dialog box.**

   This value tells Bill how many days in advance you want to be reminded of unprinted checks. The value tells Quicken how many days in advance you want to be queried about scheduled transactions and Investment reminder messages.

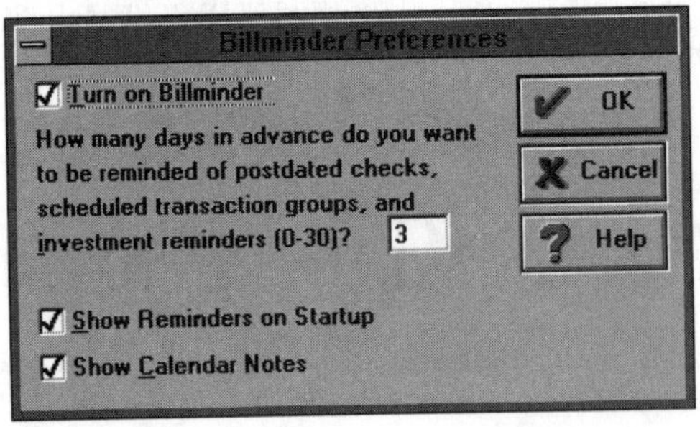

Figure 16-8:
The
Billminder
Preferences
dialog box.

Billminder Preferences

☑ _T_urn on Billminder

How many days in advance do you want to be reminded of postdated checks, scheduled transaction groups, and investment reminders (0-30)? `3`

✓ OK

✗ Cancel

? Help

☑ _S_how Reminders on Startup
☑ Show _C_alendar Notes

5. Mark the Show Reminders On Startup check box.

Marking this box tells Bill that you want to be reminded of the checks after you start up Quicken. If you don't mark this box, by the way, Bill checks whether you've got checks to print, but he doesn't come right out and say whether you've got checks to print. To find out about unprinted checks, you need to choose the Reminders command from the Activities menu.

6. Select OK.

When you start Quicken the next time, you'll see a window like the one shown in Figure 16-9. It'll tell you whether you've got checks to print, scheduled transactions that need to be entered, and any calendar notes you should probably be reading.

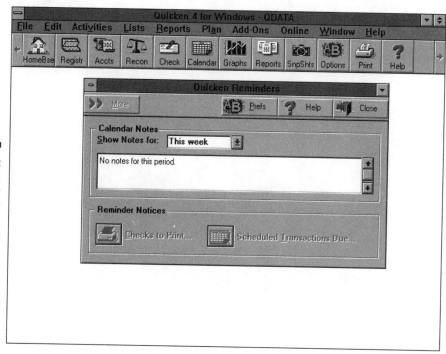

Figure 16-9:
The Quicken Reminder window. If you turn Billminder on, you'll see this window every time you start Quicken.

To actually see the checks that should be printed or the scheduled transactions that should be entered, you just click the Checks to Print button or the Scheduled Transactions Due button. Any calendar notes you've created will show in the list box at the top of the window.

Well, that about wraps up the main part of tonight's show. If you're thinking that it's still a little too early to go to bed, flip through the following chapters. They provide lists of a bunch of eclectic topics: ten things to do when you visit Acapulco, ten things you should never do during a commercial airline flight, and so on. Time flies when you're having fun, doesn't it?

Part V

The Part of Tens

In this part...

As a writing tool, laundry lists aren't something high school English teachers encourage. But you know what? The old laundry list format is pretty handy for certain sorts of information.

With this in mind (and, of course, deepest apologies to my high school English teacher, Mrs. O'Rourke), the next and final part simply provides you with ten-item lists of information about Quicken: answers to ten commonly asked questions about Quicken, ten things every business owner using Quicken should know, ten things you should (or shouldn't) do if you are audited, and so on.

Chapter 17
Ten Questions I'm Frequently Asked about Quicken

*W*hen people find out that I've written a book about Quicken, they always ask a question or two. In this chapter, I list the most common questions and their answers.

Does Quicken Work for a Corporation?

Sure. But let's talk for a minute about what's unique — at least from an accountant's perspective — about a corporation.

In addition to recording assets (like bank accounts and receivables) and liabilities (like mortgages and trade payables), a corporation needs to *track,* or keep records for, the stockholders' equity.

Stockholders' equity includes the amount people originally paid for their stock, any earnings the corporation has retained, cumulative income for the current year, and sometimes other stuff, too.

"Ugh," you're probably saying to yourself. "Ugh" is right. Accounting for stockholders' equity of a corporation is mighty complicated at times. So complicated, in fact, that Quicken can't track a corporation's stockholders' equity.

I'm not saying that you can't use Quicken if you're a corporation, and I'm not saying that you shouldn't. (I do business as a corporation and I use Quicken.) Just remember that someone — probably your poor accountant — periodically needs to calculate your stockholders' equity.

Fortunately, the financial information you collect with Quicken provides, in rough form, much of the information that your poor accountant needs in order to do things manually.

What Happens to Stockholders' Equity in Quicken?

Quicken doesn't exactly ignore a corporation's stockholders' equity. In an Account Balances report, the difference between the total assets and the total liabilities actually represents the total stockholders' equity. (Quicken labels this total Net Worth. So, to the extent that your total assets and total liabilities figures are correct, you know your total stockholders' equity.)

Does Quicken Work for a Partnership?

Yep, it does. But a partnership that uses Quicken faces the same basic problem as a corporation that uses Quicken. In a partnership, the partners want to track their partnership capital accounts (or at least they should). A partnership capital account simply shows what a partner has put into and taken out of a business.

As noted in the preceding section, Quicken calculates a net worth figure for you by subtracting total liabilities from total assets. So, to the extent that your total assets and total liabilities are accurately accounted for in Quicken, you know roughly the total partnership capital.

To solve this problem, you — or someone else — need to track what each partner puts into the business, earns as a partner in the business, and then takes out of the business.

Can I Use Quicken for More Than One Business?

Yeah, but be very careful. *Very* careful. You must be especially diligent in keeping the two businesses' financial records separate.

Quicken provides a handy tool for keeping them straight: you can work with more than one file. Each file, in effect, is like a separate set of financial records. You can't record automatic transfers between accounts in different files; instead, you must record each side of the transaction separately. You can, however, keep truly separate business records.

To create a separate file, use the File New command.

If you've been using Quicken for a while, you can probably figure out for yourself how the File New command works. If you need help, refer to my discussion of this command in Chapter 8.

Separate bank accounts are usually a must. If you keep separate records for two distinct businesses in Quicken, you need to set up separate bank accounts for them. In fact, my attorney tells me that in the case of a corporation, you must set up a separate corporate bank account for the corporation to be truly considered an independent legal entity. Talk to your attorney if you have questions; attorneys can tell you the specifics that apply to a particular state and situation.

What Kind of Business Shouldn't Use Quicken?

You're probably saying to yourself, "Quicken works for corporations (sort of), and it works for partnerships (sort of). Does that mean that it works for just about any kind of business?"

The answer is no. Quicken is a darn good product. In fact, for many small businesses, it's a great product. But it doesn't work in every situation.

Here's a three-part test you can use to determine whether your business should use Quicken. If you answer yes to two or three of the questions, you should seriously consider moving up to a full-featured small-business accounting system.

1. Do you regularly need to produce business forms other than checks?

If you answer no to this question, you're in good shape with Quicken, which produces checks easily. And if all you need is an occasional invoice, you can create them easily enough on your computer. I, for example, produce a handful of invoices a month. I do them on my word processor and never have any problems.

If you do produce a lot of forms besides checks, you should probably consider moving up to a small-business accounting system that produces the forms you want. If you've been using Quicken, for example, take a look at QuickBooks for Windows. (If it isn't out yet, it should be soon.) Another more powerful but wonderfully designed product you might try is Peachtree Accounting for Windows.

2. Do you need to track assets other than cash or investments?

For example, do you have a long list of customer receivables that you need to monitor? Or do you buy and resell inventory? In these situations, an accounting system is usually helpful in tracking these items. Quicken doesn't do a very good job of tracking these other assets, so you may want to look at one of the other small-business accounting products — QuickBooks, for example.

3. Are you having problems measuring your profits with cash-basis accounting?

I'm not going to get into a big, tangled discussion of cash-basis versus accrual-basis accounting. It wouldn't be any fun for you. It wouldn't be any fun for me, either. Nevertheless, you should know that if you can't accurately measure your business profits by using cash-basis accounting (which is what Quicken uses), you may be able to more accurately measure your business profits by using accrual-basis accounting. To do so, use an accounting system that supports accrual-basis accounting. I should be totally honest with you and tell you that to measure your profits the right way, you (or your accountant) need to use — horror of horrors — double-entry bookkeeping.

If you are a Quicken user but realize that you're outgrowing the checkbook-on-a-computer scene, check out QuickBooks. (No, I don't get a kickback from Intuit.) Here's the deal: QuickBooks looks and feels a lot like Quicken. Plus, it uses the data you've already collected with Quicken. So you'll find that moving from Quicken to QuickBooks is only slightly more complicated than rolling off a log.

Can I Use Quicken Retroactively?

Yeah. And the idea is better than it might seem at first.

It doesn't take long to enter a year's worth of transactions in Quicken (as long as you have decent records to work with). If you're, like, a millionaire, it might take you a couple days. (Of course, in this case you can probably hire someone to do it for you.) If you're a regular, ordinary person, I bet you can get it done on a rainy Saturday afternoon.

After you enter all the information into a Quicken register, you can easily monitor your spending in various categories, track your income and outgo, and reconcile your bank accounts. I know one professional who uses Quicken records to do these things every year. Hey, it's not the most efficient way to do things. And it's not a very good way to manage business or personal financial affairs. But it works. Sort of. (Sorry, Jimbo.)

Can I Do Payroll with Quicken?

Yes. See Chapter 15 for more details.

You can also use a handy payroll utility called QuickPay to do payroll in Quicken. If you've got only one or two salaried employees who always earn the same amount — a nanny, for example — then you don't need QuickPay. But if you have a bunch of employees or even a single hourly employee, QuickPay saves you a great deal of time.

Can I Prepare Invoices?

No. This is a good example of when you should consider moving up to a full-featured small-business accounting system.

Can I Import Data from an Old Accounting System?

Someone had to ask this question, I guess. (Imagine me taking a deep breath here.) Yes, you can import data from your old accounting system. To do so, export the old system's data into a file that matches the Quicken Interchange Format, or QIF, specification. Then import this file into an empty Quicken file.

Wait until the new year to switch programs

If you're moving to Quicken, your transaction volumes probably aren't so incredibly mammoth that you have gazillions of transactions to enter anyway. Given this, it probably makes sense to convert, or switch, programs at the beginning of your fiscal, or accounting, year—usually January 1. By waiting until the next fiscal year, the only data you absolutely have to load into Quicken are the asset and liability account balances. And you can do so easily enough when you set up the accounts.

- ✔ This process isn't for the timid or faint hearted.

- ✔ I would also claim that it isn't for people who have better things to do with their time.

- ✔ My advice to you? Go to a movie. Mow your lawn. Read a trashy novel. Forget all about this importing business.

What Do You Think about Quicken?

I think it's great. But I bet your question isn't really whether Quicken is good or not. Heck, the package sells something like two million copies a year. So we both know that the package is pretty good, right? My guess is that what you really want is my opinion about using Quicken in particular business or personal situations.

It's tough to answer this question in a one-way conversation. Even so, let me give you some of the best reasons for using Quicken:

- ✔ You always know your bank account balances, so you won't ever have to wonder whether you have enough money to pay a bill or charge a purchase.

- ✔ Reconciling your account takes about two minutes. (I'm not joking. It really does take a couple minutes.)

- ✔ You get a firm handle on what you're really making and spending.

- ✔ You can budget your spending and then track your spending against your budget.

- ✔ If you're a business, you can measure your profits as often as you want by using cash-basis accounting.

- ✔ If you're an investor, you can monitor your investments and measure their actual returns.

I hope these answers help. My guess is that if you think a program like Quicken will help you better manage your financial affairs, then it probably will.

Chapter 18
Ten Tips for Bookkeepers Who Use Quicken

. . . .

In This Chapter

▶ Tricks for learning Quicken if you're new on the job

▶ How and why you cross-reference

▶ Why you shouldn't use a suspense account

▶ Why you should reconcile promptly

▶ What you should do at the end of every month

▶ What you should do at the end of every year

▶ How Quicken handles debits and credits

▶ How to convert to Quicken from some other system

▶ What to do if you're (unwittingly, of course) a party to income tax evasion

▶ What you should know about payroll taxes

. . . .

An amazing number of people use Quicken for small-business accounting: dentists, contractors, lawyers, and so on. And, not surprisingly, a great number of bookkeepers use Quicken.

If you're jumping up and down, waving your hands, saying, "I do, I do, I do," this chapter is for you. I tell you here what you need to know to make your use of Quicken smooth and sure.

Tricks for Learning Quicken if You're New on the Job

First of all, let me congratulate you on your new job. Let me also remind you how thankful you should be that you'll be using Quicken and not one of the super-powerful-but-frightening, complex accounting packages.

If you're new to computers, you need to know a thing or two about them. Don't worry. This task isn't as difficult as you may think. (Remember that a bunch of anxious folks have gone before you.)

Turning on the computer

Before you use the computer, you need to:

1. **Find and flip on the computer's power switch (usually a big red switch).**

2. **Push a switch to turn on your monitor (the television-like screen).**

3. **Flip a switch to turn on the printer.**

Even if you're a little timid, go ahead and ask your boss how to turn on the computer and its peripherals. This won't be considered a stupid question. Different computers get turned on in different ways. For example, the computer and its peripherals may already be on and plugged into a fancy-schmancy extension cord called a *power strip* — but this power strip thing is turned off.

By the way, the word *peripherals* refers to things that work with the computer, such as the printer.

Starting Windows and Quicken

After you turn on the computer, you should see something on the screen that looks like this:

```
C:>
```

This "something" is called the *DOS prompt,* but you don't have to remember this bit of trivia. To start Windows, type **win** and then press Enter. Windows will start.

You use Windows to start Quicken. If you don't "do" Windows, refer to Appendix B for a quick and dirty overview.

Learning Quicken

When you know how to turn on the computer and how to start Windows and Quicken, you're ready to rock. Give Part II of this book a quick read. Then carefully read those chapters in Part IV that apply to your daily work.

One last thing. Remember when you learned how to drive a car? Sure it was confusing at first: all those gauges and meters . . . the tremendous power at your fingertips . . . traffic. After you gained some experience, though, you loosened your death grip on the wheel. Heck, you even started driving in the left lane.

Give yourself a little time. Before long you'll be zipping around Quicken, changing lanes three at a time.

Cross-Reference and File Source Documents

Be sure to cross-reference and file (neatly!) the source documents (checks, deposit slips, and so on) you use to enter transactions. I won't tell you how to set up a document filing system. There's a pretty good chance you can do this better than I — in fact, I usually use a crude, alphabetical scheme.

Check forms (the check source documents) are numbered, so you can cross-reference checks simply by entering check numbers when recording a check transaction. But be sure to do the same for deposits and other withdrawals, too.

Cross-referencing enables you to answer any questions about a transaction that appears in a register. All you have to do is find the source document you used to enter the transaction.

Always Categorize

Always categorize a transaction. In an account transfer, specify the account to which an amount has been transferred.

A favorite but sloppy accounting trick is to assign funny transactions to a *suspense account.* Suspense accounts, however, often become financial landfills where you (and anyone else using Quicken) dump transactions you don't know what to do with.

The suspense grows and grows. And pretty soon, it's a huge mess and no one has the energy to clean it up.

By the way, you can tell Quicken to remind you to enter a category every time you enter a transaction. Here's how to get this reminder:

1. **Choose the P̲references command from the E̲dit menu.**

   Quicken displays the Quicken For Windows Options dialog box.

2. **Choose the R̲egistr button.**

   Quicken displays the Registr Preferences dialog box.

3. **Specify that you want Quicken to warn you if a transaction has no category.**

   Move the selection cursor to the W̲arn Before Recording Uncategorized Transactions check box and press the spacebar. Or just click the check box with the mouse.

4. **Select OK.**

   Quicken redisplays the Quicken For Windows Options dialog box.

5. **Select Close.**

Reconcile Promptly

This is a pet peeve, so bear with me if I get a little huffy.

I think you should always reconcile, or balance, a business's bank accounts within a day or two after you get the bank statement. You'll catch any errors that either you or the bank has made.

You also minimize the chance that you'll suffer financial losses from check forgery. Here's why: if a business or individual promptly alerts a bank about a check forgery, the bank rather than the business suffers the loss in most cases.

Reconciling in Quicken is fast and easy, so there's no good excuse not to reconcile promptly. Chapter 7 describes how to reconcile accounts in Quicken.

Things You Should Do Every Month

In a business, everyone has some routine tasks: Go through the In basket. Return phone messages. Clean the coffee machine.

Here are six bookkeeping chores you should probably do at the end of every month:

1. **If the business uses a petty cash system, replenish the petty cash fund. Make sure that you have receipts for all withdrawals.**

2. **Reconcile the bank and credit card accounts.**

3. **If you're preparing payroll, be sure to remit any payroll tax deposit money owed.**

   For businesses in the United States, you can get information about how this system works from the Internal Revenue Service.

4. **Print a copy of each of the account registers for the month.**

   Set these copies aside as permanent financial records. Chapter 5 describes how to print reports, including the account registers.

5. **Print two copies of the monthly cash flow statement and the P&L statement.**

   Give one copy to the business's owner or manager. Put the other copy with the permanent financial records.

6. **If you haven't done so already during the month, back up the file containing the Quicken accounts to a floppy disk.**

   You can reuse the floppy disk every other month. Chapter 8 describes how to back up files.

Don't view the preceding list as all-inclusive. There may be other things you need to do. I'd hate for people to say, "Well, it doesn't appear on Nelson's list, so I don't have to do it." Yikes!

Things You Should Do Every Year

Here are the things I think you should do at the end of every year:

1. **Do all the usual month-end chores for the last month in the year.**

   See the list in the preceding section.

2. **Prepare and file any state and federal end-of-year payroll tax returns.**

   Businesses in the United States, for example, need to prepare the annual federal unemployment tax return (Form 940).

3. **Print two copies of the annual cash flow statement and the annual P&L statement.**

   Give one copy to the business's owner or manager. Put the other copy with the permanent financial records.

4. **If the business is a corporation, print a copy of the Business Balance Sheet report.**

   This report will help whoever prepares the corporate tax return.

5. **Back up the file containing the Quicken accounts to a floppy disk.**

   Store the floppy disk as a permanent archive copy.

6. **If the business's accounts are full — you notice that Quicken runs slower — use Quicken's Year End command to shrink the file.**

Quicken creates a new version of the file, keeping only the current year's transactions. See Chapter 8.

Again, don't view the preceding list as all-inclusive. If you think of other things to do, do them.

About Debits and Credits (if You're Used to These)

If you've worked with a regular small-business accounting system, you may have missed your old friends, debit and credit. (Is it just me, or do *debit* and *credit* sound like the neighbor kid's pet frogs to you, too?)

Quicken is a single-entry accounting system and, as a result, doesn't really have debits and credits. Double-entry systems have debits and credits. (As you may know, the two entries in a double-entry system are your old friends: debit and credit. For every debit, you have equal credit.)

Quicken does supply a sort of chart of accounts, which you can use to describe accounting transactions. The Category & Transfer List window (which you can usually display by pressing Ctrl+C) actually parallels a regular accounting system's chart of accounts.

Accordingly, when you record a transaction that increases or decreases one account, you record the offsetting debit or credit when you categorize or transfer the account.

Converting to Quicken

If you're converting to Quicken from a manual system or from another more complicated small-business accounting system, here are two important tips:

1. **Start using Quicken at the beginning of a year.**

The year's financial records are then in one place — the Quicken registers.

2. **If it's not the beginning of the year, go back and enter the year's transactions.**

Again, the year's financial records are then in one place — the Quicken registers. (This task will take time if you have a bunch of transactions to enter. In fact, you may want to postpone your conversion to Quicken.)

Income Tax Evasion

A nice fellow wandered into my office the other day and told me that he had inadvertently gotten entangled in his employer's income tax evasion. He didn't know what to do.

He had (unwittingly, he said) helped his employer file fraudulent income tax returns. Then, already sucked into the tar pit, he had lied to the IRS during an audit.

I didn't have anything good to tell him.

I never did get the fellow's name, so I'll just call him *Chump*.

It really didn't make any financial sense for Chump to help his employer steal. Chump didn't get a share of the loot; he just helped his employer commit a felony. For free. (What a guy!)

Although Chump didn't receive (supposedly) any of the booty, he probably still is in serious trouble with the IRS. The criminal penalties can be enormous. Prison, I understand, is not fun.

I'm not going to spend anymore time talking about this. But I do have a piece of advice for you. Don't be a Chump.

Segregating Payroll Tax Money

While I'm on the subject of terrible things the IRS can do to you, let me touch on the problem of payroll tax deposits — the money you withhold from employee checks for federal income taxes, Social Security, and Medicare.

If you have the authority to spend the money you withhold, don't — even if the company will go out of business. If you can't repay the payroll tax money, the IRS will go after the business owners and also after *you.*

It doesn't matter that you're just the bookkeeper; it doesn't matter whether you regularly attend church. The IRS doesn't take kindly to those who take what belongs to the IRS.

By the way, I should mention that the IRS is more lenient in cases where you don't have any authority to dip into the payroll tax money while the business owner or your boss dip away. If you find yourself in this situation, however, be darn careful not to get involved. And start looking for a new job.

Chapter 19
Ten Tips for Business Owners

*I*f you run a business and you use Quicken, you need to know some stuff. You can learn these things by sitting down with your certified public accountant over a cup of coffee at $100 an hour. Or you can read this chapter.

Sign All Your Own Checks

I have nothing against your bookkeeper. In a small business, however, it's just too darn easy for people — especially full-charge bookkeepers — to bamboozle you. By signing all the checks yourself, you keep your fingers on the pulse of your cash outflow.

Yeah, I know this can be a hassle. I know this means you can't easily spend three months in Hawaii. I know this means you have to wade through paperwork every time you sign a stack of checks.

By the way, if you're in a partnership, I think you should have at least a couple of the partners co-sign checks.

Don't Sign a Check the Wrong Way

If you sign many checks, you may be tempted to use a John Hancock-like signature. Although this makes great sense if you're autographing baseballs, don't do it when you're signing checks. A wavy line with a cross and a couple of dots is really easy to forge.

Which leads me to my next tip . . .

Review Canceled Checks Before Your Bookkeeper Does

Be sure you review your canceled checks — before anybody else sees the monthly bank statement.

This chapter isn't about browbeating bookkeepers. But a business owner will discover whether someone is forging signatures on checks only by being the first to open the bank statement and reviewing each of the canceled check signatures.

If you don't take this precaution, unscrupulous employees — especially bookkeepers who can update the bank account records — can forge your signature with impunity. And they won't get caught if they never overdraw the account.

Another thing: if you don't follow these procedures, *you* will probably eat the losses, not the bank.

How to Choose a Bookkeeper if You Use Quicken

Don't worry. You don't need to request an FBI background check.

In fact, if you use Quicken, you don't need to hire only people who are familiar with small-business accounting systems. Just find people who know how to keep a checkbook and work with a computer; you shouldn't have a problem getting them to understand Quicken.

Of course, you don't want someone who just fell off the turnip truck. But even if you do hire someone who rode into town this way, you're not going to have much trouble getting him up to speed with Quicken.

But when you hire someone, find someone who knows how to do payroll — not just the federal payroll tax stuff (see Chapter 15), but also the state payroll tax monkey business.

Get Smart about Passwords

In Chapter 8, I got all hot and bothered about passwords. Let me add here that I suggest you use a password to keep your financial records confidential if you use Quicken in a business and it's you who does the Quicken *thang*. (Especially if you have employees who know how to operate a PC and have access to the PC you use for Quicken.)

Leave Your Password Record at Home

To assign a file password, see Chapter 8. But be sure that you don't lose your financial records by forgetting your password. (I think it's a good idea to keep *at home* a record of the password you use for the computer at work.)

Cash-Basis Accounting Doesn't Work for All Businesses

When you use Quicken, you employ an accounting convention called *cash-basis accounting* to measure your profits. When money comes in, you count it as revenue. When money goes out, you count it as expense.

Cash-basis accounting is fine when a business's cash inflow mirrors its sales and its cash outflow mirrors its expenses. This isn't the case, however, in many businesses. A single-family home contractor, for example, may have cash coming in (by borrowing from banks) but may not make any money. A pawn-shop owner who loans money at 22 percent may make scads of money even if cash pours out of the business daily. As a rule of thumb, when you're buying and selling inventory, accrual-basis accounting works better than cash-basis accounting.

So this news isn't earthshaking. It's still something you should think about.

When to Switch to Accrual-Basis Accounting

If tracking cash flows doesn't indicate whether your business is making a profit or a loss, then you probably need to switch to accrual-basis accounting. Almost certainly you need to switch accounting systems.

What to Do if Quicken Doesn't Work for Your Business

Quicken is a great checkbook program. In fact, my friends at Microsoft won't like me saying this, but Quicken is probably the best checkbook program.

However, if Quicken doesn't seem to fit your needs — for example, you need accrual-basis accounting (see preceding section) — you may want one of the more complicated but also more powerful small-business accounting packages.

If you like using Quicken, look at QuickBooks for Windows. (Although QuickBooks for Windows wasn't available when I wrote this, I hear it will be ready soon.)

You also should look at other more powerful programs, such as the full-featured Windows accounting programs. Today the big boys are Microsoft Profit from you-know-who and Peachtree Accounting for Windows from Peachtree. I think Peachtree is probably the better package.

I am amazed that PC accounting software remains so affordable. You can buy a great accounting package — one you can use to manage a $5 million or a $25 million business — for a few hundred bucks. This deal is truly one of the great bargains.

Keep Things Simple

Let me share one last comment about managing small-business financial affairs. *Keep things as simple as possible.* In fact, keep your business affairs simple enough that it's easy to tell if you're making money and if the business is healthy.

This advice may sound strange, but as a CPA I've worked for some very bright people who built monstrously complex financial structures for their businesses, including complicated leasing arrangements, labyrinth-like partnership and corporate structures, and sophisticated profit-sharing and cost-sharing arrangements with other businesses.

I can offer only anecdotal evidence, of course, but I strongly believe that these super-sophisticated financial arrangements don't produce a profit when you consider all the costs. What's more, these super-sophisticated arrangements almost always turn into management and recordkeeping headaches.

The 5th Wave **By Rich Tennant**

"IT SAYS HERE IF I SUBSCRIBE TO THIS MAGAZINE, THEY'LL SEND ME A FREE DESK-TOP CALCULATOR. DESKTOP CALCULATOR?!! WHOOAA - WHERE HAVE I BEEN?!!"

Chapter 20
Ten Things You Should Do If You're Audited

● ●

In This Chapter

▶ Leave Quicken at home

▶ Print Summary Reports for tax deductions

▶ Collect all source documents

▶ Call a tax attorney if the agent is "special"

▶ Don't volunteer information

▶ Consider using a pinch hitter

▶ Understand everything on your return

▶ Be friendly

▶ Don't worry

▶ Don't lie

● ●

*B*ecause you may use Quicken to track things like your income tax deductions, I want to mention some of the things you should do if you get audited.

Leave Quicken at Home

Don't bring Quicken with you to an IRS audit. Even if you're really proud of that new laptop.

Here's the problem: Quicken's reporting capabilities are incredibly powerful. If you've been using Quicken diligently, you own a rich database describing almost all your financial affairs. When you bring Quicken (and your Quicken file) to the IRS, you're spilling your financial guts.

Now I'm not one who recommends sneaking stuff by the IRS. But it is dumb to give an IRS agent the opportunity to go on a fishing expedition. Remember, the agent isn't going to be looking for additional deductions.

I know of a young, inexperienced CPA who took Quicken to an audit. After the IRS agent asked a question, the CPA would proudly tap a few keys on the laptop, smile broadly, and then show the agent on-screen, for example, all the individual entertainment expenses claimed by the taxpayer in question.

Funny thing, though, the IRS agent also saw some other things. Such as money that should have been claimed as income. Reporting requirements the taxpayer failed to meet. Obvious out-of-line deductions.

Print Summary Reports for Tax Deductions

Ol' Quicken can be your friend, though, if you're audited.

Before you go to the audit, find out what the IRS is questioning. Print a summary report of every questioned deduction: charitable giving, medical expenses, travel and entertainment, and so on. You'll have an easy-to-understand report explaining how you came up with every number the IRS wants to examine.

By the way, I know a very clever tax attorney who used Quicken in this manner. The audit lasted half an hour.

Collect All Source Documents

After you print a summary report of every questioned deduction, collect all the source documents — usually canceled checks — that prove or indicate a transaction in question.

For example, if you claim $600 in charitable giving, the report summarizing this deduction may show twelve $50 checks written to your church or to the local United Way agency. To verify this report, find the twelve canceled checks.

Call a Tax Attorney if the Agent Is "Special"

An IRS *special agent* isn't an agent endorsed by Mr. Rogers. Internal Revenue Service special agents investigate criminal tax code violations. If a special agent is auditing your return, you're in a heap of trouble. So get a tax attorney.

In my mind, being audited by a special agent is like being arrested for murder. Call me a scaredy-cat, but I'd want legal representation even if I were innocent.

Don't Volunteer Information

Loose lips sink ships. Don't volunteer any information — even if it seems innocuous. Just answer the questions you're asked.

Again, I'm not suggesting that you lie. The agent, however, is looking for income you forgot or deductions you overstated. The more information you provide, the more likely you'll reveal something damaging.

For example, if you offhandedly tell the agent about your other business — where you knit socks for golf clubs — you may wind up debating whether that cute little business is really a business (and not a hobby) and whether knitting golf socks entitles you to deduct those country club dues and green fees.

Consider Using a Pinch Hitter

I don't think an audit should terrify you. And I'm someone who's scared of everything: dinner parties where I don't know anyone, stormy nights when the neighborhood seems particularly deserted, driving on bald tires. You get the idea. Nonetheless, if you used a paid-preparer, think about sending that person in your place.

You'll pay for this service, of course. But it may help if the person who prepared your return does the talking.

Understand Everything on Your Return

Be sure you understand everything on your return. You won't help yourself if you tell an agent that you don't have a clue about some number on your return.

Be Friendly

Be nice to the IRS. Remember, the agents actually work for you. In fact, the more taxes that the agents collect from people who owe the federal govern-ment, the less the rest of us have to pay. (An article in *Money* magazine a few years ago suggested that we end up paying several hundred dollars more a year in income taxes because so many people cheat.)

Don't Worry

If you've been honest and careful, you've got nothing to worry about. Sure, maybe you made a mistake. Maybe the agent will find the mistake. And maybe you'll have to pay some additional taxes.

If you haven't been honest and careful, I offer my condolences. Sorry.

Don't Lie

Don't lie; it may be perjury. You could go to jail and share a cell with someone named Skull crusher.

You get the picture. And it's not pretty.

So don't lie.

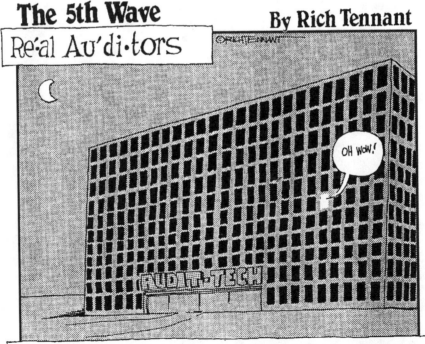

Real Auditors always do their best work between 1 and 5 a.m.

Appendix A
How to Install Quicken in Ten Easy Steps

· ·

1 f you haven't already installed Quicken, let's get it over with right now:

1. **Turn on your PC.**

   Find and flip on the computer's power switch (usually a big red switch).

2. **Get the Quicken floppy disks.**

   Rip open the Quicken package and get out the floppy disks (those plastic 5¼-inch or 3½-inch squares).

3. **Insert the first floppy disk.**

   Stick the floppy disk that's labeled "Install Disk 1" into your floppy drive slot. (If you have a choice, stick it into the top floppy drive slot, which is usually, but not always, drive A. The bottom one is usually drive B.)

4. **Start Windows.**

   If Windows isn't running yet, type **win** at the DOS prompt:

   ```
   C:\>win
   ```

   Then press Enter. The Windows Program Manager window appears (see Figure A-1). Your window will look a little different because your computer probably isn't cluttered with a bunch of other programs.

5. **Choose the Run command from the File menu.**

   You can do this procedure by pressing Alt+F and R. In other words, press the Alt and F keys at the same time and then press R. Windows displays the Run dialog box shown in Figure A-2.

6. **Tell Windows which program you want to run.**

   If you stuck the Install Disk 1 floppy disk into the top floppy drive slot (usually drive A), type **a:install**. If you stuck the Install Disk 1 floppy disk into the bottom slot (usually drive B), type **b:install**. Whatever you type appears in the *text box,* shown in the middle of the Run dialog box (see Figure A-3). You probably don't need this figure, but a few of your fellow Quicken users will.

Figure A-1: The Windows Program Manager.

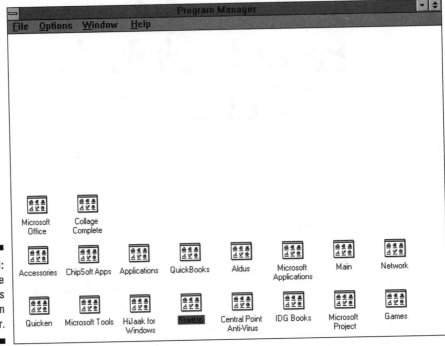

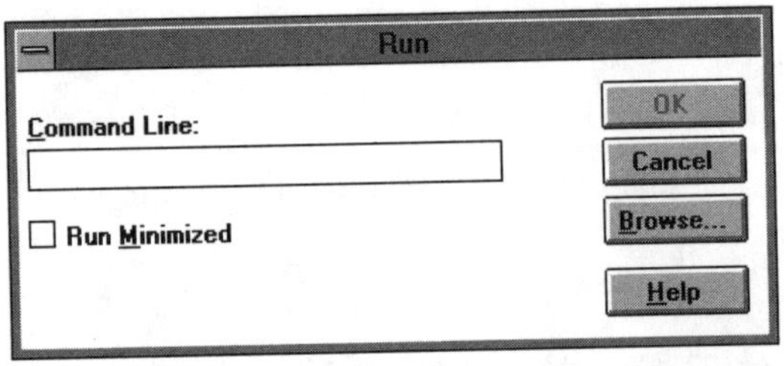

Figure A-2: The Run dialog box.

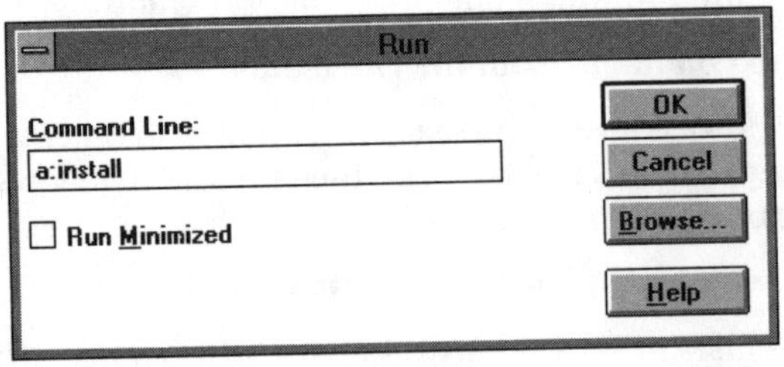

Figure A-3: The Run dialog box after you type **a:install** into the text box.

7. **Press Enter to start the Install program.**

   You should hear the floppy disk drive whirl and grind; then you should see a new window that tells you the Quicken installation program is ready to start (see Figure A-4).

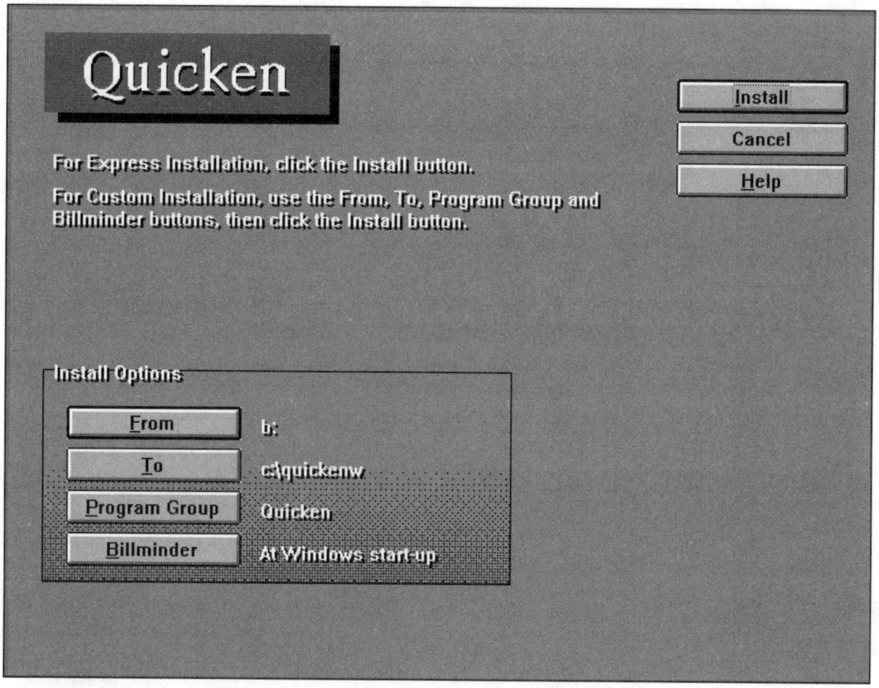

Quicken

Install

Cancel

Help

For Express Installation, click the Install button.

For Custom Installation, use the From, To, Program Group and Billminder buttons, then click the Install button.

Install Options

From   b:

To   c:\quickenw

Program Group   Quicken

Billminder   At Windows start-up

Figure A-4:
The Quicken Install window.

8. Click the Install button with the mouse's left button.

When you click the button labeled "Install" — you should find the button in the window's upper right corner — you tell the installation program that you want to install Quicken the easy way. As the installation program runs, you should see messages like decompressing. Don't worry.

At some point, the installation program will ask you to insert the Install Disk 2 floppy disk. Insert the disk and then click the OK button or press Enter.

When the Install program finishes, you should see the message box shown in Figure A-5. Congratulations, dude. You're done with the installation.

Figure A-5:
The message box that tells you Quicken has been installed.

Quicken Install

Quicken is installed on your computer.

To start Quicken:

   1) Click OK to close this dialog.

   2) Double click on the Quicken program item icon on the Program Manager desktop.

OK

If you've used a previous version of Quicken, the install program will display a message box that asks whether you want to move the existing Quicken files to the new Quicken directory. Go ahead and do this step — click the Move button on the message box.

9. Press Enter (or click the OK button).

You should see the Quicken program group on the Program Manager window. (See Figure A-6.)

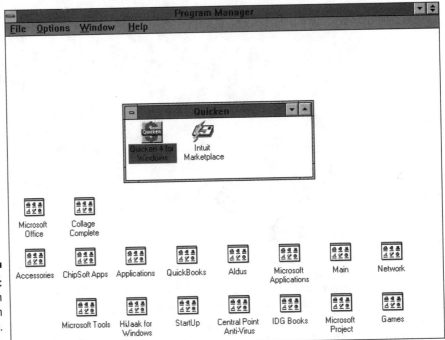

Figure A-6:
The Quicken program group.

10. (Optional) Celebrate.

Stand up at your desk, click your heels together three times, and repeat the phrase, "There's no place like home, Toto, there's no place like home."

Appendix B
Quick and Dirty Windows

. . . .

*I*f you're new to the Microsoft Windows operating environment, you need to learn a few things about Windows. Although this appendix doesn't reveal anything earthshaking, it provides a quick and dirty overview of what you need to know to get around.

If you've used other Windows-based applications, you probably don't need to read this appendix because you already know the material it covers.

I won't bore you with technical details. The information here, though, will allow you not only to operate Quicken, but also to converse easily about Windows at cocktail parties, over lunch, or with the guy at the computer store.

If you want to learn more, read a good book like Andy Rathbone's *Windows For Dummies*, published by IDG Books Worldwide.

What Is Windows

Windows is an operating environment that, along with DOS, manages your *system resources* — things like memory, monitor, printer, and so on.

Applications (programs like Quicken) run on top of Windows. In other words, you start Windows first; then, after Windows is running, you can start applications like Quicken.

Windows provides a standard graphical interface. In English, Windows provides a common approach for using *visual elements* — things like icons, buttons, check boxes, and so on. (This appendix describes how the major pieces of this graphical interface work.)

Windows lets you run more than one application at a time. You might, for example, run Quicken, a tax preparation package, and even a Windows accessory program like the Calendar. Sure, you don't need to do this stuff. But, hey, you can if you want.

Starting Windows

Starting Windows is easy. Type **win** (which stands for Windows) at the DOS prompt; then press Enter.

What's that? You want to know what *the DOS prompt* is? It's the letter, colon, and greater-than symbol combination. It looks like this:

```
C:>
```

After you press Enter, the Windows copyright screen appears briefly. Then the Program Manager window appears (see Figure B-1).

The top line of the Program Manager shows the window title, "Program Manager." Underneath the window title is the menu bar — something I'll talk about more in the next section.

Just to clear up any initial confusion, let me say that a menu bar is *not* where menus from all walks of life gather after work for a drink and friendly conversation.

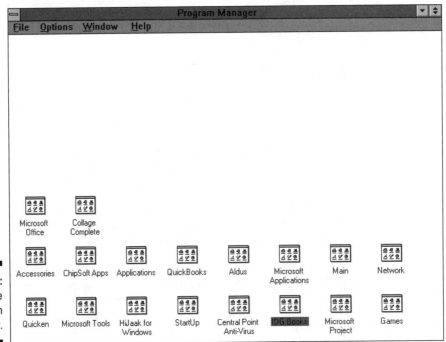

Figure B-1:
The
Program
Manager.

Beneath the window title and the menu bar, the Program Manager window displays *icons* (pictures), representing the various Windows program groups. In Figure B-1, for example, the Program Manager window shows a bunch of different program group icons. The Quicken program group icon is the upper left icon.

"What are program groups?" you ask. Good question. Windows creates *program groups* to organize your applications. Each program group contains one or more applications. As you install the Windows software, for example, Windows automatically creates three program groups: Main, Accessories, and Games. When you install Quicken, Windows creates a Quicken program group. (If you haven't already installed Quicken, refer to Appendix A.)

Come to think of it, these program groups are really just like the dresser drawers you use to organize your underwear, socks, and T-shirts.

Choosing Commands from Menus

To set in motion something in Windows, you usually need to choose *commands* from menus.

I don't know why they're called commands. Perhaps because you often (but not always) use them to command Windows and Windows applications to do things. "Windows, I command thee to start this application," or "Quicken, I command thee to print this report."

The Program Manager, the program group windows, and most application windows have a *menu bar* — a row of menus across the top of the window. Predictably, not every Windows menu bar contains the same menus. But they're often darn similar. Some of the commands on Quicken's menus, for example, mirror commands on Microsoft Word for Windows (a word processor) menus.

This isn't some nefarious conspiracy, though. At least, I don't think so. In fact, the common command sets make things easier for us. And that's kind of cool, don't you think?

As you read the next section, don't worry about what particular commands or menus do. Just focus on the mechanics of choosing commands.

Choosing commands with the furry little rodent

I think that the easiest way to choose a command is to use the mouse.

To select one of the menus using a mouse, move the *mouse pointer* — the small arrow that moves across your screen as you physically roll the mouse across your desk — so that it points to the name of the menu you want to select. Then click the mouse's left button: Windows displays the menu. (Pointing to some object like a menu name and then pressing the mouse's left button is called *clicking* the object.) Now click the command you want to choose.

If you inadvertently display a menu, you can deselect it (that is, make it go away) by clicking anywhere outside the menu box.

Choosing commands with the Alt+key combinations

Another way to choose a command is to use an *Alt* key (cleverly labeled Alt, these keys are usually at either end of the spacebar):

1. Press the Alt key.

This action tells Windows that you want to choose a command.

2. Press the underlined letter in the menu you want to select.

This action tells Windows which menu contains the command you want. Windows proudly displays the menu in question. Figure B-2 shows the Window menu, for example.

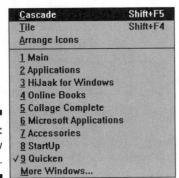

Figure B-2:
The Window
menu.

3. Press the underlined letter in the command you want to choose.

This action tells Windows which command you want. For example, press T to choose the Tile command from the Window menu.

Windows offers yet another way to choose menu commands. After you press the Alt key, use the left- and right-arrow keys to highlight the menu you want to select. Then press Enter. Windows displays the menu. Use the up- and down-arrow keys to highlight the command you want to choose. Then press Enter.

For example, press Alt to activate the menu bar. Press the right-arrow key twice to highlight the Windows menu. Press Enter to display the Windows menu of commands. Press the down-arrow key once to highlight the Tile command. Then press Enter.

If you want to deselect a menu but still leave the menu bar activated, press the Esc key once. To deselect the displayed menu and, at the same time, deactivate the menu bar, press the Esc key twice.

Using shortcut-key combinations

For many menu commands, Windows offers *shortcut-key combinations*. When you press a shortcut-key combination, Windows simultaneously activates the menu bar, selects a menu, and chooses a command.

Windows (and Windows applications like Quicken) display the shortcut-key combination that you can use for a command on the menu beside the command.

Take another look at Figure B-2, for example. Next to the Cascade command are the words Shift+F5; next to the Tile command are the words Shift+F4. So you can press Shift+F5 to choose the Cascade command, and you can press Shift+F4 to choose the Tile command.

Disabled commands

Not every menu command makes sense in every situation. In fact, Quicken disables commands that would be just plain kooky to choose.

Quicken displays disabled commands in gray letters. In comparison, commands you can choose show up in black letters.

In Figure B-3 (the File menu), for example, notice that the Move and Copy commands appear in gray letters. All the other File menu commands — New, Open, Delete, Run, Properties, and Exit Windows — appear in black letters. Move and Copy are disabled commands.

OK, do you feel pretty comfortable with this menu and command business?

Figure B-3:
The File
menu with
disabled
commands
in gray.

New...	
Open	Enter
Move...	F7
Copy...	F8
Delete	Del
Properties...	Alt+Enter
Run...	
Exit Windows...	

Good. Now let me tell you why Windows is called Windows.

Working with Windows

Windows is called Windows because information in Windows gets displayed on-screen in rectangular chunks, or *windows*.

Figure B-4 shows the Program Manager window. Inside the Program Manager window is the Quicken program group window, which shows the Quicken for Windows application program icon. (Remember that these icons aren't religious images characteristic of the Eastern Orthodox Church. These icons are just little picture symbols.)

Windows lets you do a bunch of things with its windows. In the following

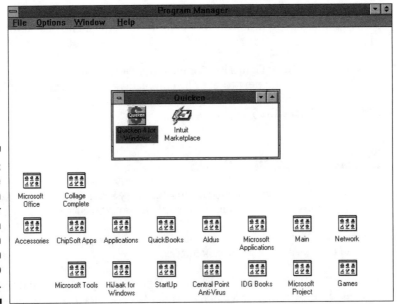

Figure B-4:
The
Program
Manager
window with
the Quicken
program
group
window.

sections I describe how to move windows, change windows' size, activate and deactivate windows, and even remove windows from the screen.

Using the Control menu to change windows

In the upper left corner of every window is a small box with a hyphen. If you click this box, called the *Control menu box*, or if you press Alt+spacebar, Windows displays the Control menu (see Figure B-5).

Figure B-5:
The Control menu.

The Control menu lists commands (Restore, Move, Size, Minimize, Maximize, Close, and Switch) for managing the windows you see on your screen. Not every Control menu has all these commands, though; some menus list only two or three. But I will talk about each Control command.

By the way, windows aren't the only things with control menus. Dialog boxes have short control menus, too.

Moving windows with the Control menu

The Control menu's Move command lets you change a window's location. When you choose the Move command, Windows changes the mouse pointer to a four-way arrow. Now you can move the window incrementally by pressing the arrow keys.

If you're sitting at your computer, take a minute to experiment with the Move command.

Changing window sizes with the Control menu

Four Control menu commands let you change a window's size: Size, Minimize, Maximize, and Restore.

When you choose the Size command, Windows replaces the mouse pointer with a four-way arrow (like the one displayed by the Move command). Use the left- and right-arrow keys to move the window's right border; use the up- and down-arrow keys to move the window's bottom border. The left arrow, for example, moves the window's right border to the left — thereby decreasing the window's size.

This sounds a great deal more complicated than it is. If you're bewildered, bedazzled, or bewitched, just noodle around with window resizing. You should get the hang of it quickly.

The Minimize command reduces a window to an icon. In Figure B-1, for example, each icon actually represents a minimized program group window.

After you minimize a window, you can't see the Control menu box. To enlarge a window, click the icon to display the Control menu. Then choose the Maximize command, which enlarges the window to fill the entire screen.

The Restore command reverses the most recent Minimize or Maximize command.

Removing windows with the Control menu

To remove a window from the screen, use the Close command.

If you close an application's window, you exit that application. If you close the Program Manager window, you exit the Windows operating environment. Closing other windows — for example, program group windows — usually minimizes them.

Switching between applications with the Control menu

You can use the Switch command when you're running more than one application. After you select the Switch command, Windows lists the applications currently open, including the Program Manager.

To switch to a different application or to display the Program Manager window so that you can start another application, point (with the mouse, not your finger) to the application you want and then quickly click the mouse's left button twice.

If you want more information about the Switch command or Window's multitasking capabilities, refer to a Windows book like *Windows For Dummies* or to the Microsoft Windows Users Guide.

Using the mouse

You can use a mouse to do most of what you accomplish with Control menu commands. You can move a window. You can change a window's size. You may even be able to switch between applications.

Moving windows with the mouse

Hey, dude, computer stuff doesn't get much easier. Point to the window title bar, hold down the mouse's left button, and drag the mouse in the direction you want the window moved.

By the way, this process — pointing to some object, holding down the left mouse button, and then dragging the mouse — is called *dragging* the object.

Changing window size with the mouse

You can change a window's size with the mouse by using the Minimize and Maximize/Restore buttons, which appear at the right end of each window's title bar. The Minimize button is the square containing the down arrow. The Maximize/Restore button is the square containing the up arrow or the double-headed arrow.

To minimize a window, simply click the Minimize button. To maximize or restore a window, click the Maximize/Restore button. If the Maximize/Restore button shows an up arrow, clicking it maximizes the window. If the Maximize/Restore button shows a double-headed arrow, clicking it restores the window to its previous size.

If a window's border shows, you also can change the window's size by dragging a border (or a border corner). When you point at a window border, the arrow becomes a double-headed arrow; then hold down the mouse's left button and drag the window to its new location or size. This sounds more difficult than it really is. If you are worried, take a few moments to try resizing a window.

Knowing the difference between active and inactive windows

You know that you can display more than one window on-screen at the same time (Figure B-4, for example, shows both the Program Manager window and the Quicken program group window). OK, here's a problem for you to ponder for a millisecond or so: Suppose that you choose the Arrange Icons command from the Window menu (this command neatly organizes a window's icons into rows). In which window will Windows arrange icons?

"Yikes," you say. "I don't know — that's why I'm reading this appendix." Oh, yeah, I forgot. Well, commands act on the active window.

"The active window," you say. "Double yikes! What's that?"

The *active window* is the window at the top of the stack. If you can't tell which window is on top, display the Window menu. Windows puts a checkmark beside the name of the active window. In Figure B-6, the checkmark is next to the first program group listed, Quicken.

Multitasking

If you want to switch to another application (such as to Quicken from the Program Manager), use the S<u>w</u>itch command. If you want to switch to another program group window or, after you're in an application, to another document window, use the <u>W</u>indow menu commands. I talk about Quicken document windows in Chapter 1.

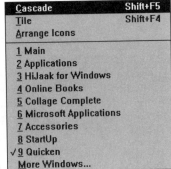

Figure B-6: The <u>W</u>indow menu tells you which window is active.

By the way, the active window's title bar is a brighter color than all the others; the inactive windows' title bars are dimmed.

To change the active window, you can use the mouse, the Control menu's S<u>w</u>itch command, or the <u>W</u>indow menu's commands.

If you can see the window you want to activate, click the window with the mouse. Easy, right?

If you can't see the window you want to activate, use either the S<u>w</u>itch command or the <u>W</u>indow menu command name that represents the window.

Working with Dialog Boxes

Windows (and Windows applications like Quicken) use a special type of window, called a *dialog box*, to communicate with you. In fact, after you choose a command, Windows and Windows applications often display a dialog box to get the information they need to carry out the command.

Which commands display dialog boxes

It is easy to tell which menu commands display dialog boxes: command names that prompt dia-log boxes are followed by an ellipsis, as shown in the File menu in Figure B-3.

Dialog boxes have five unique design elements: text boxes, option buttons, check boxes, list boxes, and command buttons.

Text boxes

Text boxes provide a space into which you can enter text. To see what a text box looks like, choose the Run command from the File menu. Windows, responding nicely to your deft touch, displays the Run dialog box (shown in Figure B-7). The text box is the box under the words Command Line:.

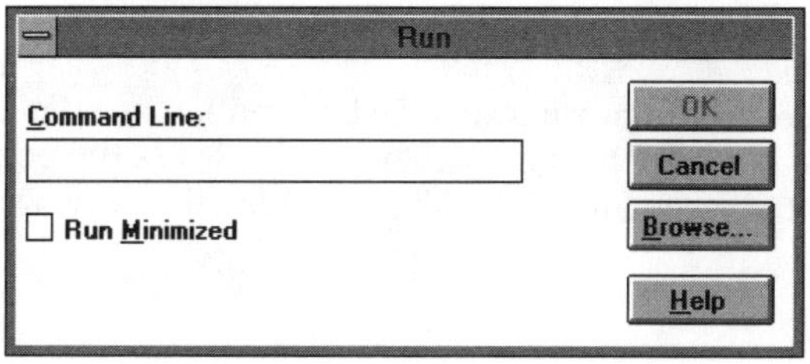

Figure B-7:
The Run
dialog box.

```
┌─────────────────────────────────────────┐
│ ─            Run                          │
├───────────────────────────────────────────┤
│ Command Line:              ┌───────────┐ │
│                            │    OK     │ │
│ ┌─────────────────────────┐├───────────┤ │
│ │                         ││  Cancel   │ │
│ └─────────────────────────┘├───────────┤ │
│ ☐ Run Minimized            │ Browse... │ │
│                            ├───────────┤ │
│                            │   Help    │ │
│                            └───────────┘ │
└─────────────────────────────────────────┘
```

To use a text box, move the *selection cursor* — the flashing line or outline that marks the active element of a dialog box — to the text box. Then type in the text.

You can move the selection cursor several ways:

   ✔ Click the text box.

   ✔ Press Tab or Shift+Tab until the selection cursor is in the text box (pressing Tab moves the selection cursor to the next element; pressing Shift+Tab moves the selection cursor to the preceding element).

   ✔ Press the Alt+key combination (for example, press Alt+C to move the selection cursor to the Command Line: text box).

If you make a mistake typing in the text box, use the Backspace key to erase incorrect characters. There are some other editing tricks, but I won't describe them here. Remember that this is just a quick and dirty overview of Windows.

You also can move the *insertion bar* — the vertical line that shows where what you type gets placed — using the left- and right-arrow keys. The left-arrow key moves the insertion bar one character to the left without deleting any characters. The right-arrow key moves the insertion bar one character to the right without deleting any characters.

Figure B-8 shows the Command Line: text box after I typed some text.

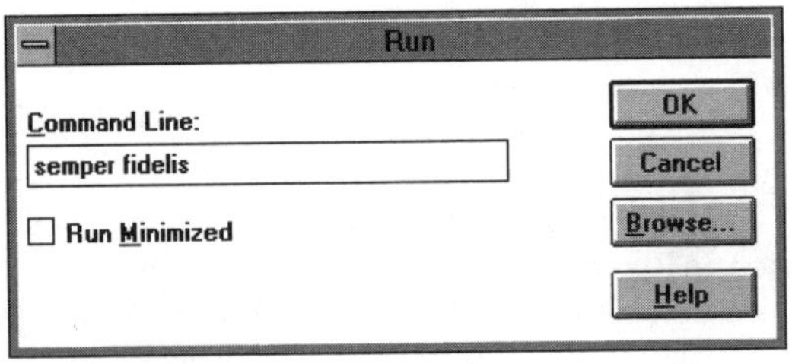

Figure B-8:
A text box
with text.

Run
Command Line:
semper fidelis
☐ Run Minimized
OK
Cancel
Browse...
Help

Fields

A field is a space reserved for storing specific information in a database program. When you see a spreadsheet on-screen, the fields are the boxes within the spreadsheet that you can fill in. You fill in a field in the same way that you fill in a text box.

Check boxes

Check boxes work like on-off switches. A check box is "on" if the box is marked with an X. A check box is "off" if the box is empty (Figure B-8 shows the Run Minimized check box turned off).

To turn a check box on or off with the mouse, click the check box. If the check box is on, your click turns the check box off. If the check box is off, your click turns the switch on.

You also can use the spacebar to mark and unmark a check box. After you move the selection cursor to the check box, press the spacebar to alternatively mark and unmark the check box. Toggle, toggle, toggle.

Command buttons

Every dialog box includes command buttons. *Command buttons* tell Windows or a Windows application what you want to do after you finish with a dialog box.

Figure B-8, for example, shows two command buttons: OK and Cancel. If you want the Run dialog box to enact the Run command, choose OK. If you change your mind and don't want to enact the Run command, choose Cancel.

To choose a command button, either click it or move the selection cursor to a command button and press Enter.

You also can use an Alt+key combination to choose a command button. For the Run dialog box (see Figure B-8), you can press Alt+B to choose the Browse command button and Alt+H to choose the Help command button.

Of course, if a command button doesn't have an underlined letter in its name, you can't use the Alt+key approach. Darn it.

Option buttons

Option buttons are sets of buttons representing mutually exclusive choices. To see what these babies look like, select the New command from the File menu. Windows displays the New Program Object dialog box (see Figure B-9), which has a set of option buttons, New. The set includes two buttons: Program Group and Program Item.

Figure B-9:
The New
Program
Object dialog
box uses
option
buttons.

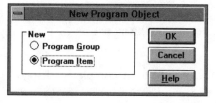

You can select only one button in a set. Windows identifies the selected button by putting a *bullet,* or darkened circle, inside the button. In Figure B-9, for example, the Program Item button is selected.

The easiest way to select an option button is to click the button you want. You can use the keyboard, however. Move the selection cursor to the option button set; then use the up- and down-arrow keys to move the bullet so it marks the option button you want to select. You also can type the underlined letter of the option button you want to select.

If you're at your computer, take the time to try all three methods. When you finish, remove the New Program Object dialog box by choosing the Cancel command button.

List boxes

List boxes list a series of possible choices. To see a list box, first verify that the Quicken program group window is displayed. Then choose the Copy command from the File menu. Windows displays the Copy Program Item: dialog box (shown in Figure B-10).

Figure B-10:
The Copy Program Item dialog box.

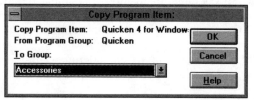

Windows uses two types of list boxes: a regular list box, which is always displayed, and a *drop-down* list box, which Windows won't display until you tell it to. Drop-down list boxes look like text boxes with a down-arrow button at the right end of the box.

To activate a drop-down list box, click the down-arrow button (or you can move the selection cursor to the list box and then press Alt+down-arrow key). Figure B-11 shows the Copy Program Item: dialog box's To Group: drop-down list box.

Once activated, a drop-down list box works the same as a regular list box. After you select an item from the list box (using the mouse or the arrow keys), press Enter.

Unfortunately, a list is sometimes too long to be completely displayed in the list box — see Figure B-11. When this minor tragedy occurs, you can use the PgUp and PgDn keys to page through the list.

You also can use the *scroll bar* — the vertical bar with arrows at either end. Just drag the square scroll bar marker up or down. You also can click the arrows at either end of the scroll bar, or you can click the scroll bar itself (this last trick moves the scroll bar marker toward the place where you clicked).

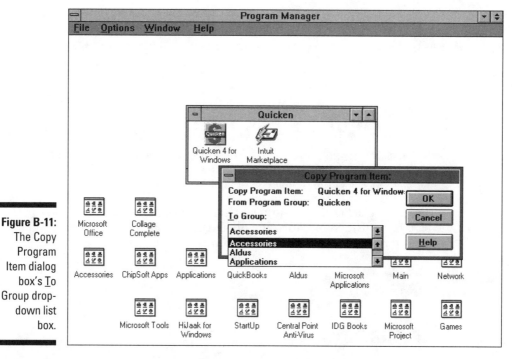

Figure B-11:
The Copy
Program
Item dialog
box's To
Group drop-
down list
box.

Starting and Stopping Quicken for Windows

After you install Quicken and start Windows, starting the Quicken application is
a snap. Just display the Quicken program group window and then double-click the
Quicken program item. Windows starts the application. (I talk more about this
feature in Chapter 1 — including what Quicken asks when you start it the first
time.)

To stop a Windows application, either close the application window or choose
the Exit command from the application's File menu. (Most Windows applications have File menus with Exit commands.)

If you exit Quicken the wrong way

If you exit Quicken by turning off (or resetting)
your computer, the index file Quicken uses to
organize your financial records gets, well, wasted.

Quicken will rebuild the index when you restart,
but this process takes a few seconds.

Don't exit Quicken or Windows by turning off your computer. This action may not cause serious problems (let me say, though, that Windows isn't as forgiving as Quicken), but it is bad form — akin to eating the last potato chip or leaving the gas tank empty in your spouse's car.

A Yelp for Help

Help, a separate application within Windows, has a number of powerful tools to help you learn about Windows and Windows applications like Quicken. To access Help, select the <u>H</u>elp menu or click the ? icon.

The <u>H</u>elp menu (see Figure B-12) lists five commands: Quicken Help, How to <u>U</u>se Help, <u>T</u>utorials, <u>S</u>how Qcards, and <u>A</u>bout Quicken. In the following paragraphs, I briefly describe how each command works.

Figure B-12:
The Quicken
Help menu.

The Quicken Help command

Choosing the Quicken <u>H</u>elp command starts the Help program and loads the Quicken Help file. The first window shows a list of the major help topics for the Account register window (see Figure B-13). Each topic is displayed in color — green is the default — on a color monitor.

If you want to learn more about entering a new transaction, for example, click the Enter a transaction help topic. (When you point to a help topic, Help changes the arrow pointer to a picture of a small hand with a pointing index finger.)

Help next lists the specific help topics within the selected category. For example, if you pick the Enter a transaction help topic, Help lists other related help topics (see Figure B-14).

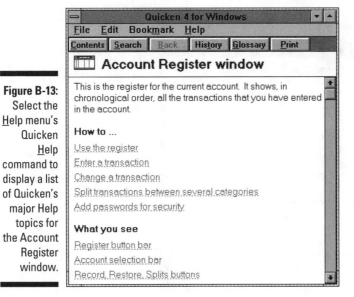

Figure B-13:
Select the
Help menu's
Quicken
Help
command to
display a list
of Quicken's
major Help
topics for
the Account
Register
window.

Figure B-14:
After you
select one
of the major
topic
categories,
Help lists
other
related
topics and
provides
information.

Finally, pick the specific help topic for which you want more information.
(Remember, help topics appear in green letters.) For example, if you want more
information on filling out a check, click that topic from the Add a transaction to
the register help topics list. Help displays the first page of help information on
the selected topic (see Figure B-15).

Often there's more than a single page, or window, of help information on a
particular topic. To page through a help topic, use the PgDn and PgUp keys
(you also can use the mouse and scroll bars).

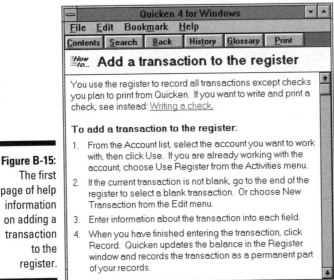

Figure B-15:
The first
page of help
information
on adding a
transaction
to the
register.

With Help, you can learn everything you want to about a Quicken topic.

By the way, Help also provides several special tools that should make it easier to learn. Specifically, Help provides a menu bar with four menus of commands (File, Edit, Bookmark, and Help), as well as nine command buttons. I don't describe these commands here. But try learning about the Help program using the Help program.

The How to Use Help command

Use the How to Use Help command to get help with the Help program. For example, if you're angry that I won't talk about the Help menus and commands, use the How to Use Help command.

The Tutorials command

The Tutorials command displays a submenu with two additional commands that let you see Quicken's Introduction to Windows and Quicken's Introduction to Quicken.

You don't need that stuff, though. You should learn what you need to know in this book.

The Show Qcards command

The Show Qcards command turns on and off Quicken's Qcards. What are Qcards, you ask. Good question. There are actually two answers. Answer #1: If you're a new user and like the idea of a bit of handholding, Qcards are these truly nifty pop-up boxes that display helpful information and useful nuggets about the Quicken window or dialog box you're using. Answer #2: If you're already comfortable with Quicken and pretty much know your way around town, Qcards are these really irritating pop-up boxes that hide portions of the Quicken window and tell you a bunch of obvious things you already know.

When you start to get irritated by a Qcard you see for one of Quicken's windows, you can click its control-menu icon. This is like a secret message to Quicken saying, "I pretty much know everything I need to know about what I'm doing right now. Give me a break, will you?" If you do the clicking thing for a Qcard displayed with the Account register window, for example, Quicken won't display Qcards with the Account register window anymore — but it will display them for other stuff — like the Investment portfolio window.

If you get truly irritated by each and every Qcard you see, you should, however, use the Show Qcards command. This tells Quicken enough is enough.

By the way, if the Show Qcards command is checked with a checkmark, it means Quicken's Qcards are on. If the command isn't checked with a checkmark, it means all the Qcards are off.

By the way, if you turn off the Qcards for a particular window and then later decide the backseat driving they do isn't such a bad thing, you can turn them back on. Here's how. First, turn off all the Qcards by choosing the Show Qcards command. Then turn on all the Qcards by choosing the Show Qcards command.

The About Quicken command

The About Quicken command displays a dialog box that gives the application's complete name, Quicken For Windows. To remove the About Quicken dialog box, press Esc.

Quitting Windows and Windows Applications

To quit a Windows application, choose the Exit command from the application's File menu. You also can use the Control menu's Close command to remove the application program's window.

To quit Windows, choose the Exit Windows command from the Program Manager's File menu. You also can choose the Close command from the Program Manager's Control menu. Windows displays a dialog box asking you to confirm that you want to exit Windows. Simply choose OK if you want to exit.

What about Chicago

What I've talked about in this chapter is how things work in Windows 3.x. As I'm writing this book, however, there's quiet rumbling going on down the street at Microsoft concerning the newest version of Windows, code-named Chicago. (Yes, the monstrously huge Microsoft campus really is right down the street from my small, modest, unassuming office.

This puts me in a bit of a pickle because Quicken 4.0 for Windows will precede the new version of Windows by several months. Yikes. But it gets even messier than that. Even though Microsoft does give advance copies of new Windows versions to people, they make these people promise they won't talk about the product before it's really available in stores. Double Yikes. Yet, the next version of Windows changes a lot of stuff. So what should I do? And, more important, what should you do?

Hmmm. Here's what I think. When Chicago is available, get it. Then, if you have questions about it after you've noodled around with it a bit, get the newest version of Andy Rathbone's book, *Windows For Dummies*. That's all I better say for now. Like I said, Mr. Bill is right down the street.

Appendix C
Glossary of Business and Financial Terms

1-2-3

The Lotus 1-2-3 spreadsheet program. The original "killer" application, 1-2-3 almost single-handedly turned IBM-compatible personal computers into standard business and financial management tools.

940 Payroll Tax Form

The annual federal unemployment tax return. There's also a 940EZ version that is supposed to be EZ-er to fill out.

941 Payroll Tax Form

The quarterly federal payroll tax form that tells the IRS what federal employee payroll taxes (Social Security and Medicare) you've collected and remitted.

942 Payroll Tax Form

The quarterly payroll tax form that tells the IRS what domestic employee payroll taxes you've collected and remitted. (Use the 942, for example, if you employ a nanny and you want to be the U.S. Attorney General someday.)

Account

In Quicken, a list of the increases and decreases in an asset's value or in a liability's balance.

Account Balance

The value of an asset or the outstanding principal owed for a liability. For example, the value of a checking account is the cash value of the account. The balance of a mortgage liability is the principal you still owe.

Account Transfer

An amount you move from one account (such as a checking account) to another (such as a savings account).

Account Type

Quicken provides several versions, or types, of accounts: four for keeping records of the things you own and two for keeping records of the amounts you owe.

- Bank accounts — for tracking checking and savings accounts
- Cash accounts — for tracking the cash in your pocket or wallet
- Investment accounts — for tracking mutual funds and brokerage accounts
- Other asset accounts — for tracking anything else you own
- Credit card accounts — for tracking your plastic
- Other liability accounts — for tracking everything else you owe

Accounts Payable

In a business, the amounts you owe your trade creditors — your landlord, the office supplies store, the distributor from whom you purchase your inventory, and so on. People who prefer monosyllabic speech often refer to accounts payable as A/P.

Accounts Receivable

In a business, the amounts your customers or clients owe you. People who prefer monosyllabic speech often refer to accounts receivable as A/R.

Amortization

The itsy-bitsy principal payments you make over the course of repaying a loan. Eventually, these principal reductions pay off the loan.

ASCII

An acronym standing for the American Standard Code for Information Interchange. People usually use the term to refer to files — in other words, ASCII files — that contain just regular old text: letters, numbers, symbols from the keyboard, and so on.

Backing Up

Making a copy. If something terrible happens — fire, hard disk failure, thermonuclear exchange — you still have a copy on floppy disk.

Balancing an Account

The steps you take to explain the difference between what your records show as a balance and what the bank's records (statement) show. Also referred to as "reconciling an account."

Billminder

A program that comes with Quicken. When asked by you, Billminder looks through your postdated checks whenever you start your computer. If there's a check that needs to be paid, Billminder tells you.

Bookkeeper

Someone who keeps the "books," or financial records.

Brokerage Account

An account specifically set up to track a brokerage account you use to invest in securities. Unlike a mutual fund account, a brokerage account includes a cash element.

Budget

A plan that says how you plan to make and spend money.

Capital Accounts

The money a sole proprietor leaves in or contributes to the sole proprietorship. Also, the money a partner leaves in or contributes to a partnership.

Capital Gain

What you earn by selling an investment for more than you paid for it.

Capital Loss

What you lose by selling an investment for less than you paid.

Category

In Quicken, how you summarize income and outgo. For example, you might use a category such as "Wages" to summarize your payroll check deposits. And you might use categories such as "Housing," "Food," and "Fun" to summarize your checks.

Category List

The list of categories you can use. While setting up the first account in a file, Quicken suggests category lists for home users and for business users.

Certified Public Accountant

Someone who's taken a bunch of undergraduate or graduate accounting courses, passed a rather challenging two-and-a-half-day test, and worked for at least a year or two under a CPA doing things like auditing, tax planning and preparation, or consulting.

Chart

A picture that shows numbers. In Quicken, you can produce pie charts, bar charts, line charts, and so on.

Check Date

The date you write your payment instructions, or check. Technically, the check date is the date on which your payment instructions to the bank become valid.

Check Form

The preprinted form you use to provide payment instructions to your bank: "OK, Mammoth National, pay Joe Shmoe $32 from my account, 00704-844." Theoretically, you could use just about anything as a check form — a scrap of paper, a block of wood, and so on. In fact, rumor has it that someone once used a cowhide. It's easier for your poor bank, though, if you use check forms that follow the usual style and provide OCR characters along the form's bottom edge.

Circular E

Instructions from the Internal Revenue Service to employers. This publication tells how much federal income tax to withhold and other stuff like that. Call the IRS and request a copy if you need one.

Cleared

When a check or deposit has been received by the bank. An *uncleared* transaction hasn't been received by the bank.

Click

The process of pointing to something on a screen with a mouse and then pressing the mouse's left button. Occasional secondary usage (spelled "clique") refers to a snobbish group of adolescents.

Commands

What you use to tell Quicken what it should do. For example, "Quicken, I command thee to print a report."

Controller

A business's chief accountant — and usually the brunt of most accountant jokes. Also known as a *comptroller.*

Corporation

A legal business entity created by state law, owned by shareholders, and managed by directors and officers. As a business entity, a corporation has unique advantages and some disadvantages. Ask your attorney for more information.

Credit Card Accounts

An account specifically set up to track credit card charges, payments, and balances.

Cursor

Someone who uses vulgar language habitually. Also, the little blinking line or square (mouse pointer) that shows where what you type will go.

Deleted Transaction

A transaction that Quicken has removed from the register. *See also **Voided Transaction.***

Directory

Basically, a drawer (like a filing cabinet drawer) that DOS uses to organize your hard disk.

Disk

The thing-a-ma-jig in your computer on which DOS stores your programs (like Quicken) and your data files (like the Quicken file for your financial records). A hard disk (inside your computer) can store a great deal of information; floppy disks (5¼-inch or 3½-inch), which can be removed, store less data than a hard disk.

DOS

An acronym standing for Microsoft's Disk Operating System. Quicken uses DOS to handle the hardware (things like the screen, the keyboard, and so on). Because this book is about financial stuff, I should mention that DOS is one reason why Bill Gates became America's richest man.

Double-Click

Two clicks of the mouse in quick succession.

Exit

To shut down, terminate, or stop a program.

Field

Where bunnies hop around. Also, input blanks on a screen.

File

Where data is stored. Your Quicken financial records, for example, are stored in a file.

File Assistant

A clever program within a program that asks a few questions and then sets up a new Quicken file. You almost certainly used the File Assistant when you set up Quicken.

Filename

The name of a DOS file in which Quicken stores data. Actually, what Quicken calls a filename is actually the name used for several files.

Financial Wizards

People who believe that they know so much about the world of finance that it is actually their God-given duty to share their expertise with you.

Find

A tremendous bargain, as in "At $22,000, the five-bedroom house was a real find." In Quicken, also an Edit menu command that you can use to locate transactions. *See also* **Search Criteria.**

Fiscal Year

A fiscal year is just the annual budgeting year. Most of the time, a fiscal year is the same as the calendar year, starting on January 1 and ending on December 31. But some businesses use a different fiscal year. (Why they do is way, way beyond the scope of this book.)

Formatting

Hey, this is too complicated for a book like this, isn't it? Let's just say that formatting means doing some things to a disk so that you can write files to that disk. It can also mean setting up some nice typesetting "looks" in your printed documents.

Graphics Adapter Cards

A chunk of circuitry inside your computer that Quicken and other programs need to draw pictures on your monitor. The acronyms EGA, VGA, CGA, and SVGA all refer to graphics adapter cards. But you really shouldn't have to worry about this stuff. Heck, you really don't need to know the difference between an EGA and the PTA (as in Harper Valley — get it?). Also needed for playing neat computer games.

Help

A program's on-line documentation — which can almost always be accessed by pressing F1. Also a verbalized cry for assistance.

Homebase

The homebase is Quicken's alternative interface. It organizes menu commands into sets of related financial management tasks rather than into Windows menus. You can turn on and off the homebase window by choosing the Homebase command from the Activities menu.

IntelliCharge

A credit card especially for Quicken users that lets you receive your monthly statement on disk or via a modem. As a result, you need not enter your monthly credit card charges.

Internal Rate of Return

An investment's profit expressed as a percentage of the investment. If you go down to the bank and buy a certificate of deposit earning 7 percent interest, for example, 7 percent is the CD's internal rate of return. I don't want to give you the heebie-jeebies, but internal rates of return can get really complicated really fast.

Liability Accounts

An account specifically set up for tracking loans, payments, the principal and interest portions of these payments, and the outstanding balance.

Memo

A brief description of a transaction. Because you also give the payee and category for a transaction, it usually makes sense to use the Memo field to record some other bit of information about a check or deposit.

Menu

In Quicken, a list of commands. In a restaurant, a list of things you can order from the kitchen.

Menu Bar

Although it sounds like a place where menus go after work for a drink, a menu bar is a horizontally arranged row, or bar, of menus.

Missing Check

A gap in the check numbers. For example, if your register shows a check 101 and a check 103, check 102 is a missing check. The term also refers to missing persons of Czechoslovakian ancestry. (In this case, however, the usual spelling is "missing Czech.")

Mouse

A furry little rodent. Also, a pointing device you can use to select menu commands and fields.

Mutual Fund Account

An account specifically set up to track a mutual fund investment.

Partnership

A business entity that combines two or more former friends. In general, each partner is liable for the entire debts of the partnership.

Password

A word you have to give Quicken before Quicken will give you access to a file. The original password "Open sesame" was used by Ali Baba.

Payee

The person to whom a check is made payable. (If you write a check to me, Steve Nelson, for example, I'm the payee.) In Quicken, however, you can fill in a Payee field for deposits and for account transfers.

Power User

Someone who's spent far more time than is healthy fooling around with a computer. Power users are good people to have as friends, though, because they can often solve your worst technical nightmares. However, note that most people who describe themselves as power users aren't.

Quicken Quotes

Quicken Quotes is an on-line service you can use to grab up-to-date price information on stocks and bonds. The book doesn't talk much about Quicken Quotes.

Register

The list of increases and decreases in an account balance. Quicken displays a register in a window that looks remarkably similar to a crummy old paper register — your checkbook. To print a copy of the register you see on your screen, press Ctrl+P and then Enter.

Report

An on-screen or printed summary of financial information from one or more registers.

Restore

Replace the current version of a file with the backup version. You may want to do this after a fire, hard disk failure, or thermonuclear exchange. *See also* ***Backing Up.***

QIF

An acronym standing for Quicken Interchange Format. Basically, QIF is a set of rules that prescribes how an ASCII file must look if you want Quicken to read it. If you're a clever sort, you can import category lists and even transactions from ASCII files that follow the QIF rules.

Quicken

The name of the checkbook-on-a-computer program that this book is about. You didn't really need to look this up, did you?

QuickFill

A clever little feature. If Quicken can guess what you're going to type next in a field, it'll type, or QuickFill, the field for you. QuickFill types in transactions, payee names, and category names.

QuickPay

An extra program you can buy from Intuit, the maker of Quicken, to make payroll a snap.

QuickZoom

A clever big feature. If you have a question about a figure on an on-screen report, highlight the figure and choose QuickZoom from the File/Print menu. Quicken then lists all the individual transactions that go together to make the figure.

Savings Goal Accounts

The last couple versions of Quicken have included this pseudo-account called a savings goal account. In effect, a savings goal account is a compartment in a banking account where you can "hide" or set aside money you're saving for a special purpose. A new car. A boat. A trip to Montana. Whatever.

Scroll Bars

The vertical bars along the window's right edge and the horizontal bars along the window's bottom edge. Use them to scroll, or page, through your view of something that's too big to fit on one page.

Search Criteria

A description of the transaction you want to locate. *See also* **Find.**

Sole Proprietor

A business that's owned by just one person and that doesn't have a separate legal identity. In general, businesses are sole proprietorships, partnerships, or corporations.

Spacebar

An intergalactic cocktail lounge. Also, the big long key on your keyboard that produces a blank space.

Split Transactions

A transaction assigned to more than one category or transferred to more than one account. A split check transaction, for example, might show a $50 check to the grocery store paying for both groceries and automobile expenses.

Stockholders' Equity

The money that shareholders have contributed to a corporation or allowed to be retained in the corporation. You can't track stockholders' equity with Quicken.

Subcategory

A category within a category. For example, the suggested Quicken home categories list breaks down utilities spending into a Gas and Electric subcategory and a Water subcategory.

Tax Deduction

For an individual, an amount that can be deducted from total income (such as alimony or Individual Retirement Account contributions) or used as an itemized deduction and deducted from adjusted gross income (such as home mortgage interest or charitable contributions). For a business, any amount that represents an ordinary and necessary business expense.

Tax-Deferred Account

Some accounts aren't taxable — Individual Retirement Accounts for one example and 401(k) Plans for another. To deal with this real-life complexity, Quicken lets you tag any account as being a Tax-Deferred one. As a practical matter, however, it'll probably only be investment accounts and the occasional bank account that are tax-deferred.

Techno-Geek

Someone who believes that fooling around with a computer is more fun than anything else in the world.

Transposition

Flip-flopped numbers — for example, 23.45 entered as **24.35** (the 3 and 4 are flip-flopped as a 4 and 3). These common little mistakes have caused many bookkeepers and accountants to go insane.

Voided Transaction

A transaction that Quicken has marked as void (using the Payee field), marked as cleared, and set to zero. Void transactions appear in a register, but because they are set to zero, they don't affect the account balance. *See also **Deleted Transaction.***

W-2 and W-3

A W-2 is the annual wages statement you use to tell employees what they made and to tell the IRS what your employees made. When you send in a stack of W-2s to the IRS, you also fill out a W-3 form that summarizes all your individual W-2s. W-2s and W-3s aren't much fun, but they're not hard to fill out.

Windows

The Microsoft Windows operating system. Quicken 3.0 for Windows relies on Windows to do a bunch of system stuff, such as print. Refer to Appendix B for more information.

X

What Quicken uses in the Clr (or cleared) field to show that a transaction has cleared the bank and been processed by you in a monthly reconciliation.

Zen Buddhism

A Chinese and Japanese religion that says enlightenment comes from things like meditation, self-contemplation, and intuition — not from faith, devotion, or material things. I don't really know very much about Zen Buddhism. I did need a Z entry for the glossary, though.

Index

• C •

Notes

Notes

Notes

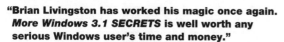
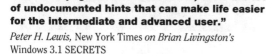

Order Form

Order Center: (800) 762-2974 (8 a.m.-5 p.m., PST, weekdays) or (415) 312-0650

For Fastest Service: Photocopy This Order Form and FAX it to: (415) 358-1260

Quantity	ISBN	Title	Price	Total

Shipping & Handling Charges

Subtotal	U.S.	Canada & International	International Air Mail
Up to $20.00	Add $3.00	Add $4.00	Add $10.00
$20.01-40.00	$4.00	$5.00	$20.00
$40.01-60.00	$5.00	$6.00	$25.00
$60.01-80.00	$6.00	$8.00	$35.00
Over $80.00	$7.00	$10.00	$50.00

In U.S. and Canada, shipping is UPS ground or equivalent.
For Rush shipping call (800) 762-2974.

Subtotal _____

CA residents add applicable sales tax _____

IN and MA residents add 5% sales tax _____

IL residents add 6.25% sales tax _____

RI residents add 7% sales tax _____

Shipping _____

Total _____

Ship to:

Name _____

Company _____

Address _____

City/State/Zip_____

Daytime Phone _____

Payment: ❏ Check to IDG Books (US Funds Only)   ❏ Visa   ❏ Mastercard   ❏ American Express

Card# _____ Exp._____ Signature_____

Please send this order form to: IDG Books, 155 Bovet Road, Suite 310, San Mateo, CA 94402.

Allow up to 3 weeks for delivery. Thank you!

IDG BOOKS WORLDWIDE REGISTRATION CARD

Title of this book: **QUIKEN 4 FOR WINDOWS FOR DUMMIES, 2E**

My overall rating of this book: ❏ Very good [1]   ❏ Good [2]   ❏ Satisfactory [3]   ❏ Fair [4]   ❏ Poor [5]

How I first heard about this book:

❏ Found in bookstore; name: [6]   ❏ Book review: [7]

❏ Advertisement: [8]   ❏ Catalog: [9]

❏ Word of mouth; heard about book from friend, co-worker, etc.: [10]   ❏ Other: [11]

What I liked most about this book:

What I would change, add, delete, etc., in future editions of this book:

Other comments:

Number of computer books I purchase in a year: ❏ 1 [12]   ❏ 2-5 [13]   ❏ 6-10 [14]   ❏ More than 10 [15]

I would characterize my computer skills as: ❏ Beginner [16] ❏ Intermediate [17] ❏ Advanced [18] ❏ Professional [19]

I use ❏ DOS [20] ❏ Windows [21] ❏ OS/2 [22] ❏ Unix [23] ❏ Macintosh [24] ❏ Other: [25]

                                                       (please specify)

I would be interested in new books on the following subjects:

(please check all that apply, and use the spaces provided to identify specific software)

❏ Word processing: [26]   ❏ Spreadsheets: [27]

❏ Data bases: [28]   ❏ Desktop publishing: [29]

❏ File Utilities: [30]   ❏ Money management: [31]

❏ Networking: [32]   ❏ Programming languages: [33]

❏ Other: [34]

I use a PC at (please check all that apply): ❏ home [35]   ❏ work [36]   ❏ school [37]   ❏ other: [38]

The disks I prefer to use are ❏ 5.25 [39]   ❏ 3.5 [40]   ❏ other: [41]

I have a CD ROM: ❏ yes [42]   ❏ no [43]

I plan to buy or upgrade computer hardware this year: ❏ yes [44]   ❏ no [45]

I plan to buy or upgrade computer software this year: ❏ yes [46]   ❏ no [47]

Name: Business title: [48]   Type of Business: [49]

Address (❏ home [50] ❏ work [51]/Company name:)

Street/Suite#

City [52]/State [53]/Zipcode [54]:   Country [55]

❏ **I liked this book!** You may quote me by name in future
   IDG Books Worldwide promotional materials.

My daytime phone number is _____

IDG BOOKS

THE WORLD OF
COMPUTER
KNOWLEDGE

 # YES!

Please keep me informed about IDG's World of Computer Knowledge.
Send me the latest IDG Books catalog.